GENERATIONS OF GIVING

GENERATIONS OF GIVING

Leadership and Continuity in Family Foundations

Kelin E. Gersick
with Deanne Stone, Katherine Grady,
Michèle Desjardins, and Howard Muson

LEXINGTON BOOKS
Lanham • Boulder • New York • Toronto • Oxford

Published in association with

**NATIONAL CENTER FOR
FAMILY PHILANTHROPY**

Washington, D.C.

LEXINGTON BOOKS

A division of Rowman & Littlefield Publishers, Inc.
A wholly owned subsidary of The Rowman & Littlefield Publishing Group, Inc.
4501 Forbes Boulevard, Suite 200
Lanham, MD 20706

Estover Road
Plymouth PL6 7PY
United Kingdom

NATIONAL CENTER FOR
FAMILY PHILANTHROPY

A publication of the National Center for Family Philanthropy
1818 N. Street, NW, Suite 300, Washington D.C., 20036

British Library Cataloguing in Publication Information Available

The hardback edition of this book was previously cataloged by the Library of Congress as follows:

Gersick, Kelin, E.
    Generations of giving : leadership and continuity in family foundations / Kelin E. Gersick.
        p. cm.
    Includes bibliographical references and index.
    ISBN-13: 978-0-7391-0924-3 (cloth : alk. paper)
    ISBN-10: 0-7391-0924-3 (cloth : alk. paper)
    ISBN-13: 978-0-7391-1863-4 (pbk. : alk. paper)
    ISBN-10: 0-7391-1863-3 (pbk. : alk. paper)
    1. Family foundations—United States—Management. 2. Family foundations—Canada—Management.
I. Title.
HV97 .A3G475 2004
361.7'6—dc22   2004010608

Printed in the United States of America

♾™ The paper used in this publication meets the minimum requirements of American
National Standard for Information Sciences—Permanence of Paper for Printed Library
Materials, ANSI/NISO Z39.48–1992.

CONTENTS

TABLES AND FIGURES

TABLES

FIGURES

FOREWORD

For almost a century, the practice of philanthropy by families across several generations has been considered an inevitable part of our charitable history. It was rarely if ever noted and certainly not an event for close observation or careful study. Transferring the mantle of philanthropic stewardship to the founder's children and grandchildren simply "happened." We had little sense that the effectiveness of family philanthropy might be a function of making those often-difficult transitions as successful as possible.

This view persisted even as we began to realize almost twenty years ago that leadership of the post–World War II foundations (created between 1946 and 1960) would pass from generation to generation over the next several decades. Indeed, these years represented what was, until recently, the greatest period of foundation formation in American history. Seemingly overnight, hundreds of families started looking for resources to prepare them for truly uncharted philanthropic journeys—journeys of great consequence for the nation and the families themselves.

Since 1980, this already significant trend took on even more urgency as the numbers of new foundations and other philanthropic structures literally exploded. New donors brought bold ideas about the focus and format of their giving and, we learned, very often planned to involve their children and grandchildren in the philanthropy.

Multigenerational philanthropy on a grand scale had to be seen as a great deal more than "inevitable." It had to be recognized as a highly generative phenomenon demanding studied attention. The National Center for Family Philanthropy turned serious attention to determining how well prepared we were—as an organization and a field—to inspire, inform, and embrace the new generation of grant-makers. As we cast about for ideas and data, we found very little to guide the practice of family giving or our own work in service to donor families. To be sure, there was much discussion about the prospect of the unprecedented generational transfer of wealth, fairly estimated at trillions of dollars. There was nothing on the generational transfer of philanthropic leadership.

As a new organization serving philanthropy, we had the unique advantage and good fortune to have the guidance of many philanthropic families. All had been characteristically generous in sharing their time and experience, in telling the stories of their hopes, accomplishments, foibles, and frustrations. We sensed in those remarkable stories an extraordinary wisdom. If we could mine those stories through first-rate social science research, we might identify a road map for what might be ahead for other families.

But how were we to proceed when there was little, if any, research on these kinds of questions at the scale and level of thoughtfulness we envisioned? We looked at the research of those who had studied the participation and impact of families working together in other kinds of shared endeavors. We found research efforts similar to what we were hoping for in other areas of family enterprise—principally around family businesses.

We felt very fortunate to have initiated what has turned out to be an extraordinarily productive working relationship with two of the most accomplished and credible researchers and consultants in that area—Kelin Gersick and Ivan Lansberg of Lansberg, Gersick & Associates. Kelin's work on *Generation to Generation: Life Cycles of the Family Business* had caught our attention early on and we were anxious to see if the principles uncovered in that work could apply to family foundations.

When the National Center's president, Ginny Esposito, first sat down with Kelin and Ivan more than seven years ago, they discovered a shared interest in developing the first-ever social science study of the organizational life and development of family foundations. Kelin was particularly enthusiastic about taking on this formidable task.

The National Center and Kelin defined a shared vision: To make philanthropy and philanthropic participation more meaningful and successful by understanding what is implied and likely to happen when families choose to work together in philanthropy. We wanted philanthropic families (and those who wanted to better understand this area of private grantmaking) to know why this knowledge is so important. Finally, we wanted to offer grounded suggestions for how the decisions founders were making about family participation and grantmaking could be reflected both in the near term and the more distant futures of these important institutions.

The National Center convened a small advisory team under the leadership of Alice Buhl, one of our founding board members and a consultant to numerous family foundations. Her colleagues on that group include Judith Healey, a highly experienced staff and consultant to family foundations; Curtis W. Meadows Jr., former president and trustee of the Meadows Foundation and a member of the National Center board; and Colburn Wilbur, trustee and former president of The David and Lucile Packard Foundation. The goals they fashioned for what would come to be known as the *Generations of Giving* project mirrored the early vision for this project and many of the values and goals of the National Center for Family Philanthropy itself:

- To help donors and families understand the implications of the decisions they make regarding family involvement and to help them establish appropriate governance and management structures for their philanthropy;
- To help families work together as productively as possible to ensure a positive experience for themselves and those that work with them in this effort; and that those groups and causes served by the grantmaking will benefit to the greatest extent possible; and
- That, where intended, donors and families can build on and pass along the tradition of philanthropy with integrity and purpose.

While it was important to address both the stunning growth in family foundations and to identify a discreet, credible research sample, all of the families studied in this project have a private family foundation (although all had other avenues and structures for their giving as well). We are struck, however, by the themes and lessons that emerged and their applicability for all kinds of family giving programs, including donor advised funds. We believe all who participate in and work with family giving programs of any kind will find something of astonishing value in this book.

The ongoing intellectual and practical guidance as well as the emotional support offered by the Advisory Committee over six years cannot be overstated. Nor can the confidence and steady hand of the National Center's Board of Directors, led during the launching of the National Center and this project by Tom Lambeth and now by Curtis Meadows.

We are indebted to Serena Leigh Krombach and her colleagues at Lexington Books for their belief in this material and their guidance throughout every phase of the publication process.

It is difficult, surprisingly, to find funding for research in the field of family philanthropy, even for a study we knew would be groundbreaking and have very practical applications. We are, then, most appreciative of the vision and generosity of the Surdna Foundation for launching the work with our first major grant and, later, with funds to ensure its proper completion. And we could not have succeeded without the support of The William Penn Foundation, the Phoebe Haas Fund, the Frey Foundation, the Walter and Elise Haas Fund, and the Lynde and Harry Bradley Foundation.

Particularly encouraging was the participation of a number of foundations, many of which consider themselves to be "smaller foundations." There is one school of illogic that says that such foundations don't get involved in projects of this scope, scale, and focus. The Nord Family Foundation, Flora Family Fund, Putnam Foundation, Towsley Foundation, and the Seaver Institute defy such illogic by understanding the power of leverage and a great idea.

We are also indebted to Joel Fleishman and Atlantic Philanthropies for their early support of both the National Center for Family Philanthropy and the mandate to take on studies like *Generations of Giving*. Our thanks in this volume to all of these funders only begins to express our gratitude for their support and confidence.

Finally, our sincere appreciation and admiration is warmly extended to Kelin Gersick, his research team of Deanne Stone, Katherine Grady, Michèle Desjardins, and Howard Muson, and his colleagues at Lansberg, Gersick & Associates. This is a dedicated, talented, and committed team and, without question, Kelin is their special leader.

Kelin's vision and insight reveal important new understandings of the challenges and contributions of philanthropic families—and that may well be the true phenomenon uncovered in this work. He instinctively cares about these families and he wants to see their giving be remarkable for families and grantees alike.

Kelin would agree that it is, ultimately, the participating families who made this work possible. We are indebted to those interviewed for this study and the hundreds of families who have been our inspiration and teachers over many years. It is to these families, their advisors, and grantees—past and future—that we offer *Generations of Giving*.

Alice C. Buhl
Chair, Advisory Committee
Generations of Giving

Virginia M. Esposito
President
National Center for Family
    Philanthropy

ACKNOWLEDGMENTS

Every book is a group effort; some more than others. In the case of *Generations of Giving* there were actually three sets of collaborators: the research team, the National Center for Family Philanthropy, and the family participants. All of them deserve more than pro forma recognition, because in each case their contributions went far beyond the norm.

This was a great research team. Each member brought a special expertise that fundamentally changed the final product.

Deanne Stone is one of the best-known chroniclers of American philanthropy. Her case studies and articles are the standard for the field. In this project she was the voice of experience, and the firm advocate of telling the truth, good and bad.

Katherine Grady and I have known each other since she came to Yale as a psychologist in 1977. Katherine brought a very deep understanding of families, and each of her case write-ups for this project was a compelling novella of family dynamics and collaborative dreams.

Michèle Desjardins is the team's analyst of organizational behavior and culture. She took on some of the most complicated cases in the sample. Her insightful comments in the middle of long discussions frequently brought us back to the core issues: how these complicated families do philanthropy, and why.

It took some perseverance to convince Howard Muson to join this project. He has been the leading editor in the field of family business for more than a decade, and he has a journalist's "no nonsense" approach to data and writing. Without him this book might be a 2,000-page jumble.

Finally, although not included as an author, Ivan Lansberg was certainly a member of the team. His understanding of family enterprise is unique in our field. This project would have fallen off the tracks a dozen times without his encouragement and good judgment.

The second group of partners was the National Center for Family Philanthropy and our advisory committee. Ginny Esposito is the person most responsible for this project existing at all. It was her idea—she framed it, funded it, guided it, and protected it. When we first met to discuss a comprehensive, in-depth, international, social science study of enduring family foundations, there was no one else in the field willing to invest in that kind of effort. She has tolerated delays, downturns in the economy, and my academic obsessiveness with equanimity.

Jason Born was the person who actually kept the project moving. He was both kind and demanding, and extremely helpful in very practical ways. And he managed to get the job done while keeping everyone in agreement that he is one of the really nice people in the world.

The Advisory Committee did much more than legitimize the study. In practice as well as in title, they were most valuable advisors. The experience of Curtis Meadows and Cole Wilbur was invaluable in strengthening the project at every stage. Judy Healey provided that rare combination of support, critique, persistence, and good humor that saved us from some serious miscalculations in both concept and prose.

I cannot thank Alice Buhl enough. As Chair of the Committee she managed all the coordinating responsibilities with ease. For me, she alternated the kick in the butt and the pat on the back with amazing insight and timing. There would be no *Generations of Giving*—at least not one authored by me—without her.

The final group that must be mentioned is the families, and I cannot name them. Many of them had bad experiences in the past with sensationalist press and envious commentators. Some knew that their histories were mixed, exposing flaws and embarrassing shortcomings. Others valued their privacy above all else. And yet they said "yes," because they were convinced that they could make a contribution. Their openness is additional good evidence of their generous cultures.

Others made significant contributions at special times. Colleen Kaftan was a dream of an editor. We thought we were just hiring her to clean up the text, and instead she reconstructed the entire book—all for the better. And Terry Carrasco was unflappable through hundreds of revisions, meetings, and project management logistics.

Lastly, my family. Connie, my wife and partner, was, as always, my most valuable sounding board and editor. Her mark is all over this volume in ways I cannot enumerate or even identify. And our children—Andy and Jen, Sarah and James—provide the unconscious fuel for my fascination with families of all kinds and my hope to help us understand them better. We are not a family of wealth, so my work—teaching, research, and writing—is my philanthropy. I thank them for being my inspiration.

Kelin Gersick
March 22, 2004

Pile up money for your children and grandchildren—
They won't be able to hold onto it.
Pile up books for your children and grandchildren—
They won't be able to read anything.

No, the best thing to do
is to pile up merit,
quietly, in secret,
And pass on this method to your descendants:
it will last a long, long time.[1]

Hakuin Ekaku
(1685–1768)
Artist and teacher

1. Adapted from a translation by Jonathan Chaves in Stephen Addiss, *Zenga and Nanga: Paintings by Japanese Monks and Scholars* (New Orleans: New Orleans Museum of Art, 1976).

INTRODUCTION

This volume is based on a study of family foundations in the United States and Canada that have survived through at least two generations. It uses the histories of thirty such foundations to examine continuity and leadership over time. Our analysis asks questions about why the foundations were started, what they looked like at the beginning, how the families of the founders came to be involved, and how they have organized themselves to do their work from year to year and decade to decade.

The cases are varied. Some foundations are entering their second decade, and others are approaching their second century. Some remain committed to the local communities where they started, and others are funding programs across the country and around the world. Some look very much the same as they did when the founder opened the doors and wrote the first checks to grantees. Others are so changed that the only remaining link to the early years is the foundation name on the letterhead.

But with all of their diversity, they have all had to confront and survive a common set of challenges. They make choices, once a year or every month, to support some requests and deny others. They must manage their assets, and comply with laws and regulations. Most of all, they need people willing to do the work. Some of the tasks are demanding, some are rewarding, and still others are mind-numbing and mundane. Enjoyable or not, the organization depends on their completion.

In that way, family foundations are actually the beneficiaries of two types of gifts. The first, and most obvious, is the gift of funds. Before a foundation can give, it must receive. Someone, or many "someones," have taken assets that they owned and put them into the foundation's hands. Their fundamental generosity is the irreducible heart of philanthropy.

The second type of gift is equally essential. Whether or not there are paid staff and director compensation, these are primarily voluntary organizations. They depend on individuals willing to give of themselves—to contribute their time, attention, and effort. The longer a family foundation has existed, the more generations and family members have been asked to make that contribution.

This study is about the "why" and the "how" of those two gifts, each essential to the survival of the foundation. We do not need to be reminded of the nobility of private philanthropy. These are exemplary "good works," representing a combination of generosity and social responsibility that makes us feel the best about our society and our future.

But we cannot allow ourselves to focus only on the goodness of foundations. We also need to be clear and objective about the organizations themselves. How are they doing? Where can they improve? Which organizational designs, leadership styles, and governance systems make family foundations most effective, efficient, and rewarding at the different stages of their development?

Finally, we also want to be practical. How can the experience of some be used to improve the plans of others? What concepts and models can we extract from particular cases to guide the future? We must not only appreciate philanthropy, we must increase our understanding so that we do it better. That is the reason for this study, and the purpose for this book.

FAMILY FOUNDATIONS, FAMILY BUSINESSES, AND THE CONCEPT OF SUCCESS

One realization that has helped us understand the unique qualities of family foundations has been the distinction between them and family businesses. While there are many similarities—and often overlaps—between the two types of enterprise, there are also fundamental differences that derive from each organization's ultimate purpose.

The family company, like any business venture, is performance-driven. Success is determined in part by outside forces (the market, manufacturing systems, the overall economy) and is measurable by performance metrics (sales, profit, market share, stock price, equity growth).

In contrast, the foundation is value-driven. It sets its own purpose and, within limits, is the creator of its own criteria of success. There are willing potential grantees for almost any program area. The legal requirements are minimal. It is, in short, hard to "fail" if failure is defined as the involuntary death of the organization.

In a family business the market is the ultimate arbiter of differing strategies, styles, and governance systems. In the foundation, there is no outside arbiter. As long as they comply with the law, families can set their own standards and adopt their own agendas without deferring to outside influences.

For this reason, we have come to the conclusion that the concept of "success" in a family foundation has been severely under-explored in our field, and the discussion has often been looking in the wrong place for answers. Leaders have been striving for years to raise the overall level of performance expectations. It is not easy; the difficulties of tracking impact and evaluating outcomes are well documented.

For many foundations, if the grants are made on time, the required 5 percent distributed, the general guidance of the mission statement or the current interpretation of donor intent complied with, the year was a success. Other foundations put more effort into strategy and planning, and only feel satisfied if they have focused their grantmaking and generated some evidence of impact. Still others are exemplary in their use of program evaluation and benchmarking.

But for family foundations, that is only one part of the issue. Family foundations have other purposes besides program. Based on the case histories in this book, we have come to believe that success must also be measured by the family members' commitment to the foundation's work, the satisfaction they take in doing that work together, and the foundation's ability to evolve and remain vital from one generation to the next. In this sense, a foundation's success will be measured in the eye of every family member.

DEVELOPMENTAL STAGES AND TRANSITIONS IN FAMILY FOUNDATIONS

One essential factor in this broader view of success in family foundations is time. This research is a study of continuity, but that does not imply a value position on the dilemma of perpetuity versus spending out. There is nothing inherently superior about intergenerational philanthropy or foundations that continue beyond lifetimes and across generations. That is a choice that every family must make. But those who want to remain must cope with the passing of time, and its impact on living systems.

It is easy to see an underlying evolution in families and in all their enterprises—including family foundations—toward more complexity, inclusion, and diversity over time. The life cycle of most institutions resembles an expanding pyramid, from founders to successors and on to larger and larger groups of stakeholders. That was certainly true in general in our sample of foundations. Most of them began with one or two individuals, grew to a somewhat larger group in the second generation, and then gradually involved more and more people from multiple branches and generations.

This evolution is not a gradual expansion, bit by bit, year after year. The important changes tend to be distributed more unevenly. Most models of organizational change now endorse the concept of a "punctuated equilibrium"—moments of dramatic change that mark the transitions between longer periods of relative stability.[1] We found that pattern of evolution in the foundations in this sample.

The transition from the first stage to the second was more dramatic and difficult than expected. At that point, to move to a true family foundation, both the governance structure and the operating processes of the foundation were redesigned. Some foundations prepared for it and spread the work of the change over months and even years. Others avoided even thinking about the departure of the founder until it happened, and then they had to respond. Either way the foundation that emerged was fundamentally different from its earlier form.

Our understanding of equilibrium and evolution in family foundations is enhanced by referring to basic conceptual models, developed from research on family businesses but applicable to foundations and other family enterprises.[2] When considering the various ways to organize clusters and subgroups within the sample, we thought a lot about the applicability of the principal models for family businesses to these foundation cases,[3] as well as other models for foundation development.[4] Since this was a longitudinal, retrospective study, we concluded that a developmental typology made the most sense.

In the stories of these foundations we found three distinctive types of governance organization. All of the cases fit in one of the three, or were in transition from one to another:

Controlling Trustee Foundations
Collaborative Family Foundations
Family-Governed Staff-Managed Foundations

These types represent loosely defined "stages," because a foundation could start in any one, stay in any one, or move back and forth. Nevertheless, we found a tendency for foundations to begin in the first type and to move at some point to the second, and sometimes to the third, over time. The types were often associated with generations in the family—first (parents) to second (siblings) to third and beyond (cousins)—but not necessarily. Part II of this book includes a detailed description of each type, including the challenges they must meet in order to successfully fulfill their organizational mission in that stage.

TRANSITIONS: CHALLENGE AND OPPORTUNITY

From our studies of the stages of development of family businesses, we have learned that to understand continuity, it is particularly important to focus on the periods of change between stages: the transitions. They are the most critical and challenging moments in the histories of family enterprises.

Transitions in family organizations, including foundations, are not just changes in the people who are in charge, from one generation to the next, although that is often an important part of what is happening. They also mark fundamental changes in the organizations themselves. Transitions are often periods of uncertainty when the decision makers feel most anxious and vulnerable—understandably so, because that is when the organization makes critical choices that will profoundly shape its future.

By calling attention to the transitions, we do not mean to imply that periods of "stability" within each stage should be taken for granted. The transitions between stages are opportunities for reassessment of the course the foundation is following, and *fundamental change.* The middle of a stage, when the enterprise (in this case, the foundation) is committed to a particular governance structure or organizational design, is the major opportunity for *focus and growth.*

Both change (transition) and growth (stability) are essential for success and continuity, although they require different kinds of work. The tasks of transition periods are exploratory and strategic; the tasks during periods of stability are operational and tactical in nature.

Put another way, during the transition we may consider all options and decide which mountain to climb—often while the army cools its heels in the valley and waits. Then, during the stable period that follows, all our efforts are focused on climbing the chosen peak, without a moment's wasted thought about the other mountains not chosen. Understanding these differences, and the essential alternation of change and stability, is critical for the effective management of a family enterprise over time.

SIX COMPONENTS OF TRANSITIONS

The overall time span of a transition may be a few months or several years, depending on the type of transition and the complexity of the system. But we believe that all transitions from one stage to the next, such as the one from the Controlling Trustee Foundation to the Collaborative Family Foundation, follow the same basic pattern. Our research suggests that there are six distinct components of transitions, beginning with the continuous accumulation of developmental pressures, and ending with the steps to implement a new governance system (see figure I.1).

Preparation: The Accumulation of Developmental Pressures

One metaphor that captures the nature of the forces that propel transitions is the glacier. A glacier, like a family foundation, is a growing, working system—constantly interacting with its environment,

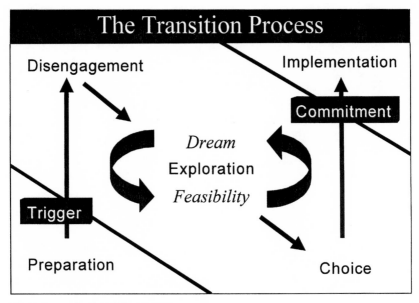

Figure I.1.   The Transition Model

and balancing movement with stability. The forces at work in a glacier as it moves across the landscape are powerful and complex, but
they are largely invisible. Over time, as the pressure builds in the river
of ice, it is preparing for change. Then suddenly, when it has reached
a state of "readiness," it may only require a momentary trigger to initiate the calving of huge sections from the edge of the glacier into the
sea, giving the glacier itself a new shape.

In the same way, the developmental pressures that accompany
families and their foundations are constantly at work—creating the
need for, and a readiness for, change. Individuals age, generations and
family dynamics evolve, assets grow and shrink, and the environment
is continually in flux. Like the glacier, family foundations normally resist change for as long as they can, protecting their habits and routines.
But sooner or later the pressure to change becomes irresistible. At
those moments of "readiness," important changes most often happen
in concentrated bursts, initiated by a trigger—one action or event.

The Trigger

The trigger that sets the transition in motion can be either a
temporal "alarm" (such as an important birthday), an event (such as a

health crisis or a dramatic conversation), or a change in the environment (new legislation or a shift in the grantee network). It is surprising that the trigger may seem insignificant in itself. This is because, in Shakespearean terms, "the readiness is all." The energy for the change comes from the accumulated developmental pressures in the system; the trigger is just the spark that starts the action.

To return to the metaphor, a glacier can be under such internal pressure that the shout of a tourist from a passing ship can be enough to trigger the splitting off of hundreds of tons of ice. In the family foundation, it can be an event in the life of one of the key leaders, a meeting of the board, or a sudden new perspective by one of the next generation (from attending a conference, reading an article, or talking with a friend), that sets the transition in motion.

Sometimes the senior generation experienced the buildup of pressure to a point of readiness, and as soon as some event triggered them to action they were quickly able to move toward implementing change. In other cases, the younger generation felt much more pressure than their parents, and they needed to wait for the seniors to be "ready." Either way, no trigger can be effective until enough tension has built up in the system, and, conversely, once the system has reached the state where the pressure is unsustainable, almost any trigger will do.

Once the transition has been "triggered," the actual work begins. The change process in transitions is composed of three sequential tasks.

Disengaging

This is the first task, to acknowledge that the era of the old structure is coming to an end, and a new one must be found. In governance transitions, disengagement is often symbolized by a public commitment to a new membership plan for the board, a retirement date for current leaders, or the scheduling of a retreat or a project with a consultant to design the future.

Exploring Alternatives

This is the most critical work of the transition. It involves considering different forms for the new governance structure, and then measuring their viability against the dreams, talents, and capabilities of the participants. This is a process of testing, learning, and revision. It may happen quickly, or be prolonged over several years. Managing this exploration phase is the most important leadership challenge of transitions.

Transitions are opportunities for change, not guarantees of improvement. Transitions raise anxiety. Many family members and directors may wish for a premature decision. They would like to move directly to "commitment" without spending enough time exploring alternatives and evaluating experience.

Leaders need to avoid the pressures to choose a new structure too early. More than anything, transitions are rare opportunities when it is acceptable to ask difficult questions and to challenge routines. Leaders can increase the chances of long-term success if they open the process to a range of possibilities, test the feasibility of each option, and make decisions based on adequate, reliable data. If a choice is made prematurely, it may not stand the pressure of implementation, and in the end the organization will pay dearly if it has to undo a poor choice and start again to find a better one.

Choosing

At some point, one alternative must be selected and the rest put aside. While this task is often given the most attention, it is actually only one step in the process, and can only be successful if it follows an adequate preparation.

These three tasks may happen quickly and in sequence. Alternatively, some families move back and forth among tasks. They may announce an impending change, but delay exploring alternatives. In those cases the "developmental pressures" continue to build, and since the transition has already been triggered, the force of the pressure is enhanced and the system usually experiences uncomfortable and disruptive stress.

Other families begin to explore a limited set of alternatives, and may even make a preliminary choice, but then become aware of important flaws in the chosen path. This may send them back to the exploration task, casting the net more broadly this time. Whatever the sequence, a successful transition ends with some clear choice, when competing alternatives are put aside, and the system moves to the final transitional stage.

This is the other side to the "premature closure" issue. Exploration of options is essential, but so is ending the exploration and making a decision. Foundations and families do not operate effectively in an environment of unending provisional status. Leaders need to recognize when it is time to bring the transition to a close, and commit the system fully to the chosen future. Choosing and implementing the new governance system signals to the family, the foundation, and the environment that the torch has been passed, and the new era has begun.

Commitment to the New Structure, and Implementation

The choice does not mark the end of the transition, but instead must be solidified with a closing phase of commitment and implementation. At this time, the family foundation formally declares itself ready to operate differently. It involves actually implementing the changes in the structure, and helping (or requiring) the environment to deal with the new system. These tasks often include the withdrawal of the prior leaders from critical roles in operations, important changes in support systems and individuals, and the implementation of new policies and routines. For a moment, immediately after the transition, the new shape of the glacier is in temporary equilibrium. The forces are relieved, and everyone takes a deep breath. And then, the developmental pressures begin again, starting the process over which will ultimately lead to the next transition—perhaps far in the future.

People who find themselves in these transitions often feel like they are in the middle of a circus. This is not far from reality. Things are very complex. But they can be understood and managed in such a way as to make the most of the opportunity for change that is inherent in transitions, and to emerge stronger at the transition's close. In the chapters that follow, we will explore and draw lessons from the varied transition experiences of the foundations that so generously participated in our study.

STRUCTURE OF THIS VOLUME

The remainder of this book uses the model of stages and transitions to present data from the research cases along with conclusions, observations, and implications for people who care about the future of family foundations. Some sections represent more traditional social science, with graphs, charts, and statistical analysis. Those pages will be reassuring to some readers and irrelevant to others.

We made the decision to include the description of the research design and the analyses in the text where appropriate and to present an expanded review of the data in an appendix. Readers who are interested in the quantitative data can refer to appendix D whenever they seek more detailed information.

Part I (chapters 1 and 2) provides a description of the study and some historical context.

Part II (chapters 3 through 5) presents the primary data from the cases, exploring in detail each of the three typical stages of foundation development and the transitions from one stage to another.

Part III (chapters 6 through 10) explores the four themes that we found most essential to continuity:

mission and dream
family dynamics
organizational structure
successor development

In these chapters we present conclusions from the data and implications that may guide the actions of current and future foundation leaders.

In chapter 10, we step back to speculate on the overall meaning of the results of the study.

We have included as many vignettes and case examples in each chapter as possible. No one tells the story or makes a point as eloquently as the participants themselves. In addition, readers can draw their own conclusions from the situations and points of view of the interviewees. In some cases those conclusions may differ from ours, and that will only enrich the ongoing learning from the study.

Different audiences may want to approach this book in different ways. Colleagues in academia may focus on this as a research report. We have included some citations from the small literature on foundation governance and some of the basic method, although this was not written as a publication for a professional journal. We would be happy to provide more background to readers who are interested.

Individuals currently involved in foundations, including family members, staff, and advisors, may be interested in both the developmental typology and the chapters presenting themes and tasks. We hope that they will have many moments of recognition as they read the case vignettes, and at least some "A-ha!" responses to the concepts and interpretations.

Kurt Lewin was famous for arguing that "there is nothing so practical as a good theory," and that is our hope—that our perspective will be a useful tool for readers as they address the specific situations of their own foundations. In particular, we would be pleased if our readers find themselves considering the critical questions:

- Did the founder or the present leaders/members consciously choose an appropriate form and articulate the foundation's mission and dream?
- Does the form of the foundation fit the stakeholders' needs and the family's purpose today?
- Do the structure, leadership, governance, systems, and processes of the foundation fit with the family dynamics in a mutually constructive way?
- Is the organization capable of preparing for the inevitable transitions of the future?
- What individual choices and behaviors can enhance both the foundation and the family's experience—in periods of stability and during transitions?

These are difficult questions, and readers looking for clear answers may be frustrated—as are the authors. We wish the challenges these foundations face lent themselves more easily to *solutions.* Instead we can present *options* and, at best, lessons from the experience of other foundations that have traveled the same path. For today's foundations, raising and addressing the questions is a courageous first step.

Finally, we hope that readers who are considering establishing a foundation will use this book to anticipate possible paths for your charitable future, and to help you decide whether the private family foundation is, in fact, the best vehicle for your philanthropy and your family. We suggest that you use this book more as a reference than a recipe. If you note the themes, you can return to them as they emerge in your foundation's development.

Today's founders and donors are starting on a new path. It remains to be seen how much they can improve on the experience of the past century, how much they can learn from the successes and mistakes of their predecessors, and how they will respond to the changing realities of the world of resources that they represent and the world of need that they serve. Perhaps someday in the near future, social scientists will aggregate and analyze their experience as we have done with their parents' and grandparents' efforts. Then we will all be able to see how far we have come.

NOTES

1. See Tushman, Newman, and Romanelli (1986); Nadler and Tushman (1989); and, in particular, Gersick (1991).

2. An earlier version and a fuller description of this model can be found in K. Gersick et al. (1999). It is also developed further in Murray (2003).

3. See K. Gersick et al. (1997) and I. Lansberg (1999).

4. Remmer (2000), and Gersick et al. (1990).

I

FAMILY FOUNDATIONS
IN CONTEXT

The chapters in this section introduce the study and portray some aspects of the world of family foundations in the past century. Taken together, these chapters present the social science base for the book.

Chapter 1 is an executive summary of some of the key themes in the research. It also describes the scientific method used for the study.

Chapter 2 is historical. Understanding the development of family foundations across generations requires an understanding of the economic and social environment that supports them. Unlike personal private philanthropy, which can occur completely away from public awareness, a foundation must exist in a social context. Tax laws affect the financial transactions. Other laws make demands on reporting and grantmaking policy.

Many different events can affect the availability of family members for participation. Technology creates new opportunities for impact, and makes other traditional programs obsolete. The ups and downs of the economy strongly affect the status of grantees, the press of need, and the appeal of different program areas.

All of these forces and many others are "in the room" when the foundation meets to do its business. Chapter 2 outlines some of the key factors that affected these foundations across their early decades, and suggests some general conclusions and consequences.

1

UNDERSTANDING FAMILY
FOUNDATIONS

Kelsey and Liz Wilson created a foundation as a convenient vehicle to support charities that had always interested them. The corporate attorney from their family business drew up incorporation papers, and Kelsey's secretary provided clerical support. They made annual contributions to traditional organizations (social service agencies, the United Way, their alma maters, and the local hospital). The grantmaking did not change year after year, in this case for three decades. When they reached their seventies and began spending much of their time in another state, they turned things over to their three children. The offspring each took responsibility for giving away one-third of the required disbursements. They met once per year at their Club for a couple of hours, informed each other what they had done, and that was that.

Over the following decade the pressure began to build for a more formal structure. Most importantly, as the parents died and their estates were settled, the foundation endowment grew suddenly to nearly ten times its original size. The second generation was moving through middle age, and the family was becoming much more complex with multiple marriages and many offspring in the third generation who were already adults.

The family was also dispersing geographically, and the range of opinions about appropriate grantmaking was very broad. The second and third generation began to evolve the foundation into a more formal organization. Staff were hired and gradually assumed more responsibility. The board was expanded several times to accommodate spouses and siblings, and eventually nonfamily community representatives.

By the foundation's fiftieth anniversary, it had become a complex, professionally managed organization. Its governance was overseen by a board that represented the second, third, and fourth generations of all family branches. Grantmaking was managed by an executive director and the staff.

Is this a success story? How should we, or the extended Wilson family, judge that? Are the Wilsons doing good work, and doing it well? Are they fulfilled? Are they fulfilling their responsibilities?

Is it anybody's business but their own?

We have arrived at a moment in history when two specific and typically invisible phenomena—wealth management and private philanthropy—suddenly are in view, illustrating many of the themes that are currently "hot" in our culture. The public seems equally fascinated with *values* and with *value*. A focus in the news, in popular culture, and in private conversations in recent years has been about economics—from personal to global. We are preoccupied with getting, having, and enjoying wealth, and the pleasures and purchases that wealth brings.

But not without ambivalence.

The other half of our attention is on families and parenting, health, spirituality, security, and meaning—the very things that wealth alone cannot provide. Moreover, we seem to be confused and uneasy about the links between the two themes: wanting more and more, but increasingly disenchanted with the benefits that money can offer, and distrustful of the people who have accumulated a lot of it.

Part of the current fascination is undoubtedly due to the expansion at the top of the economic pyramid. Demographics and economic development have brought us to a new territory. A series of wealth-generating waves has swept through the economy. The financial success stories of the post–World War II years have led to new twenty-first-century legacies. At the same time, in the most recent decades the journey from inspired or fortunate entrepreneurship to enormous wealth has been shortened from multiple generations to a handful of years (and in the most extreme cases, to months).

In 1900 there were fewer than 5,000 millionaires in the United States (one-tenth of 1 percent of households). By 2000 the number of millionaires had increased more than a thousand-fold, to over

6,000,000 (somewhere between 3.5% and 6% of households). Even taking into account inflation, the percentage of American families that have considerable wealth has increased between 5 and 10 times over the course of the twentieth century.[1] They are, in fact, next door, and behind many doors, and the ups and downs of the economy have only added to the mix. As a result, confusion about the consequences of wealth has become a very personal preoccupation for a whole new sector of our society.

There is great agitation and energy surrounding wealth, but little clarity or comfort.

Philanthropy is at the intersection of these complex social currents.[2] Private charitable giving in 2002 topped $240 billion in the United States, an all time record. Yet this is certainly not the first experience of landmark philanthropy in American history. Beginning a century ago, the charitable agendas of wealthy families like the Carnegies and the Rockefellers have shaped our communities and our social systems in dramatic ways.

Now the new wealthy families of this new century are trying to figure out for themselves how philanthropy fits into their values, their dreams, and their lifestyles. They are looking for lessons from the experience of the past decades that can be adapted to current realities.

Many of those families choose to demonstrate and manage their philanthropy through family foundations. There are approximately 40,000 family foundations in North America today, and they are being formed at the rate of more than 5,000 per year. They collectively oversee more than $175 billion in assets, and they disburse more than $8 billion per year in grants. Even though they are a relatively new category of charitable foundation, they are the fastest expanding category. They have grown from less than a quarter of the membership of the Council on Foundations in 1992 to 40 percent a decade later, and they make up the vast majority of the Association of Small Foundations' more than 3,000 members.

Some of them are famous and household words: Ford, Mellon, Pew, and lately Gates and Turner, Hewlett and Packard. They manage endowments of hundreds of millions or billions of dollars, and they have the grantmaking power to single-handedly address significant health and social issues.

But these megafoundations are only the tip of the iceberg. Ninety-nine percent of all family foundations have less than $100 million in assets; 60 percent, under $1 million. Large and small, these foundations share a central role in the world of private philanthropy. Family foundations are the cutting edge of social venture funding and entrepreneurial philanthropy, and they provide the lifeblood for countless thousands of agencies across the country.

We have heard many of their stories. And yet we know very little about them *as organizations.*

When the National Center for Family Philanthropy initiated the "Leadership and Continuity Research Project" in 1998, its basic purpose was to enhance our core understanding of multigenerational family foundations. At that time, everyone acknowledged that there was a good body of stories, opinions, and anecdotal learning about family foundations, but almost no well-documented social science research on these organizations. The project was designed to fill that gap.

As the study progressed, the initial findings began to generate a new conceptual understanding of family foundations. A picture emerged of an industry at a crossroads. Driven partly by economic factors, partly by the natural evolution and maturation of these philanthropic families over the past several decades, and partly by current events, even the most successful family foundations are feeling challenged—and sometimes threatened—as never before.

The experienced foundations in this sample were eager to make sense of their histories, to address their current frustrations, and to move into the future with a more confident assurance that their model is fundamentally strong.

At the same time, we hear from all corners of the field that new foundations, and potential donors, are impatient to have access to the experience of others, so as not to reinvent the wheel or make the same mistakes.[3] Across the board, philanthropic families are looking for guidance. As a result, we broadened the scope of the study to integrate the analysis of this sample with our broader experience with family foundations, new and old. Our goal is to elaborate the conceptual model of developmental stages and transitions in family foundations. In so doing, we will examine the implications for today's foundation leaders and families of wealth.

We must emphasize that this study and this report are *not* primarily about grantmaking. Many professionals, practitioners, and academics have done wonderful work over the past several decades on program development, monitoring and evaluation, relationships with grantees, venture philanthropy, ethical and legal requirements, and all of the skills that are essential in doing grantmaking well.

Our concern is with *governance and continuity*: the ways that families organize themselves to accomplish their philanthropic goals. Why are these families engaged in philanthropy? What does it mean for them? What is the relationship between the family and its philanthropic organizations? How do they think about their collaborative future, and what steps are they taking to achieve it?

PROJECT DESCRIPTION

The findings in this volume come primarily from a five-year study of governance and continuity in family foundations, sponsored by the National Center for Family Philanthropy. This project used interviews and site visits to create comprehensive case histories of multigenerational family foundations in North America. The research team, assembled by Lansberg, Gersick & Associates, included psychologists, organizational specialists, and interviewers and writers with extensive experience in the field of philanthropy. The study was designed to address two core questions:

> How do families effectively structure their philanthropic organizations?
> How do families plan for and accomplish continuity of involvement in these foundations over time and across generations?

In order to evaluate the reliability and validity of our conclusions, it is important to know how the research was conducted. We wanted to use traditional qualitative research techniques to generate good social science data, not just good stories. At the same time we wanted the research team to explore our respondents' experiences in all their depth and complexity. Therefore we decided to conduct extensive interviews and site visits instead of surveys. After much discussion we determined that comprehensive case studies would provide enough variety to cover the basic issues of multigenerational family foundations, and still allow an in-depth analysis of each case.[4]

The primary data are case analyses of thirty family foundations established between 1920 and 1990 in North America. They all currently involve at least two generations; many involve three. Their current endowments range from under $10 million to well over $1 billion. (Table 1.1 summarizes the demographic characteristics of the sample.)

We promised our respondents complete anonymity—the only possible way to get this kind of access to these families and organizations. In all we talked with almost 300 individuals, in thirty-five states and three Canadian provinces. We met with individuals, couples, and family groups, attended meetings, interviewed professional advisors, and reviewed by-laws, articles of incorporation and trust agreements, grantmaking guidelines, and trustee handbooks.

The cooperation and interest of the participants was universally excellent. We were invited into trustees' offices, their homes, and, most importantly, their memories. As a result, we have detailed case notes, foundation histories, family histories, and financial records. The data are very rich and somewhat formidable. The analysis continues and will for some time, even as we begin to disseminate findings.

Sample Selection

We generated lists of appropriate foundations from the National Center for Family Philanthropy, the literature on family foundations, and colleagues in the field of philanthropy. The data gathering was accomplished in two phases. In 1999, we approached an initial sample of four foundations to test the interview protocol and the research procedures. Since no modifications were made, we combined the test sample with the larger group we recruited in 2000.

We established the following baseline criteria for inclusion in the pool:

1. a formal foundation;
2. having completed at least one generational transition of participation and leadership;
3. governance control in the hands of one extended family, and at least four family members currently involved;
4. a willingness to participate and to talk about the family's philanthropy; and
5. geographic dispersal across North America.

Table 1.1. Sample Characteristics

Decade Founded	Legal Form	Gens. Currently Involved	Mission Statement	Endowment US $ (millions)	Annual Giving US $ (thousands)	Senior Staff Position	Total Staff (paid and volunteer) FTE	Board Members	In-laws ok?	% of Giving in Discretionary Funds
1920s	Corp.	3, 4, 5	Specific	40	1,300	Nonfamily	2	1, 2, 4	Yes	0
1930s	Corp.	2, 3, 4	Specific	17	850	Family	1.75	1	No	1
1930s	Corp.	2, 3, 4	Specific	340	10,000	Nonfamily	11	1, 2, 4	Yes	5
1930s	Trust	3, 4	Specific	470	17,000	Nonfamily	13	1	No	2
1940s	Trust	3, 4	None	53	2,500	Nonfamily	3	1, 4	No	0
1940s	Corp.	2, 3	Specific	9	500	Family	1	1	No	0
1940s	Corp.	3, 4	Specific	1,169	64,000	Family	24	1, 3, 4	Yes	10
1940s	Trust	2, 3, 4	Specific	154	7,000	Nonfamily	11	1, 3	No	8
1940s	Trust	2	General	100	3,700	Nonfamily	2.5	1, 2, 4	No	10
1940s	Trust	2, 3	Specific	177	8,000	Nonfamily	2.5	1, 3	No	0
1940s	Corp.	2, 3	None	53	2,200	Nonfamily	3.5	1, 4	No	0
1940s	Corp.	2, 3, 4	None	150	7,000	Family	2	1, 2, 3	Yes	35
1950s	Corp.	2, 3	General	44	2,500	Family	2	1, 3	No	0
1950s	Corp.	2, 3	General	55	1,900	Nonfamily	2	1, 2	Yes	15
1950s	Trust	2, 3, 4	General	97	2,600	Family	1	1	No	10

(continued)

Table 1.1. Sample Characteristics (continued)

Decade Founded	Legal Form	Gens. Currently Involved	Mission Statement	Endowment US $ (millions)	Annual Giving US $ (thousands)	Senior Staff Position	Total Staff (paid and volunteer) FTE	Board Members	In-laws ok?	% of Giving in Discretionary Funds
1950s	Corp.	2, 3	Specific	34	1,700	Nonfamily	2	1	No	0
1950s	Trust	2, 3	Specific	204	10,000	Nonfamily	7	1	No	1
1950s	Trust	2, 3, 4	Specific	87	5,000	Nonfamily	6	1, 2, 4	Yes	0
1950s	Trust	1, 2	General	9	500	Family	0.25	1	No	10
1950s	Corp.	2, 3	Specific	34	1,500	Family	1.5	1, 3, 4	No	15
1950s	Corp.	3, 4	General	42	2,000	Nonfamily	2	1, 3, 4	No	10
1950s	Corp.	2, 3	General	160	8,000	Nonfamily	3	1, 2	Yes	0
1950s	Corp.	2, 3	Specific	80	3,000	Family	1	1, 3	No	2
1960s	Corp.	2, 3, 4	Specific	39	1,500	Nonfamily	2	2	Yes	20
1960s	Corp.	2	Specific	35	1,700	Family	1	1, 3	No	33
1970s	Trust	2	General	67	4,000	Nonfamily	1.5	1, 3	No	0
1980s	Trust	1, 2	None	34	1,400	Family	0.5	1, 2	Yes	0
1980s	Trust	1, 2	Specific	8	350	Family	1	1, 2	Yes	50
1980s	Corp.	2, 3, 4	Specific	98	3,200	Nonfamily	4	1	No	15
1990s	Corp.	1, 2	None	7	300	Family	0	1	No	0
Range = 1921–1990	Corp = 18 Trust = 12	1st = 4 2nd = 24 3rd = 23 4th = 8 5th = 1	None = 5 General = 8 Specific = 17	Mean = $129 million Median = $54 million	Mean = $5.9 million Median = $2.5 million	Family = 11 Nonfamily = 19	Mean FTE = 3.3 Median = 2	1 = Direct desc. of founder 2 = Extended. fam. 3 = Advisors 4 = Comm. Reps.	No = 20 Yes = 10	Mean = 8.4%

Table 1.2. Target Distribution

	Founder to 2nd Generation	2nd to 3rd Generation	3rd Generation and Beyond	Total
<$30 million	3	3	2	8
$30–100 million	2	6	7	15
>$100 million		3	4	7
Total	5	12	13	30

We did not attempt to randomize our sample on any dimensions. However, we determined a target distribution on two criteria: generation of family participants, and current size of the endowment (see table 1.2).

Foundations were contacted by letter and phone in waves of approximately twenty, to invite their participation. The recruitment process was often prolonged. A few foundation leaders eagerly accepted the invitation very quickly. Others brought it to their boards for lengthy discussions which took weeks, months, and in a few cases almost a full year. As the sample was filled in, we adjusted our second and third wave of invitation letters to focus on the underrepresented cells. In all we made initial contact with about seventy-five foundations, and had at least one conversation with fifty, to reach the sample of thirty participants. Only one foundation began the project and then withdrew, requiring a replacement. The final sample was a very close approximation to the target. (Table 1.3 summarizes the actual distribution for the sample.)

It is important to emphasize that this is not a study of exemplary foundations, chosen according to any measure of performance excellence. *Continuity is not the same thing as success.* All of the foundations in this research sample are survivors, but only some of them define themselves as successes. Nearly all of the trustees, directors, and staff feel like they are doing "good work," but a smaller percentage feels that they are "doing their work well," that the foundation captures their best ideas and efforts as individuals and weaves them into an exceptional collaborative enterprise. The most important lessons from

Table 1.3. Actual Sample Distribution

	Founder to 2nd Generation	2nd to 3rd Generation	3rd Generation and Beyond	Total
<$30 million	3	1	1	5
$30–100 million	2	8	6	16
>$100 million		3	6	9
Total	5	12	13	30

this research are about the choices that each of these foundations has made along its path, and the distinctions between those foundations that are thriving and those that are merely enduring.

Data Gathering and Policy Decisions

The data gathering continued throughout 2000 and 2001. Interviews were scheduled at the convenience of the participants, and took from one to four hours. We assembled detailed information about each foundation's demographics, organizational characteristics, history, mission, continuity planning, asset management, staffing, governance and leadership, grantmaking procedures, family dynamics, and issues of special concern. (Appendix A presents the complete interview protocol.) At the conclusion of the set of interviews, a lead researcher summarized each case and the team met several times to refine and aggregate the case material.

We needed to make a few policy decisions during the data gathering that shape and somewhat restrict the generalizability of the results.

1. The size of the sample foundations is skewed to the larger foundations in the population. Overall less than 5 percent of family foundations have endowments greater than $30 million, but they represent 80 percent of our sample. We did that because, with such a limited group, we wanted to maximize the learning that each case provided. Larger and older foundations offer the most complex governance and leadership situations. In addition, the stories of older foundations yield historical data on their experiences as start-ups, and on all their stages of development since. That is not to say that all small foundations are on the way to growth. But since many of the smaller foundations will over time become older and larger, we hope that our findings may be a guide to the path ahead of them.

2. After much debate, we restricted the study to formal family foundations. We talked with these families at some length about other philanthropic vehicles. In fact, most of them were charitable in many ways—individually, through corporate donations, and in some cases, through a network of founda-

tions. However, without the central axis of a single foundation, it would have been nearly impossible to make sense or
aggregate our learning across cases.

3. Within each case, we tried to interview every family trustee[5]
who was willing and reasonably available. This led to five to
fifteen interviews per case. We were careful to talk to at least
one person in each family branch, and to oversample the senior generation—two preferences that all the families strongly
supported.

4. Our experience in this study confirmed our general approach
to research on families, which emphasizes how important it is
not to accept the perspective of *any* individual or branch as
the "real truth" about the family or the foundation. Each new
point of view adds dimension and understanding. For example, it proved important to try to reach at least one "outlier"
in each family, who was not deeply involved in family or
foundation governance. You always learn new things from
people on the margin, although they are sometimes the very
relatives that the high-status family members argue will have
nothing valuable to add.

5. In addition, one important lesson we learned in the first pi-
lot cases was how essential the professional staff were as information sources. In fact, in the staffed foundations, we
found that it worked best to talk to the executive director or
head staff person first. They provided a broad overview of the
foundation and the family, and they were extremely committed to the goals of the research.[6] In some cases they had taken
some risk to encourage the family to join the study, so they
were very motivated to help us make it work well. Of course,
starting with the executive directors did not mean we were
"captured" by their perspective. Staff members have a particular point of view, with its own subjectivity, and proved most
helpful as we "triangled in" on the story of each foundation
from more than one angle.

Overall, these families were amazingly open and eager to tell their
stories. Half the families were enthusiastic about participating from
the beginning; in the other half, one or more family members

expressed some ambivalence even as they agreed. The initial hesitation seemed to be largely due to a concern about two areas: old family rifts, or embarrassing grantmaking inadequacies. Once the interviews began and they became reassured that we were respectful and not looking for exposés, we had no trouble getting respondents to answer questions.

In fact, many of them were thrilled to be asked, and very interested in having conversations about philanthropy and their foundation in particular. They often asked for feedback and advice. The dilemma for the interviewers was how to protect the neutrality and objectivity of the research without being unnecessarily withholding. We ended up choosing a firm policy of nonintervention; we did not advise or give feedback to the foundations in any way until all the data gathering on their case was completed.

Once a family agreed to participate, we were generally welcomed into all parts of the family and the foundation. Nevertheless, about 10 percent of our requests for an individual interview were denied. Most of the reasons given were logistical; people told us they were too busy, or unavailable for other reasons. Only five individuals said they did not like the idea and refused on principle.

In addition to the interviews, we compiled financial and legal data on each case. Annual financial reports and the most recent 990 forms were reviewed. We carefully read articles of incorporation, trust documents, and bylaws. Some families had commissioned formal histories or biographies of leaders. Most had reasonably complete minutes of board meetings. A large number also had clipping files and collections of descriptions, notices, articles, and pictures from other sources about the foundation and the family. We read whatever was available—before, during, and after the interviews.

There are, of course, limitations to the applicability of this work. We only looked at older foundations in North America. The sample is drawn according to principles of qualitative field research, not large-sample survey research or controlled laboratory experimentation. For this type of study, thirty case histories is a reasonable number. We certainly would have heard other stories if we had done more cases, but we are confident that the major themes are represented here. In fact, after the first ten to fifteen cases, we were impressed that the core concepts began to circle back again and again. In general, when faced with design decisions we consistently opted for depth and more complex understanding instead of breadth and a larger, more representative sample. The resulting data reflects both the strengths and the limitations of that choice.

Data Analysis

As the interviews were completed, the data was compiled into thirty case reports. Each report included:

- demographic data on the family, the foundation, and the business or other parts of the family enterprise;
- a narrative summary of the interviews, aggregated according to the protocol;
- a timeline of key events from the founding of the family enterprise to the present;
- a genogram (family tree) of the extended family;
- an interpretive summary of the key themes; and
- additional questions and themes raised but not answered in the case.

This qualitative material was compiled, aggregated, discussed, and reanalyzed by the research team. Summaries and excerpts were prepared. A database was created which compiled all of the demographic, historical, economic, and organizational data for all thirty cases.

At the end of the data analysis, we also created a set of performance ratings by the researchers. In the absence of data from grantees, we needed to summarize and quantify in some form our impressions of the relative strengths of each foundation in key areas related to continuity. Each lead researcher completed a set of rankings, from 1 (very low) to 5 (exemplary) on the following characteristics:

Clarity of program
Grantmaking vitality
Degree of staff control
Family collaboration
Likelihood of continuity
Successor development
Asset management
Next generation enthusiasm

Conflict avoidance
Quality control
Clarity of mission
Organizational structure
Positive family dynamics
Resource adequacy

After the series of meetings and discussions of each case, the project director completed his own set of ratings. The two sets were compared, and discrepancies were resolved in discussion, leading to one set of ratings which were used in the analysis and reported throughout this volume.

The conclusions reflected in this report come from both the quantitative and qualitative data. (A complete list of variables in the database is presented in appendix B.)

Anonymity and Case Examples

In keeping with our promise of anonymity, we will not release the identity of the foundations that participated. We made a commitment to the participants to remove identifying names and labels from the stories that are reported, and to disguise unique situations or characteristics. (A copy of the Understanding on Anonymity is included as appendix C.)

At the same time, it is important to note that the case examples are true, and not made up to fit a predetermined conclusion or theory. Therefore in all of our case examples we tell the story as accurately as possible, with some nonessential facts changed. In some vignettes we use disguised names; in the others we simply omit all names. The members of particular families may recognize themselves, or think they do (although our experience has shown us over and over that respondents most often misidentify their own stories), but others could only guess at the sources of our examples.

Sample Demographics and Summary Facts

The first generation is still involved as trustees or directors in four of the foundations (13%); the second generation in twenty-five (83%);

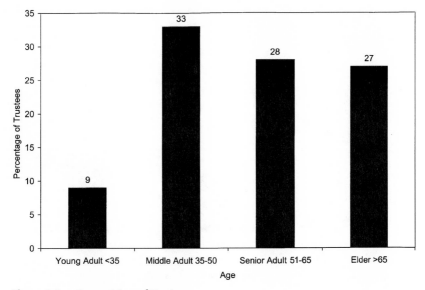

Figure 1.1.   Current Age of Trustees

the third in twenty-three (77%); and the fourth in thirteen (43%). Three of the foundations currently have only second-generation members as trustees. The rest have at least two generations currently working together; eight of the foundations (27%) have three generations currently involved.

The ages of the trustees vary widely, but overall the trustees and directors are concentrated in middle, senior, and elder adult categories (see figure 1.1).

Only twelve of the foundations have any trustees under 35 years old, and for the sample as a whole about 10 percent of the trustees are younger than 35. One-third of the trustees are between 35 and 50, and all but four foundations have at least some trustees in this age group. Nearly a third are between 50 and 65, with all but six foundations having at least one trustee in this age group. Finally, 27 percent of the trustees are over 65 years old. Twenty-seven of the 30 foundations have at least one trustee in this age group, and in five foundations the majority of trustees are over 65.

Only thirteen (40%) of the foundations began with an original endowment. The range was from $8,000 to $60 million, with a median just under $1 million. (Those figures are in dollars for the year

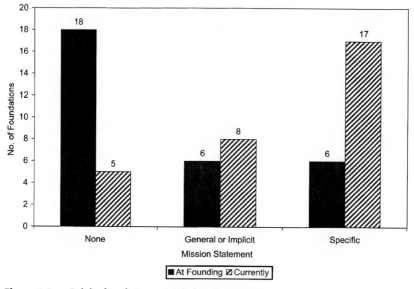

Figure 1.2.   Original and Current Mission Statement

of founding. Converted to 2003 dollars, the range was from $38,000 to $90 million, with a median of $18 million.) Seventeen of the foundations (60%) began without any endowment, but were funded annually out of operating revenues of a company or personal contributions. Today all of the foundations have their own assets, and the endowments of the foundations in the sample range from $9 million to over $1 billion (see table 1.3 above).

At founding, only six of the foundations began with a clear and specific mission statement or programmatic focus. Six more had a general statement of purpose that provided some guidance or priorities; eighteen had no mission statement at all, or a legal statement of purpose that provided no programmatic guidance ("to support such organizations as the board shall from time to from time designate"). As a whole, the clarity of the foundation's mission seems to increase dramatically with age; currently seventeen of the foundations have a specific mission (e.g., "to support treatment facilities for the elderly and those suffering from chronic diseases"); eight have a general statement (e.g., "to improve the quality of life for families and children in our area"), and only five have no stated programmatic focus (figure 1.2).

Currently only two of the foundations operate without any paid staff, relying on family volunteers exclusively. The average staffing level is about three FTE (full-time equivalents) per foundation, and six of the foundations (20%) have four or more FTE staff. The range here is truly remarkable, from zero to twenty-three FTE. While size makes a difference (the correlation between asset size and staff size is .9), it does not tell the whole story. For example, in this sample foundations of comparable size ($150 million) vary from one to eleven FTE of paid professional staff.

About half of the families are still involved in an operating business, and one-third (10) have at least one other foundation. We will discuss this phenomenon later concerning governance of the complex family enterprise, but it is clear that the foundation is not an isolated activity for most of these families. Instead it operates in a network of family structures, all of which play a role in the on-going generation, management, and/or dispersal of the family's wealth.

So what is a picture of the typical foundation in our study? It is fifty years old, begun with less than $1 million and now managing an endowment of about $75 million. There may be one or more members of the founders' generation still alive, but the control of the grantmaking rests with the second generation and the older members of the third. The trustee group or board of directors, numbering about eight, meets three times per year, considers several hundred proposals, and disperses 100 grants totaling about $4 million. There is a professional executive director (sometimes a family member, but typically not), a program officer, and a clerical person. Some of our foundations are older, some younger, some smaller, some much larger—but if you imagine this group as you read the stories in this book, you will not be far off.

THEMES RAISED IN THE DATA

At one level, the accomplishments of the thirty foundations in our research sample are remarkable. Their aggregate annual giving exceeded $150 million in 2000, and they are significant shapers of the quality of life in their varied communities. Every one of them points to programs, agencies, services, and public institutions that would be hard pressed to continue without their support. They pay close attention to legal requirements and the ethical guidelines of professional associations. The level of voluntary effort in most of these organizations is very high. They have continued for good reason.

But the current challenges are glaring. In our work over the past decade we have found it useful to focus on four critical concerns which come to the fore as organizations develop and evolve: mission and dream, family dynamics, organizational structure, and succession planning. While there is great variation across foundations, in each area we found significant uncertainty in the majority of the research sample.

- *Mission and Dream.* A high percentage of these foundations are feeling strong pressure to revisit their mission, particularly in anticipation of, or response to, a current generational transition in leadership. They are caught between honoring their legacy from the past and present, and maintaining commitment for the future. Most of them do not see a clear pathway to resolution.
- *Family Dynamics.* Open conflict, destructive rivalry, angry battles and withdrawals, and other acute dysfunction in family dynamics per se are serious problems in only a small segment of this sample. On the other hand, *avoidance* is a major and widespread danger, particularly as it interferes with a straightforward attack on the problems in mission, structure, and succession planning. The culture of politeness and a fear about rocking the boat have prevented some of these foundations from debating the fundamental changes that are needed in the other three areas. That is how challenges become crises.
- *Organizational Structure and Policies.* The organizational structures of these foundations have characteristically not kept pace with their growing endowments and families. Their grantmaking skills far exceed their governance abilities. Most have gone through a first round of formalization following the death or withdrawal of the founder. However, there is more to be done. Only a few have completed the changes in structure and procedure that are needed to accomplish more complex grantmaking, make best use of professional staff and advisors, and deal with larger pools of potential trustees. There is also great reluctance (or at least ambivalence) about spending the funds necessary to modernize and upgrade the organizational infrastructure.
- *Succession Planning.* Some of these foundations take the preparation

of their next generation very seriously, but most avoid or delay serious efforts toward successor development. Even those that have had good discussions about the selection of future trustees often procrastinate on implementing a succession process. It is surprising that despite the success that some exemplary foundations across the country have had in recruiting, training, and selecting successor trustees, the dissemination of their experiences has been poor. As a result most of these foundations go about reinventing the wheel of succession planning.

We will return to these four challenges several times in this book, reporting data and suggesting responses. In general, our findings suggest that these foundations are doing good work, operating honorably and conscientiously, and giving voice to the philanthropic dreams of a large number of family members. However, many of them need considerable attention to their governance structures and processes.

The data from this project describe a system coming to a plateau after nearly half a century of enormous growth. These mature foundations are at a historical turning point. They have evolved from first-generation start-ups, implementing the personal philanthropic values of their founders, through second generations of formalization, professionalization, and dramatic expansion. Now they are struggling with the challenges of creating permanent collaborative family institutions. Their special strength and their most critical dilemma both come from their unique character as organizations: a value-based agenda of service and social intervention, in contrast to a business's economic purpose of wealth creation. They are an incubator of intense family process, because they are inherently voluntary working systems with substantial resources, controlled by social and interpersonal norms rather than financial rewards. For that reason and others they are potentially a rich source of understanding about the deep values of families and the enterprises they create.

NOTES

1. These are estimates, and economists disagree over the details. However, everyone agrees about the trend, and we have used some conservative figures. Popular

discussions of new wealth include Stanley and Danko (1998) and Moore and Simon (2000).

2. Peter Karoff has been one of the most thoughtful, creative analysts of the meaning of philanthropy in the lives of individuals and in our culture. His latest book, *Just Money: A Critique on Contemporary American Philanthropy* (2004) continues his contribution.

3. Sometimes that awareness comes only with experience. In an article on new megadonors, John Byrne quotes new philanthropists who "have gone off course by assuming they had nothing to learn from those who went before. . . . 'We thought we had all the answers and wanted to do it ourselves. We should have been more respectful of the people who have done this all their lives'" (Byrne 2002).

4. There is an extensive literature on qualitative field research. We were guided in our design by sources such as E. Lawler et al. (1985).

5. Half the foundations in the sample were trusts, so the official title of the governance role is "trustee." The other half were corporations, using the title of "director." We decided it would be too awkward to use the combined form every time in the text, so we will use them interchangeably. While it is true that the legal rights and responsibilities are quite different, in terms of their role in governance, there were no systematic differences in this sample.

6. Only one nonfamily executive director opposed the family's decision to participate in the research. The family leader in that foundation suggested to us that the director was apprehensive about our focus on their governance process, since the family had become very passive and the executive was operating with a free hand. We discuss that type of "renegade" staff role in chapter 5.

2

FAMILY PHILANTHROPY IN NORTH AMERICA

Institutionalized family philanthropy is an American phenomenon. Nowhere else in the world is it practiced on such a broad scale, in such an organized fashion. Foundations have been part of the North American landscape for the past century. In the early years, they were the domain of the spectacularly wealthy, but by the close of the twentieth century the field of organized philanthropy had been profoundly democratized.

Today, donors represent a spectrum of success stories—family business owners, corporate executives, pioneers in new technologies, investors in the stock market and real estate—and their diversity is reflected in the variety of family foundations. The smallest family foundations—by far the majority—have assets of less than $1 million, give primarily in their local communities, and are run by family volunteers, often out of their homes. The largest have assets worth billions of dollars, corporate-sized professional staffs, and grantmaking programs that extend around the world.

Over the past two decades the number of family foundations has increased dramatically, even though donors can choose other charitable options that have more favorable tax benefits, lower start-up costs, and fewer responsibilities. If present trends continue, family foundations will exceed $500 billion in assets over the next decade. There are more than 60,000 private foundations in the United States and Canada, and by some counts, at least two-thirds of them are controlled by families.[1]

Their essential role in so many aspects of society (education, health, arts and culture, economic development, social welfare) and in private wealth management makes it important for us to understand them better. However, in spite of their scope and importance, they are largely unstudied organizations. Like all nonprofits, their functioning and structure have not attracted much analysis from business schools and organizational scientists. In addition, the tendency of families to protect their privacy, especially around financial matters, has helped keep all but the very largest family foundations invisible.[2]

Before we could use the research on this sample to bring family foundations into focus, we needed to understand the history of family philanthropy in general. Current trustees need to see how they fit into the broader economic picture in order to fully understand the particular choices and challenges facing their own foundations. The historical trends in private philanthropy, the ups and downs of public funding for social and cultural services, and the role of families as philanthropic sponsors, all help today's decision makers to understand the context of their stewardship and grantmaking. That context should inform the deliberations about their organization's mission, structure, leadership style, and plans for continuity.[3]

EARLY FAMILY PHILANTHROPY IN AMERICA

Philanthropy stems from a variety of beliefs, impulses, and aims, but history reveals three major motivational themes among founders and donors: the desire to support worthy causes, the quest for relief from taxes, and the wish to create a family legacy. We will examine each of these motivations in turn.

The Charitable Impulse

The impulse to use wealth for social purposes is the first of the core motivations that have driven the development of family philanthropy. Since the American Revolution, individuals have created small, private charitable organizations to care for the needy in their communities, reflecting the belief that private citizens share responsibility with the government to provide for the general welfare.

It wasn't until the late nineteenth century, however, that the concept of an endowed private foundation to provide sustained and systematic assistance took hold. The country had emerged from a period of rapid industrialization in which tremendous wealth was concentrated in the hands of a few bold entrepreneurs. Private foundations provided a means through which these individuals could apply the same resourcefulness and energy to solving social problems that they brought to their business enterprises.

Two pioneers, Andrew Carnegie and John D. Rockefeller, are widely credited for defining organized philanthropy and demonstrating its potential for improving the quality of life. Both set specific goals for their philanthropy, and both backed their projects with the money, talent, and follow-through to ensure their success.

The Role of Tax Policy

The search for tax relief is the second motivational theme in the history of family foundations. Whatever mixture of motives inspired the philanthropy of Carnegie and Rockefeller, avoiding paying taxes was not one of them. Both had been giving away large sums of money long before Congress passed the Sixteenth Amendment in 1913 that established the individual income tax. But beginning in the 1920s, the new income tax and related policies proved to be powerful factors throughout most of the twentieth century.

When federal income taxes were first introduced, taxpayers in the top bracket were assessed 7 percent of their income. Five years later, the top tax rate had jumped to 77 percent. Rates dropped after the stock market crash of 1929 but during the Depression and throughout World War II, Congress raised federal income taxes to what affluent individuals considered confiscatory levels. In 1945, the tax rate for the top bracket peaked at 94 percent and, throughout the 1950s and 1960s, it fluctuated between 70 percent and 92 percent. As tax rates escalated, people of means looked for ways to reduce their tax burden.

Philanthropy presented one answer. In 1917, Congress introduced the practice of allowing tax deductions on personal income for contributions to organizations set up for educational or charitable purposes. Individuals were permitted to deduct up to 15 percent of their adjusted gross income. In addition, in 1940 Congress enacted the federal estate tax. From 1940 to 1979 the largest estates were taxed at 77 percent, which meant that many families had to sell the family business or investments to pay the estate tax. However, there was no limit on the assets donors could transfer to private foundations. As a consequence, private foundations came to be seen not solely as vehicles for charitable giving but also a means for reducing income and estate taxes.[4]

The mid–twentieth century was a period of great prosperity and high taxation. Those family business owners who grew wealthy during and after World War II formed private foundations in record numbers. The Foundation Center report estimates that by the 1940s, close to 44 percent of all new foundations were family foundations. That percentage increased to almost 50 percent in the 1950s and 1960s.

For some of these business-owning founders, one primary motivator was a big tax loophole. In 1924, the Supreme Court ruled that a charitable organization could conduct a business that would be exempt from taxation as long as all the income from the business was used for charitable purposes. In practice, many donors stretched the rules by transferring ownership of their family businesses to their foundations. Donors gave stock in their companies to the foundations they established. They named themselves, family members, and close friends as trustees. In addition to receiving an immediate and full deduction on income tax, donors later saved on estate taxes. The gift of stock or property reduced their equity in their business and thus the value of their estate on their deaths.

Besides offering tax benefits, foundations also permitted donors to retain control of the investment, administration, and distribution of the endowment and income. Private foundations were likened to personal banks that paid high salaries to donors and their families, and gave them a decided advantage in exploiting business opportunities. Not only were foundation assets spared the high taxes that burdened other business owners, they also provided donors with a ready source of funds to draw on for investments—at a time when high interest rates made borrowing money expensive. Moreover, private foundations had the additional advantage of preventing outside takeovers of family corporations.

The benefits of private foundations were so generous that even newspapers and magazines of the day promoted them to readers. A *Fortune* magazine article from 1947 trumpeted the title, "How To

Have Your Own Foundation: Taxation Has Brought the Charitable Instrument of the Rockefellers and the Carnegies within the Reach of Thousands." The message was not whether individuals of moderate wealth should establish foundations but rather why anyone would choose *not* to have one. The advantages were too good to pass up.[5]

In the end, the extraordinary opportunity available to the wealthy for uncontrolled tax relief through foundations was its own undoing. With governmental oversight of foundation administration virtually nonexistent, the situation was ripe for exploitation. Although the opportunities for abuse were plentiful, most family foundation boards carried out their charitable responsibilities. However, some unscrupulous donors paid no dividends from their business to the foundation, thus leaving the foundation with no money to distribute to charities. Others used foundation funds to buy and sell stock and other property at prices beneficial to the trustees, or to make low or zero-interest loans to donors and their families. And in some instances, trustees invested foundation funds so recklessly that they jeopardized the foundation's endowment.

The glaring violations committed by a minority of donors and their families resulted in exposés by the press and investigations by Congress. The Revenue Act of 1950 was Congress's first attempt to regulate the mixture of business and charity in private foundations by requiring foundations that ran businesses to be taxed like corporations. Private foundations had existed for almost half a century without interference from the government. The Revenue Act of 1950 instituted some controls, but more was yet to come.

The most persistent critic of private foundations in the 1960s was Representative Wright Patman of Texas. He was appalled by the abuses that had been uncovered and intent on stopping them. His ten-year investigation of foundations culminated in the Tax Reform Act of 1969, a major restructuring of the U.S. tax code including a strict system of regulations that had significant consequences for private foundations. Congress set limits on the deductibility of gifts, instituted excise taxes, and imposed a penalty tax for self-dealing to stop the misuse of private foundations for noncharitable purposes.

Additionally, private foundations were prohibited from holding more than 20 percent interest in the voting stock of a corporation, and they could lose their tax-exempt status if they speculated with foundation assets. Finally, private foundations were required to make minimum annual payouts and to file information returns with the IRS that would be available to the public.

Some saw the stiff regulations imposed by Congress and the publicity surrounding the hearings as the death knell for private foundations. The number of new foundations formed in the 1970s did decrease, but the historical data suggest that the trend began well before 1969.[6] The Tax Reform Act undoubtedly frightened off some potential donors and created a dampening effect on the formation of new foundations. But the decline may also be attributed to the natural tapering off that occurs after a period of extraordinary growth and to the availability of other charitable instruments that offered savings on taxes without the administrative responsibilities of running a foundation.

Nonetheless, some donors still chose to set up foundations. The difference was that before the Tax Reform Act, the majority of foundations were established by living donors; after 1969, most were created by bequests in response to estate taxes (Boris 1987, 91–92).

Figure 2.1 charts the founding dates of the foundations in our sample, in conjunction with the key tax law changes throughout the century. The pattern of creation fits perfectly with the best data on overall foundation formation across the twentieth century (Odendahl 1987, 9, 83–85, 181).

By the early 1980s, the top federal income tax bracket had dropped to 50 percent, on its way to a low of 28 percent by the end of the decade. The tax incentive for establishing foundations was not as compelling as in the past, and researchers predicted a modest future for private foundations: donors would continue to establish new foundations, although at a slower rate, and most of the new foundations would be small (Odendahl 1987, 92).

However, far from stagnating, the formation of new foundations and, in particular, larger family foundations, soared in the last decades of the twentieth[7] century. Sixty percent of the new foundations established in the 1980s and 1990s were family foundations.

Apparently the analysts had overemphasized tax planning and ignored other factors that were motivating new generations of donors. One such factor was the increasing sophistication of the philan-

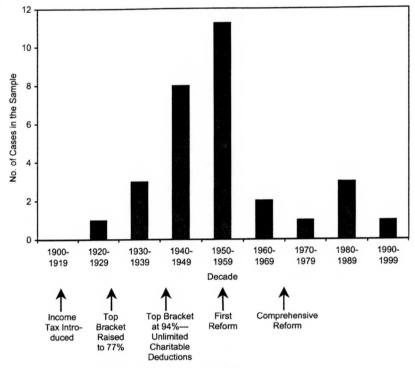

Figure 2.1.   **Sample Foundations: Year Founded**

thropic community. Although the Council on Foundations was formed in 1949, its early membership represented only a small percentage of existing foundations. Most foundations guarded their privacy, operating like islands unto themselves. As a result, there was little sense of community and a limited exchange of ideas and information.

The Tax Reform Act of 1969 gave foundations a compelling reason to come together. Alarmed by the severity of the reforms, foundation executives began to meet informally to discuss the implications of the new regulations. Over time, these groups recognized that they had other interests in common. What began as an emergency response to a new set of circumstances, gradually evolved into meetings of colleagues who came together to explore mutual concerns. Eventually these informal groups evolved into formal affinity groups such as the Regional Association of Grantmakers and many others (Nielsen 1985, 29).

In the mid-eighties, these professional organizations recognized that family foundations had different concerns from other private foundations and that family trustees were eager to learn from one another. They began organizing special conferences and workshops for family foundations and, as part of a family philanthropy initiative, educating financial and legal advisors to wealthy clients about the added rewards that could come from family members working together as grantmakers.

At the same time, the country was experiencing an extended period of unprecedented prosperity. Significant wealth was seemingly created overnight in the high-tech industries and in the soaring real estate and stock markets. The media played up stories of the new rich and made tantalizing predictions of trillions of dollars passing from one generation to the next.

Just as in the 1940s, magazine and newspaper articles promoted the benefits of charitable instruments and foundations in particular. The tax benefits were not as extreme as in earlier decades, but still they offered incentives to potential founders and donors, who could pursue their charitable interests while enjoying deductions against their income and avoiding capital-gains taxes on stock, real estate, and other appreciated investments. According to *Forbes* magazine, three-quarters of the very wealthiest Americans had their own foundations at the dawn of the new century (Barrett 2000, 104).

Philanthropy as a Collaborative Family Activity

The desire to establish a family legacy, or at least a participative family activity, is the third motivational theme. Tax minimization and the charitable impulse help explain the course of philanthropy through the last century, but why family foundations, in particular? Donors could just as easily set up donor-advised funds, charitable trusts, or simply make direct gifts to their favorite charities—as many of them did.

Those who chose to set up foundations often had another aim in mind. They wanted to make philanthropy a family activity and the foundation an enduring family institution. Families had been extolled and taken for granted in the postwar years of the 1950s, and declared "dead" by the end of the 1960s. By the last quarter of the century, there was a dramatic upsurge of attention and discussion about family vitality, and a shared social imperative to strengthen family systems.

This motivation speaks to one of the core family dilemmas of our time. Parents are simultaneously proud of the wealth they have created, and worried about its impact on their children. The role of a privileged aristocracy, inherited from Europe and expressed philanthropically in the American version of noblesse oblige, does not sit comfortably on the shoulders of the entrepreneurial successes of the late twentieth century. Many of the new wealthy fear too little time with their children, too much peer influence and television, too many "things," and too large a generation gap as a dangerous and disheartening poison. For some, family philanthropy is an antidote.

Beneficiaries of new wealth, by establishing family foundations, could simultaneously pursue a number of related goals: demonstrating socially responsible values about wealth to their children, counteracting envy and resentment in the community, and implementing their own vision of human, cultural, and environmental enhancement.

And instead of waiting to set up foundations after their deaths, more and more donors wanted to share the experience of grantmaking with their children and grandchildren. How well or poorly their organizational designs and styles of leadership match these family motivations is a major theme of the remainder of this book.

SUMMARY

The summary lesson from our historical analysis of family philanthropy is that the incentives and rewards of family foundations have changed as the economic and social environment has changed. The earliest foundations were created in an era of easily identified families of wealth, and quickly escalating taxation. Foundations were a convenient and irresistible opportunity to conserve resources within the family, and to protect the economic discretion of the generations in control. The foundations in this sample, which were established before 1950 for the most part reflect those goals focusing on tax-efficient philanthropy and community responsibility, especially connected to successful businesses.

As the century progressed, significant wealth began to emerge in a larger, entrepreneurial class, and reform legislation curtailed the most extreme advantages of foundations. Philanthropy continued to grow, but not necessarily through formal organizations. But by the end of the century, new social dynamics were ascending. The family itself was being challenged, and parents were looking for new ways to strengthen family culture and intergenerational connections. With family members scattered around the country and children growing up far from their grandparents and cousins, family foundations provided the promise of a forum in which family members could collaborate on important work, get to know one another, and deepen their connections to one another and to their shared history.

In addition, the visibility of new wealth was creating an active public dialogue about social engineering, public versus private responsibility for community enrichment, and meaningful citizenship. Among our sample foundations, those created in the later decades paid more attention to their potential as a means of inculcating family values and institutionalizing a sense of stewardship. They were more structured, more intergenerational, and prepared to be more visible.

It is interesting to ponder the current and future environment and its implications for the formation of family foundations. It is easy to predict that there will be expansions and contractions of wealth in the coming decades, and that the availability of surplus wealth for philanthropy will go up and down accordingly.

The trend toward more collaboration in the evolution of the family seems more linear, and irreversible, at least for the foreseeable future. Most sociologists agree that traditional assumptions about hierarchies of authority based on generation, gender, and birth order have been irrevocably altered.

The consolidation and transmission of wealth itself will not be a sufficient reason for collaborative action in family foundations of the future. Family foundations are being formalized as organizations, and families will be faced with the challenge of making them viable through their work and through the interpersonal negotiations among family members about obligations and rewards.

This is the great opportunity of family foundations in the decades ahead—to learn the craft of collaborative governance so that the economic, social, and psychological agendas can all be addressed in an effective and satisfying philanthropic experience.

NOTES

1. According to a recent study by The Foundation Center, even using the most conservative estimates, family foundations now make up 40 to 45 percent of all U.S. foundations (independent, operating, corporate, community). Others have put the figure closer to 70 or 75 percent. In 1998, there were close to 18,300 family foundations in the United States, and more than 5,000 were established since 1980 alone. Family foundations underwent a similar period of rapid growth in the middle of the twentieth century. Between the 1940s and 1960s, almost half the new foundations formed were family foundations. Growth tapered off in the 1970s but resumed again in the 1980s. By the end of the century, the rate at which family foundations were established exceeded even that of the middle of the century.

2. One difficulty in studying family foundations as organizations is the lack of a legal definition for family foundations. The term "family foundation" is popularly understood to denote a grantmaking institution whose policies and practices are guided by donors and/or relatives of donors. However, the government does not distinguish among foundations run by an individual, a family, or a professional staff; all are classified as private foundations. As a result, there is no governmental record of family foundations per se. When the Foundation Center, in cooperation with the National Center for Family Philanthropy, launched its recent study of family foundations, it grappled with the problem of identifying family foundations current and past. In the absence of a legal definition and precise statistical data to draw on, those researchers developed their own criteria to identify family foundations for the study:

independent foundations identified by the National Center for Family Philanthropy as "family foundations";

independent foundations that have self-identified as "family foundations" in Foundation Center surveys;

independent foundations with "Family" or "Families" in their names;

independent foundations with a living donor whose surname matches the foundation name; and

independent foundations with at least two trustees whose surname matches a living or deceased donor's name.

3. The researchers acknowledge the limitations of working with imperfect criteria, especially in identifying family foundations formed in the first half of the twentieth century. Nonetheless, the report, *Family Foundations: A Profile of Funders*

and Trends (2000), provides the most comprehensive summary of family foundations to date and the most complete picture of the "newer" family foundations.

4. Sarason was the premier social scientist on the topic of the impact of history and context in the creation of any organization. See Sarason (1972).

5. Nelson (1987) presents an excellent review.

6. See Rudney (1987).

7. Both Nelson (1987) and Rudney (1987) present data on this point, as does Boris (1987). The patterns described are explored in the broad context of American social history of the twentieth century in Robert Putnam's extraordinary *Bowling Alone* (2000).

II

THE DEVELOPMENT OF
THE FAMILY FOUNDATION

In the three chapters that follow, we identify and discuss three types of family foundations: the Controlling Trustee Foundation, the Collaborative Family Foundation, and the Family-Governed Staff-Managed Foundation. Most of the foundations in this sample began as Controlling Trustee Foundations, although none of them are still in that stage. The majority of the cases today represent some form of Collaborative Family Foundation. About one-quarter have evolved into Family-Governed Staff-Managed Foundations.

*The most important lesson from our research is that family foundations are not born as such—they **become** family foundations through a series of stages and transitions over time.* Their identity is shaped by the particular pathway that they follow, developing as both philanthropic organizations and family collaborations.

To achieve our ultimate goal of extracting practical lessons for today's foundation leaders and tomorrow's philanthropists, we used the stage and transition model at the beginning of this book to understand the developmental histories of these mature foundations. We found that their origins, the personalities and characters of the key individuals, the evolution of the family culture and the economic well-being of the family over time, and the critical events and turning points from the past, all have a great impact on governance in the present.

The stories that families tell about their ancestors and their legacies include much of what you need to know to understand their current options and, we believe, their likely futures. We also learned that, perhaps even more than in business families, actions in these foundations have very long half-lives. That is, without the ups and downs of business cycles to capture everyone's attention, the foundations tend to perpetuate core unresolved historical issues for a longer time, continually reworking and returning to the same dilemmas over and over, even as individuals change.

Chapter 3 explores in depth the experience of the founders of these foundations. They are the Controlling Trustees in the foundation's early years. In some ways this is the organization's "prehistory" as a family foundation, because true family collaboration was absent in most of them. The influence of these donors and founders is enduring, and without an understanding of how these foundations started, we could not make sense of where they are standing today.

Chapter 4 deals with the current state of most of the sample as they face the challenges of sibling and cousin collaboration. This is the heart of what makes all family enterprises special. For some, collaborative governance is a joy and for others a struggle, but for all of them it is a complex puzzle that must be solved if they are to entertain any thought of long-term continuity.

Chapter 5 looks at an extension of family governance into staff-managed foundations. This is neither the desired goal nor the inevitable destiny of all family foundations, but it is the choice of a significant subset. We look at the advantages and disadvantages of this form, and contrast it with the more hands-on family grantmaking of other cases.

3

CHOICES AND CHALLENGES FOR THE CONTROLLING TRUSTEE FOUNDATION

Nearly all of the foundations in our study started under the control of a single trustee. A few retained the Controlling Trustee form into the second generation and beyond, some more successfully than others. Since many of these foundations were formed in the first half of the 1900s, they were by definition pioneers, with few models to imitate. Therefore, their design and operations say a great deal about the imagination, personalities, goals, and skills of their founders.

At best, the Controlling Trustee Foundations provided a simple, low-cost organization though which families made significant contributions to society during the original donors' lifetime and, in some cases, for several generations afterwards. Historically, as it is today, these personal, individual donors are the "main army" of private philanthropy, and by sheer numbers their foundations overwhelm all other types. But as organizations they have drawbacks. Many were not thoughtfully designed at the start, and then expanded without a plan. At worst, some foundations became family battlegrounds, unable to move beyond a mission and a structure that no longer held meaning for many family members.

We found that the difference, to a large extent, stemmed from the founders' clarity and self-awareness about their personal philanthropic "dreams," and the degree of congruence between those dreams and the structure and procedures of the foundations they created. We can infer these dreams from what they told others about their motivation or purpose in establishing the foundation, the degree to which they included family members and future generations, the governance procedures they designed, and their skill in articulating a mission. Most importantly, as the stories of these foundations unfold over the decades, we saw how the founders' earliest decisions echoed throughout their lifespan to the present day.

THE MADISON FAMILY FOUNDATION

Peter Madison, a successful businessman widowed in his mid-fifties, began to feel ambivalent about the wealth he had created. Making it was fun, and he took pride both in his extraordinary financial success and the style, values, and reputation he engendered. The business success came at a price in his family, however. He felt positively toward his children, now grown into adults, but he didn't know them very well. They seemed to have absorbed or inherited some of his most valued characteristics: high standards for performance, high energy, and some skepticism about money as a panacea.

On the other hand, they continued to make choices—in spouses, lifestyle, politics, and career—that baffled and sometimes offended him. To some extent his offspring had all pulled away dramatically as they became adults, which he experienced as both a disappointment and a reproach.

On the advice of his attorney, Peter decided that a possible solution to his dilemmas was to start a foundation. He wanted to "walk the talk" about values and personal commitment. He had for a long time been a contributor to the local hospital and to medical research in general. For tax reasons, he could benefit from a more organized approach. He had his attorney draw up incorporation papers for his family foundation, "for the purpose of supporting cutting-edge medical research and maintaining top-quality medical service facilities throughout the metropolitan area."

He sent a packet to each of his children inviting them to join him in creating the foundation, asking them to match his $2 million endowment with a pledge of $50,000 each, representing 10 percent of their annual trust income. He also asked his children to pledge an additional $25,000 each year, and he expected to make a major additional contribution from his estate at his death. His children agreed to the proposal.

His semiretired status at the business allowed him plenty of time to meet with doctors and hospital administrators and to attend conferences, presentations, and lunches with worthy academics and practitioners in the health field. In a brief time the foundation became known as a significant resource, supporting groundbreaking research. Twice a year he distributed a notebook of the grants that the foundation had made, with vivid descriptions of the grantee programs and facilities. Then he and his children met for lunch to go over his grants and decide whether to award discretionary funds to a few new proposals. But when Peter repeatedly asked the children what they thought, they had little to say besides general support for the program areas.

After five years of this, very little had changed in the family. Peter wanted family involvement, but was not ready to share authority. His two oldest daughters had been as different as possible since they were infants, and they took opposite positions on every initiative proposed to the foundation. The sons were similarly different, except that the youngest one had very little interest in the foundation at all.

The meetings were enjoyable one-third of the time, passively quiet one-third, and openly rancorous the remaining third. Consensus was rarely reached, a problem that Peter addressed by making increasingly large continuing or capital campaign grants so that there was actually less and less discretionary money at issue each year. When a surge in the stock market led to a sudden need to double disbursements, the younger generation siblings were unable to reach any agreement after two lengthy meetings, so Peter put the new money directly into a trust fund for the local hospital.

Peter alternately encouraged attendance and "speaking up" among the offspring, and challenged their lack of preparation and fuzzy thinking. His oldest daughter, always his closest ally, began to help out in the foundation office as a volunteer after her divorce. She ended up doing most of the support staff functions and replaced her father at some external board meetings and donor functions. As Peter has withdrawn, the balance of influence and activity has begun to change slightly as the second generation has become more assertive. Still, there has never been any discussion of continuity or governance after their father's death.

This story, like many others, demonstrates the early phase of a foundation that had not yet quite found itself, although it was doing useful work and providing real help to grantees. The founder wanted to be charitable, to make a difference, and he wanted his family to join him. But his vision of how it would work was vague. He knew what he wanted to do, he knew what he hoped his children would think and feel and contribute, but he didn't know how to make it happen. His success in achieving his philanthropic goals has come at the expense of much of his family vision—at least so far.

Why has it worked out that way, and what else could Peter and his children have done?

For the Madison Foundation and for all of the others in our sample, the choices made at the very beginning proved critical. We begin with a discussion of some of the general characteristics of the founders, and then follow with a more specific analysis of the Controlling Trustee form of family foundation.

FOUNDERS AND DONORS

Why do families start foundations? Actually, for the most part, they don't. Families rarely start foundations *as families*. Individuals, or couples, start foundations. If the concept of a family foundation exists at all in the mind of a founder (and in our sample it existed only about half the time), it is—as in Peter Madison's case—a vague image of intentions, hopes, and assumptions. The transition to a family foundation in practice occurs later.

We did not select the sample based on the characteristics of founders;[1] we did not even know who the founders were until the group was complete. However, the group does parallel the "later-in-life" profile of the classic entrepreneurs of the twentieth century (Carland et al. 1984). A few were under forty, a few were over seventy, and most were in middle age (see figure 3.1).

They were overwhelmingly male. Most of the founders were married. The role of the spouses ranged from absolutely none to true partnerships. In six cases, the primary founder was a businessman who had been routinely charitable on a small scale, but his wife wanted to be more active. (We have no cases where a woman was the

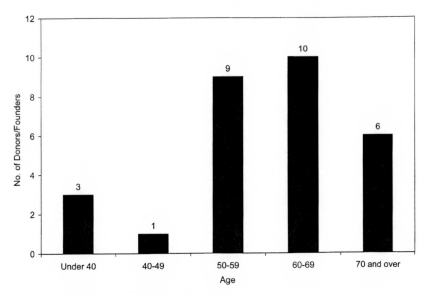

Figure 3.1.   Age of Primary Donor/Founder

primary wealth generator. There are two cases where the primary donor, of inherited wealth, was a woman, and in both cases it was her husband who was the Controlling Trustee from the start.)

In another two cases the foundation was created specifically to honor and support the wife's work, and it was assumed that she would be actively involved in the grantmaking. In seven other cases, the wife was a donor or passive trustee, but took no role in the foundation's activities. None of this is surprising, given the typical gender roles relating to business of any kind in the United States in the middle of the last century. However, in the terms of the dominant culture of that time, it does emphasize that the foundation was most often born in the "business" (man's) sphere, not the "home" or "family" (woman's) sphere.

Nearly all of the founders were business owners. Some of them represented the second or third generation in their family business, but the majority were entrepreneurs and business developers in their own right. They came from a range of religious backgrounds, but they were all white.[2] They covered the entire political spectrum, from radical social-change-oriented liberals to extreme conservatives. Some are remembered as wonderful men. Others were apparently unpleasant, cold, or nasty; the best their families can do is to acknowledge their success and their ultimate charitable actions.

FOUNDERS' MOTIVATIONS

We asked all respondents to comment on the founders' motivations,[3] and to give us evidence if they could remember anything in particular. Some of their stories are very specific. Most are vague. This is second-hand information, not self-reports of the founders themselves, so it can only be suggestive. Three broad categories stand out in these descriptions: financial incentives (mostly tax minimization), philanthropic agendas, and family closeness (figure 3.2).[4] They follow directly from the three historical themes discussed in chapter 2, but in this chapter we will address them in the order of importance as reasons cited for establishing a foundation.

Taxes

Minimizing taxes was the single most commonly identified primary reason that these foundations were started. In almost every case,

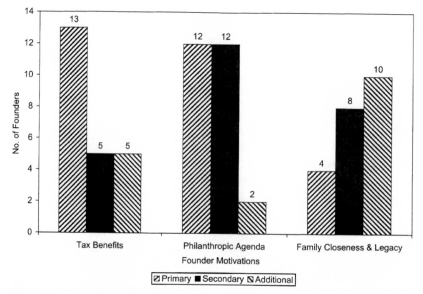

Figure 3.2.   Founder Motivations

someone brought it to the attention of the founder that a foundation would be an efficient way to use before-tax dollars for charity. The most common source of the idea was not a family member, but a business advisor. In the majority of the cases, an accountant or attorney appears to have been the first one to suggest organizing charitable activities into a foundation. Some of the founders had always been willing to pay their share of taxes but decided it would be foolish not to take advantage of this incentive in tax law. In other cases, the descendants specifically describe the donor's purpose as: "They just didn't want to give the government *any* of their money."

Philanthropic Agenda

As the respondents remember it, in this sample the motivation to enact a set of philanthropic values was equally as important as tax benefits. That does not mean that these founders were all active philanthropists. The philanthropic history of these founders is mixed (figure 3.3).

In about one-third of the thirty cases, philanthropy had been a central part of the founders' lives before the creation of the foundation, and in another third the families report that the founders had

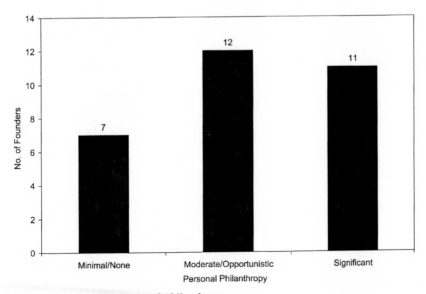

Figure 3.3.   Previous Personal Philanthropy

been making moderate charitable contributions for a long time before the foundation was begun. Family members tell stories about
grandmothers who dispensed cash at the back door to the wives of
needy employees, or executives who kept a checkbook in their draw-
ers to respond to requests from workers, who felt free to "drop in"
on the president with a request. As their enterprises were more successful, they gave away more.

For some of these long-time philanthropists, establishing the foundation was a legal technicality, barely noticed in the family. They went
on doing what they already were doing, with a different letterhead.

Kathryn and Arthur Antrim had extensive stock holdings from the sale
of family businesses. They were "opportunistically" charitable, responding to requests from friends and associates. Their attorney suggested a foundation as a tax-advantaged organizing structure, in response to recent changes in income tax rates. While they included
their two children and two advisors as directors in order to comply
with legal requirements, the others never attended meetings or participated for the thirty years until the death of the donors. Throughout
all those years the couple continued to disburse funds to traditional
grantees, primarily unchanged year after year, with an occasional
new grant if something piqued their interest.

In other cases, the formal creation of the foundation was remembered more distinctly, and fits the definition of a transition as described in the developmental model on pages 4 to 10. Often it took
place after some turning point or "trigger" in the founder's life: retirement, illness, reaching a significant birthday, or the death of a
spouse or child. Sometimes the foundation was specifically linked to
a lost relative, or created in honor of a particular purpose or cause.
In these cases, the start of the foundation represented a new decision to get serious about something that had always been important
but informal.

There are many examples in the sample: A prominent business
leader had long been well known as a prime contributor to all the
major institutions in his city: hospitals, universities, social service
agencies and general funds. The foundation was suggested by his tax
attorney at their review of his estate plan, triggered by his sixtieth

birthday. Likewise, a successful venture capitalist was stimulated to form the foundation by a health crisis. He had been informally charitable throughout his adult life. Following surgery, he was forced to cut back on his involvement in work. The foundation became his primary activity for the last decade of his life.

In seven foundations where the descendants identify philanthropic values as one of the founder's motivations, there was no personal or family history of charitable giving before the foundation was created. In these cases the donor seems to have come to a realization later in life that he had more resources than he could spend, or more than he thought would be good to leave to offspring. However, the practice of organized philanthropy—concept, mission, policies, priorities, and governance—had to be developed after the foundation already existed, and sometimes after the donor was gone.

Like many entrepreneurs, Sam Yates had been up and down financially several times in his career. He was smart, an intellectual, and involved in the community although not known as a philanthropist. When his fortunes turned up late in his life, he created the foundation at the advice of his attorney and closest friend, as a way to generate a presence and a stature in the community.

There were six cases where the founder had a specific philanthropic purpose in mind, rather than a general philanthropic value. These foundations were created to meet a particular need. When that need was fulfilled—sometimes during the donor's life, and sometimes after—the organization needed to start over and choose for the first time a mission that had a more distant horizon. (Of course, they could have spent out, but none of them chose that option.)

Family

The third reason suggested by descendants as the founders' motivation relates to family relationships and interaction. As interpreted by the current family, these donors wanted to instill the value of philanthropy in their children, and they wanted to encourage—or require—their offspring to implement that value together. Family members remember or imagine that these donors had elaborate "philanthropic dreams"—a fairly clear vision of the entire future family seated around a table (at least metaphorically), dispersing grants and bonding together as a result.

For most of the cases where family togetherness was described as an additional or secondary motivation to the financial and philanthropic agendas, it is talked about in a positive way in the interviews. In those cases the current family describe the value of nurturing family interaction as a given, in the past and in the present.

However, in other cases, it is more complicated. These founders who are described as motivated *primarily* by family goals were not among those with the highest levels of previous philanthropy before establishing the foundation. In addition, with a few exceptions, their descendants do not describe their families as particularly close. In fact, many of them seem to be compensating for concerns or regrets about a lack of family cohesiveness or powerful philanthropic values. Most surprisingly, they also were no more likely to actually include offspring in their original boards, or to be more collaborative in the grantmaking process during the early years of the foundation.

This creates a complicated paradox. When founders had an agenda—whether explicit or unspoken and assumed—to keep the family together through the foundation, they seem to have been uncertain, or ambivalent, about how to implement it. Many of these founders were strong, opinionated parents who ran their businesses with a firm authoritarian hand. Some of them clearly felt that they missed the opportunity to be more directly involved with their children, like Peter Madison in the first story in this chapter. They saw philanthropy as one place where everyone should be able to work together, because there was no personal financial gain at stake, and the work has an inherent moral quality to it.

However, these families were not skilled or experienced at collaboration, and the idea of sharing control was not easy for the parents. They also discovered that competition for status, authority, and recognition can be just as strong in the family dynamics of philanthropy as in the business or any other aspect of family life. The generous underpinning of the foundation's work does not in itself make the family any more able to act collaboratively or generously toward each other.

What resulted in many cases was a "disconnect" between the founders' imagination of family inclusion and the way the foundation itself was structured or, more frequently, the way it operated. Family members were invited to meetings, but not expected to say much. There was no demand that they prepare, or develop skills.

In some cases the offspring were young, but in most cases they were already adults. They were accustomed to being excluded from any detailed knowledge about their parents' work (except for the few who were being groomed as successors in the family business). In fact, they might not have even been aware that the foundation existed, or been any more familiar with its operation than they were with any aspects of the family enterprise. These second generation offspring remember an invitation to participate, without a clear idea about what was actually being offered. To refuse would have been insulting and ungrateful, so they complied without asking too many questions.

As the operations of these foundations took shape, the consequences of the ambivalence became more and more disruptive. As we will discuss later, particularly in chapter 7, the foundations that the family perceive as having been created with a "family dynamics" agenda have, in fact, some of the most complicated family dynamics in the generations that follow.

In the Madison Family Foundation we described at the beginning of this chapter, the second-generation siblings speculate that their father's desire in creating the trust, aside from taxes, had something to do with keeping the family together. They describe his motive as similar to that of many entrepreneurs who, late in life, try to recapture some of the family life they never had time for, and repair some of the damage done. "He sincerely wanted us to love each other and stay together. The trouble is that he knows only one way to relate to the family: by controlling us. While he has changed in recent years, enough of the control freak lingers to dampen our enthusiasm for working together."

Multiple Donors under a Controlling Trustee

We were surprised to find that, in about half of the cases, the foundation was begun with contributions from more than one donor. This includes married couples (11), parent-child combinations

(3), and extended family or family-and-company combinations (3). The married couple donors fall about evenly into a subgroup where the spouse was a silent donor, and a second subgroup where the spouses were both actively involved in the grantmaking. Both types of spousal involvement are discussed in more detail on pages 71–74.

In most of the parent-offspring combinations the offspring were invited to join in philanthropy as "donors," but not really as "founders." The younger generation experienced the call to contribute as an obligation—in fact, a payment in return for inheritance. Perhaps only through hindsight, they express little or no resentment. On the other hand, with little authority over the foundation's philanthropic activities, they felt equally little commitment. The endowment was like a tax.

For example, five offspring agreed to make an initial contribution and to commit annual funds from irrevocable trusts, created for each of them by their father when they were young. "What was our motivation? Because Dad wanted it." Their father agrees, saying that all five "were cooperative in that." In a similar case, the senior couple made 70 percent of the grants. Each of the three children contributed and controlled 10 percent, but their decisions required board approval.

Sometimes the family company joined the parents and offspring as a donor. The children contributed funds but did not expect to have any discretionary authority in the organization. Discretion over grantmaking was very specific, in keeping with the strict business protocols of the founders.

The Wyndford Foundation was created by a brilliant, exuberant entrepreneur. The initial donors were the founder and the Wyndford Corporation. Soon afterward, the company made a public offering, while remaining under family control. At that point many family members and the company began regular gifting of stock to the foundation. The large family business was the employer of all male members of the second and third generation, so the founder required all members of the first and second generations to donate 1 percent of their annual income to the foundation.

The founder's three brothers, along with some corporate officers, came and went as board members—but in name only. They met occasionally as a formality. The foundation continued to fund creative and cutting-edge programs, all initiated by the founder and implemented through his social and business community.

In a few similar cases, it was not a parent but one sibling who invited brothers, sisters, and sometimes a parent to join in creating the foundation. In all of these cases, there was a clearly identifiable "lead donor" who acted as controlling trustee.

Seven years after succeeding his father as president of the family company, John Volino invited his sister, brother, and widowed mother to join him in setting up a foundation. Each donor contributed some of his or her family business shares to create an endowment. Using the company lawyer as a fifth trustee and manager of the fund, John made annual gifts to their church and a few local charities. Once a year he called his siblings to tell them what the foundation was going to do that year. If his sister had a small request, he tried to honor it as well. Otherwise, the other three donors were silent. For seventeen years their foundation was a few-days-a-year activity, run out of John Volino's office.

In other multiple–donor foundations, the rights of discretion over grantmaking seemed to be in flux, possibly suggesting the early signs of a transition:

The Bell House Foundation has been run very informally—one might say casually—from the start. Although the second-generation have donated to it steadily, the first-generation founder was the sole signer of the trust document and remains the dominant influence, claiming the right to allocate 60 percent of annual outlays to projects he favors, since he contributed that percentage of the endowment. His offspring and codonors have always acquiesced to his preferences— even beyond a 60–40 split—but in recent years have been more assertive in defending their own prerogatives as donors.

Our general finding regarding multiple donors is that there was usually a lead founder, often the individual who was responsible for generating wealth for the family at large, or at least the designated steward of that wealth in his generation. The invitation to the other initial donors is experienced, at least in part, as an obligation. In most cases, but not all, the lead donor retained a Controlling Trustee authority—sometimes sharing discretion in proportion with the other donors, sometimes not.[5]

Childless Founders

Our sample includes four donors who established family foundations although they had no offspring of their own. Here our data is more speculative; the current successors of these donor/founders are more tentative in suggesting the donors' motivations for philanthropy, compared with the other cases where we spoke with children and grandchildren in a direct line. It makes sense that childless individuals who amass significant wealth would consider philanthropy. They do not have heirs who are depending on inheritances as a nest egg or to support their lifestyle.

Childless founders have few family options other than to involve nephews and nieces as successors, but it is interesting to speculate on their reasons for establishing a *family* foundation in the first place, beyond their desire to put wealth to good use and to avoid taxes. The descendants make some assumptions about these donors' family motivations. They portray the founders as looking for a way to get some of the rewards of parenting through nurturing the extended family, sometimes with the added edge of competing with their own siblings and demonstrating that there are other markers of a life's accomplishments besides having children. None of these childless uncles and aunts left significant inheritances directly to their extended-family heirs. This suggests that the foundations were a middle-ground solution for them. They could involve their extended family in their wealth, without overstepping an implicit boundary and treating them like offspring.

The niece of one childless founder had a very positive analysis of her uncle's motivation, and even more appreciation of the unintended result. "Uncle Bob was shrewd enough to realize that the foundation would be a way to carry on his name forever. He didn't want to give his money to the government, and he didn't want to give it to us, but he wanted us to remember who he was, so this was the perfect solution.

"He also told us, 'Don't stay together; that always leads to fights.' After all, we weren't his children, and he didn't care if we kept unified. So this has worked out contrary to his wishes, and it has been the best thing possible. Whether he wanted to or not, through his efforts he has given us the privilege of being charitable—for which he deserves recognition—and he has kept us all together, for which we are very grateful."

Whatever the motivations of these childless donors, they did not discuss them with their successors during their lifetimes. In none of these cases did the donor fully explain why the foundation existed, or what he expected of the extended family who were his successors. Perhaps as a result, the second generation in all four of these cases expressed more than the usual level of uncertainty about their obligations to the founder. Consequently, the early years after the death of a childless donor invariably entailed "starting from scratch" for the next generation of trustees and directors.

THE TRANSITION TO A FORMAL FOUNDATION

The transition model helps us understand the meaning of the creation of a formal foundation in these families. In about one-third of the cases, the founding was a nonevent—a mechanical action for tax reasons, usually initiated and carried out by a professional advisor. In these cases the organization of the foundation received little attention at the beginning. The issues of mission and operations and involvement were left to a later time. These cases still have the essential questions of founding—Why does this organization exist, and who cares enough to sustain it?—in front of them.

In another half of the cases, establishing the foundation marked an important transition in the life of the donor. In those examples, the pressures of wealth, tax policy, aging, social reputation and social responsibility, and family evolution were building in the donors. At some point, a trigger stimulated the donor's response of organizing philanthropy. It may have been an environmental change, a personal crisis, or the intervention of an outsider, such as an advisor or a friend. The foundation was the action that resulted.

Nevertheless, most of these founders stumbled when it came to the main components of the transition. The tasks of exploration and commitment to an appropriate model were often short-changed. These are the cases of personal organized philanthropy, effective and meaningful, but incomplete.

There was typically a vague dream of family involvement which was not fully articulated. The options for philanthropy were not explored. The structure and procedures of the organization were left to the attorneys' boilerplate. Rules, expectations, and processes for involving others, especially offspring, were not thought through, and almost never worked out jointly. Faced with this unfamiliar world of formalized philanthropy, the founders fell back on old patterns.

These are the foundations that faced a significant second transition at the end of the donor's life or early in the second generation's tenure. The success of that second transition, to collaborative family philanthropy, determined the success of the foundation.

Finally, there was a small group of families that fully engaged in a transition to collaborative philanthropy at the beginning of the foundation. They anticipated continuity and explored a range of designs and missions. They used the early years of the foundation to test out different ways to operate and to share authority. Those foundations set in motion the process of evolution from the beginning. All of the foundations in this sample got to their "moment of reckoning" about collaborative continuity sooner or later—but these few cases had a head start, as we will see in chapter 4.

THE CRITICAL EARLY DECISIONS

In the sections that follow, we will explore the earliest decisions made by founders in our sample as they established their foundations, and the effects of those decisions on the generations that followed. Not surprisingly, *control* appears as a major theme in these founders' critical choices.

Funding and Control

Current trustees and directors are remarkably unclear about the sources of the original funds. It appears that only about one-third of the foundations were endowed at the beginning. Even for those, the original endowments were very modest, ranging from a few thousand dollars to a few million dollars, with a very few larger endowments. Seventeen of the foundations began primarily as pass-through systems. They were funded annually by personal gifts or corporate contributions, to cover the outlays. In some of the trust structures, the dividend income from stocks deposited in the trust was available for grantmaking, although the endowment itself was not in the foundation.

The endowments were built slowly over years, with spikes of growth at the death of family members or the sale of family companies. Tax law revisions that required the liquidation of family business stock in some cases led to sudden growth, or even multiplication, of foundation portfolios. Periods of great stock market advances, especially in the last quarter of the 1900s, also changed most of these foundations from small to moderate, or moderate to very large.

This early dependence on annual contributions is more than an accounting factor for these organizations. It underscores their lack of organizational independence. Effective organizational governance requires that the leaders and policymakers have control over the organization's finances. When the level of funding each year was determined by the founder, it underscored the personal definition of the foundation operation. Any impetus toward long-term vision or mission, strategic grantmaking, or even negotiated priorities within a governance group was limited by the uncertainty about funding level and the dependence on the individual judgment of the founder. This issue is related to the distinction between donors and founders, mentioned above. When the founder continues to exercise the role of donor over and over, year after year, the foundation is more likely to remain a personal charity.

Original Structure and Control

Ten of the foundations started as trusts. Twenty began as corporations. We looked carefully at the implications of whether the original governing structure was a trustee or directors group, and found little of consequence. Both forms are evenly spread across the decades. Trusts are slightly more likely to include nonfamily trustees at the start than corporations are to include nonfamily directors, but the difference is not significant. In this sample the legal structure

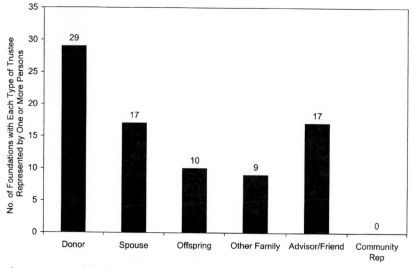

Figure 3.4.   Original Trustee/Director Categories

seems to be a function of the fashion of the time, the specific tax advantages of one form or the other, or the preferences of the legal advisors who did the paperwork.

The makeup of the original board or trustee group is presented in figure 3.4.

Spouses of the founder are included in about half of the cases. At least one offspring is included in one-third, and the same percentage have some other family members. The distribution of spouses is interesting. In seven cases, the spouse was the only family member joining the founder. Several of these were true marital partnerships, with a close collaboration between the partners. On the other hand, there are also eight cases where the spouse is not included, but offspring or other family members are.

Seven of the foundations did not include any other family besides the donor on the original board. Those seven were the most clear personal philanthropic vehicles for the donor. The other named directors in those cases were business associates or financial advisors, always as support or in name only, never with truly shared power. None of our sample actually began as full community-involved foundations, with strong nonfamily directors.

Overall, seventeen of the thirty foundations had at least one nonfamily director on the original board. In every case these outside directors were close family associates, not independent community representatives. In nine of the cases, the outside directors were directly involved in the family business. In another eight cases, it was an accountant, attorney, banker, or some other professional with a history of working for the family.

In many cases, these advisors—usually an attorney, sometimes a financial advisor—were personally connected and loyal to the founder (and often the spouse), and had little contact with the rest of the family. This was particularly true in the five cases where the board was exclusively the founder and the nonfamily directors, and there was no other family involved. Even when the family were present in a subordinated role, the family trustees recall the feeling that the nonfamily directors thought of them as "pro forma" participants—present because the founder wanted them there, but essentially irrelevant.

A granddaughter of the founder remembers her initiation into the foundation as difficult at the beginning because of the challenging style of her business-focused uncles and, particularly, the family attorney. He had been a close personal advisor to the founder and was instrumental in setting up the foundation, and he had been a director since the beginning. "We were intimidated from speaking out by the lawyer. He was always cutting down others' ideas. It was as if he couldn't get away from being an adversarial lawyer. He just didn't understand about bringing family members together and encouraging participation."

It is interesting to conjecture about the founders' reasons for including these outsiders. This is one area where the descendents did not have much to say in the interviews. In the cases where the foundation was seen as a business enterprise, it could be that the outside professionals were assumed to have more business sense or experience. They would keep things operating according to rules, budgets, laws, and other constraints. In other cases, it seems that the outsiders were recruited to be referees. The founder was worried about sitting around a table with relatives. Perhaps they thought that the family would be better behaved if a "stranger" were in the room.

A few nonfamily original directors played a very different role. They were the founder's proxy in authority. The founder relied on their leadership and decision making during his tenure. In addition, in three cases they became the senior voice for at least an interim period when the founder withdrew. The outside directors can extend the Controlling Trustee era of the foundation, even beyond the donor's death.

The founder started the foundation at age sixty, with a business associate and a distant relative as passive cotrustees. When he died twenty-five years later, the two remaining trustees continued exactly the same funding pattern for another twenty-five years. The nonfamily trustee was very explicit in deferring any changes as "not what the founder intended." The second generation only became active at the death of the nonfamily trustee.

Overall, these original outside directors provided services, they fit the founder's imagined model, they kept the lid on family process, or they provided a link with the business, but they did not set much of a precedent of community involvement or independent input. The issue of nonfamily directors returns in later generations, but in a very different context, as we shall see in chapters 4 and 5.

Governance Processes

The structure of these initial boards is important, but it can also be misleading. The key issue is not who is named in the legal documents, but what role each individual played in the foundation's work. Participation does not, in itself, mean collaborative governance. That is, being on a team is not the same thing as competently playing a team game.

While there were many particular variations in governance process, we found that governance in the Controlling Trustee period could be broken down into three main types: The Controlling Trustee Alone, Controlling Trustee and Spouse, and Controlling Trustee and Family Partner. In every case, the individual control of these founder/donors was truly astounding. In fact, in practice there was not much "governance" at all in the beginning. Most of the foundations had only one board meeting per year; the rest had two. Twenty-eight of the thirty had no staff. The grantmaking support was provided by family business employees or personal assistants in about two-thirds of the cases, and by professional advisors in the other third. We have already noted that few had articulated missions. (A typical set of incorporation papers presents the purpose as "to provide a tax efficient and orderly system for their personal philanthropic activities.") These foundations were informal, minimally organized vehicles for personal giving.

TYPE 1: CONTROLLING TRUSTEE ALONE (OR SUPPORTED BY PROFESSIONAL ASSOCIATES OR ADVISORS)

In these seventeen cases, the donor/founder operated the foundation for the most part individually. There may be other named trustees or directors (usually dominated by business associates or employees, sometimes with one or more family members in name only). Nevertheless, there was no significant sharing of involvement, discretion, or control.

A donor established the foundation late in his life, to honor his recently deceased wife. There was no stated mission, no meetings, and no grantmaking process. Business associates handled the minimal paperwork. The founder wrote checks at the end of each year, usually in the range of $25,000 to $50,000, to traditional agencies and umbrella funds.

Sometimes the very personality traits that made founders so successful in entrepreneurship and wealth generation are the most complicated in the early governance of their foundations.

Edward George ("E. G.") Quigley had a forty-year reign as the rather autocratic leader of this foundation and only began to share grantmaking with his sons when he became ill at the age of eighty-five. The second generation did not have a full shot at leadership, as E. G. remained a presence for another five years until he died. By the time of his death, they had begun the transition to the third generation.

All the interviewees described E. G. as vibrant, strong, attractive, and magnetic with a forceful, and at times erratic, will. In general, his sons commented positively on his good qualities, but also made it clear that, in their eyes, he was a difficult, ornery character as well. The sons are quick to remember his capricious decisions, such as disinheriting them, and giving the beautiful family home and furnishings to charity without consulting them.

He started the foundation for several reasons: to create a place to deposit a large chunk of corporate stock for tax reasons; as a way of handling requests for contributions (since "he was constantly being hit up for dollars from everyone"); and a desire to help the little guy and contribute to the community.

E. G. ran the operation single-handedly. He contributed family business stock to the foundation and then just gave away money. There was no staff. He selected a number of nonfamily directors, all from the family business, "to keep the family in line, since they all knew what he wanted." Three of them went on to serve for thirty to fifty years. As his son remembers it, "Father ran it like an entrepreneur, as he saw fit. He had a board only because the law said he needed to. My role was just a 'yes man'—and in fact everyone just nodded at the meetings and said fine."

This type includes the cases where the founder is clearly in control of the foundation, but invites or requires other family members (usually spouse and/or children) to be present and sometimes to make financial contributions. The message, whether explicit or implicit, is that the others are there to observe and learn, not to voice opinions.

A close associate and lawyer for this fourth-generation business owner suggested the idea of a foundation in the late 1940s following changes in the tax laws. The founder had always been very generous and civic minded. He had supported many causes and projects in the company's home town. As his daughter remembers, "My father just called in my brother, sister and mother and told them to come to the meeting and to bring $2,000. (He gave us the money for that purpose.)

"He said, 'If I can give money away and get a tax credit at the same time, this is best for everyone.' And then, he just told us about the foundation." They met three times a year, in very businesslike meetings ("Roberts Rules of Order and everything"). The lawyer for the company did legal work; the secretary of the company did the clerical work. As a result, the foundation had no operating expenses.

When asked how they felt about their involvement at the time, the son and heir to the business said, "I thought it was great," and his sister added, "I was on the board, I approved of everything, of course! My brother and sister did too—we all went with father's suggestions."

Not every Controlling Trustee went to such lengths to create a sense of camaraderie:

One nonfamily executive described the founder's response as the next generation began to speak up at meetings. "I've given you my proposal. All those in favor, say 'Aye.' All those opposed, say 'I resign.'"

TYPE 2: CONTROLLING TRUSTEE WITH AN ACTIVE SPOUSE

This was the second most common form of early governance, apparent in six cases. Most often, the husband and wife both contributed funds, either in the form of stock or cash or by designating income from holdings to be diverted to the foundation. The level of partnership varied from one active/one mostly silent, to a more equal partnership. Sometimes the children or business associates were named as trustees or directors, but in these cases they have no voice and usually did not attend meetings. Sometimes the founders managed the paperwork of the foundation themselves. In other cases, a family advisor, personal secretary, or someone from the family business provided support and clerical functions. None of these foundations had dedicated staff at this time.

Both of these spouses had significant inherited wealth from family businesses, but neither was active in those companies. They got the idea to set up a foundation from seeing the work of some foundation-supported community agencies and cultural institutions. There was no statement of mission or purpose. Two family office employees and two offspring joined the couple on the board. The meetings were held in the couple's living room, "whenever the founder thought they needed one. The father made all the decisions, the lawyer took notes, and their sons, if they attended at all, were not expected to say anything. Everybody knew this was [the founder's] foundation and he did what he wanted."

Even in the foundations where the spouse played an important role, it was mostly regarding programs and individual grants, not in overall governance. The particular interests of spouses were taken into account in granting priorities in nearly half the cases. However, there are no indications in most of the stories that spouses are also equal, or even active, participants in decisions about the appropriate size of the endowment or its management, supervising support staff, continuity planning, or policies and procedures.

In both of these two types, the founders exercised remarkable individual control. These foundations were not mission-driven but rather "discretion-driven," and the presence of other family members or outside directors did not constrain that control at all. There was little rancor or challenge. In fact, the offspring who were present were remarkably disinterested. And that seems to have been fine with the founders.

TYPE 3: CONTROLLING TRUSTEE WITH A FAMILY "PARTNER"

There were a total of seven cases that involved some form of significant shared leadership from the beginning. Four of them were father/son or uncle/nephew partnerships. They all grew out of family business working relationships. The philanthropic work was well integrated into the family's overall financial interdependence.

This father and son partnership was active in all aspects of their family enterprise, including several businesses and the foundation that they started together. They put together an endowment from family business stock, gifts from the parents, and income from several trusts. Originally the wife of the senior founder was also included, but she was never active, and after five years she resigned in favor of her daughter-in-law, who played a more involved role. The management of the foundation, the family's investments, and the businesses was a seamless structure of father/son collaboration. Grantmaking was very ad hoc: "We're sending you a check. We'll call in a few weeks to decide what it is for." As assets were sold or restructured, the pair assigned proceeds to the foundation or distributed them to other non-involved offspring. When the father died after twenty years, the second generation couple continued in an uninterrupted way, and began to involve their children.

Another father and son team designed the foundation together when the father was given a short time to live by his doctors. They saw it as an extension of their personal charitable work. The only mission was to support "worthy causes" in the geographic areas of their family businesses, and to keep the foundation's overhead costs very low. The founders did everything themselves. Although the son said he wanted his own children to be donors to the foundation and to be involved in philanthropy, he never included them in the foundation's work during his lifetime.

A father and only son, who worked together closely in the family business, started the foundation to honor their ties to the community. For fifteen years until the father's death, the foundation was run out of the President's office, managed by a series of corporate secretaries. Father and son made decisions together, informally, once per year. The father's brother-in-law was a silent, mostly absent third trustee.

Looking ahead to the transition to the second generation, there were two interesting consequences of this type of early history. In these cases where there is a two-generation founder partnership, the younger founder always maintained the Controlling Trustee form after his parent's death. Even when the second generation siblings were equal inheritors of the family business and personally close with the foundation leader, the one who had been the father's partner in the foundation did not transform it into a collaborative sibling-governed organization at the father's death, but rather replicated the senior founder's personal control.

This is in contrast to the cases that were individually controlled by a parent alone or the parents together, with only a passive role for any offspring in the first stage. Those were much more likely to change into a collaborative sibling system when the parents withdrew.

But the design of that later change was also affected by the pattern of sibling involvement in the Controlling Trustee foundation. If the first board included two generations—even if the offspring were not invited into active collaboration—it matters greatly whether all of the offspring were included or only some.

If all the second generation were included from the beginning or joined as they each reached a predetermined age, it sets a precedent of equal access and leads to later governance representation by branch. In future generations there is a very strong tendency to have equal numbers of trustees from the descendant pool of each second-generation sibling. This remains true in third and fourth generations even as the branches grow to very different sizes, with some moving completely away from the original locale.

On the other hand, if only some of the second generation were included, then the representation rules are less tied to "silos" of family branches later on. Other criteria besides equity can be used for the third and later generations.

Family Foundations and Other Family Enterprises

One aspect of family foundations that has not received the attention it deserves is the place of the foundation within the broader family enterprise. As a new field, the study of family philanthropy has naturally focused on the foundation as a stand-alone. It is clear from our sample that this is rarely the case. Twenty-four of the thirty foundations were created to stand alongside an operating family business. Many of them were household names in manufacturing, consumer products and services, and retail business. Thirteen of those families still have other business interests in common.

The grantmaking programs of nearly a third of the foundations were very closely linked to active family businesses at the beginning. Their primary purposes were community development, business public relations, and "giving back" to the populations that provided labor, services, and a home base for the business.

There was usually a business advisor or colleague instrumental in the formation of these foundations, sometimes on the board, sometimes acting as a staff director. The other family members involved in these cases were also leaders in the business. During this early stage, these foundations were handled as business and public relations operations. The grantmaking process was set up to maximize efficiency. Meetings were minimized. Reporting was essential, but only to the degree that it pushed the "bottom line" performance of the organization.

Sometimes the business and the foundation merged in their role in the community. Especially in the twelve cases where the family business was a major employer in its hometown, the foundation can be seen as just one arm of the company's and the family's expression of social responsibility.

This family company was one of the most visible manufacturers in its small town. It was considered a great place to work; employees stayed for a lifetime. The second-generation leader was described as a very soft-spoken guy who connected with everyone in the business, walking the shop floors, greeting all 500 employees by name and asking with accuracy about their children.

The current nonfamily directors easily tell stories about the company and the foundation interchangeably, pointing out that this family was well known, well respected, and had done a lot for their community and state. The foundation was formalized in the late 1960s because "it was the right thing to do," and it continued an informal style of responding to identified community needs as they arose.

The longtime administrative secretary said, "The early grantmaking was to collect letters that had been sent, and when the pile got too high they would say, 'We better look at these,' and then they would sit down and write checks." This style has persisted, even as they have turned grantmaking operations over to a professional director.

In another situation, the foundation was established as a set of trusts, each funded with company stock. The board was composed of a mix of family and company trustees. But, for over forty-five years, this "family" foundation was managed by corporate executives as a community and public relations effort. "The meetings lasted 1/2 hour per year, just to sign papers. We had no mission, no specific programs. We just added up the grants to equal the funds available and we were done." The system was forced to change when the company was sold. At that point, a third-generation successor consolidated the trusts into one foundation, created an all-family board and, after sixty years, a genuine family foundation was born.

Even when a "family business" is a sole proprietorship or an individual entrepreneurship, the foundation can replicate the business design and style and emulate the same business philosophy. In a few cases it was evident that the foundation was another opportunity for the founder to be an entrepreneur. This resulted in a kind of philanthropic venture capital fund.

Since the founder was an investment manager rather than an institution builder, the foundation followed the same model: pick projects carefully but cast your net widely, look for great ideas that have the potential to be self-sustaining, do not foster dependency. As a result the foundation does not have a central programmatic theme, but more of a philosophy of this "investment" style of philanthropy. This has proven hard to transfer across generations, since it was based on such a strong reliance on the individual judgment and entrepreneurial discretion of the founder.

As these "business integrated" foundations grew, the taken-for-granted lack of a boundary between the company and the foundation began to be more problematic. Sooner or later there was always some uncertainty about the appropriate roles for family members and for company managers in grantmaking. Demands on staff time for portfolio management, legal compliance, writing checks, public appearances, and record keeping sometimes brought the issue to a head. Usually the family was happy to benefit from the "free" service that company employees could provide. As long as the founder was leading both systems, the potential conflicts rarely surfaced. However, the lack of distinction created very interesting challenges for the family when the founder withdrew, or when the business was sold.

In addition, as the foundations grew they emerged as a significant alternative system for involvement in many of these families. That raised all kinds of "human resource" questions: Who serves in the business (by invitation or demand), and who serves in the foundation? In large, complex family enterprises, what is the authority relationship among the operating business(es), the holding company, the family office, the trustees, the senior generation, and the foundation? What happens when the public identities of the business and the foundation are in conflict? Can they have different investment policies, or political ideologies, or social networks? These dilemmas reemerge more clearly at the later stage of the transition to the Collaborative Family Foundation, and will be addressed again in chapters 4 and 5.

Grantmaking Style

Only six of the foundations had a specific goal or purpose from the very beginning: two to build a particular institution, two to support a particular church, and two to meet a specific local community need. Another six had a general mission statement or some overall guidelines for the grantmaking program. For the remaining eighteen, there was either no mission statement at all or a statement so general that it provided no guidance on program or priorities. For example: "To enrich the quality of life in [...] through grants to registered charitable organizations"; "To provide a heritage of giving to charitable causes for [the founders] and their issue"; "To create a vehicle to carry on the tradition of giving of [the founders]"; or "To provide money to deal with the pressing needs of institutions engaged in activities of particular interest to the members of the [...] family." A successful businessman saw a problem, a community need, a disease, a gap in institutional services, or a political agenda worth supporting, and applied dollars to the solution.

A husband donated some of his corporate stock to a foundation with the sole purpose of building a library to house his wife's extensive collection of art books and works. The library became a significant cultural resource for the city and the local university.

The style of grantmaking at the beginning was clearly reflected in the resources available for program research and follow-up. It appears that only three of the foundations had paid staff from the beginning. It is difficult to be sure, because the living respondents aren't always sure who paid the salaries of the secretaries and administrators who managed the details of the early grantmaking.

In most of the cases where the donor was running a business at the time, the secretaries, managers, and occasionally the financial officers of the company did the necessary support work. It is unlikely that their salaries were apportioned between the company and the foundation, but there is no way to know from this data. The rest had family members or an outside professional volunteering to complete the foundation's work.

The lack of dedicated staff support, even in those foundations that began with sizable endowments or annual giving programs, adds to the picture of these young organizations. That is, they were not really organizations at all. They were activities—serious and consequential, but not formally structured. Their articles of incorporation or bylaws were perfunctory, boilerplate, and almost never read. They had no space of their own and no infrastructure. Their boards operated only on paper. Most of them did not have annual budgets at all. The founders kept an informal record of their commitments, and they made annual contributions to the foundation sufficient to cover the outlays.

In the twelve foundations that had some form of endowment, only in seven was it large enough so that the proceeds from the investments were sufficient to support the grantmaking. In all the other cases, the donor supplemented the income with direct contributions, either of personal funds or of dividends paid directly from company stock.

However, the lack of organizational structure and resources did not, by any means, preclude significant grantmaking accomplishments. Nearly all of these founders were personally involved philanthropists. *They felt little need for formal structure to accomplish their philanthropic purposes.*

Even while observing the lack of structure, it is very important to keep in mind that, year after year, funds were distributed and grants were made. There is not much detail available in the family records of the early recipients of grants. Surprisingly, most of the foundations said they did not have records of recipients until very recent decades. But the current participants have good memories of the early grantmaking.

"Our grandfather did not put his mission into writing; he acted on it." He continued his efforts to foster the education of minorities, particularly blacks. "Having suffered discrimination as a Jew, he was sensitive to discrimination against other groups." Other cousins described a co-founder as "a powerhouse in correcting social injustices." They supported minority education in numerous ways, some institutional (such as funding scholarships and hiring a prestigious consulting group to help a local college create a strategic plan and find a strong executive) and some personal (they taught night courses themselves).

They were creative individuals in their own business, and creative in their philanthropy (they were the first to fund a program to provide free legal services to Mexican Americans in rural areas of their region). And sometimes the giving was very personal. "Our grandmother demanded contributions of money and old clothes from all the family. Then she distributed them from the back porch."

Not all the cases were as hands-on in their patterns of giving. As suggested by other writers on historical philanthropy, the initial foundation grantmaking was weighted toward institutional rather than programmatic grants. There was very strong support for traditional recipients: colleges and universities, medical and health services organizations, and local arts institutions.

A few specifically prohibited grants to religious organizations, but seven others concentrated a significant part of their grantmaking on one religious group or church. About half were completely reactive, responding to requests as they came in. Most of the others had a consistent program of institutional support, rarely varying from year to year. Only three of the foundations were "programmatic" in their grantmaking from the beginning, initiating new program ideas with local agencies, integrating related grants, or working actively with social entrepreneurs to create fundable programs.

The primary restrictions were geographic, which was consistent throughout the lives of these foundations. A comparison with current

Table 3.1.   Grantmaking Restrictions

	Grantmaking Restrictions				
	None	*Geographic*	*Program*	*Grantee Type*	*Term/Size of Grant*
At Founding	5	18	8	3	1
Current	0	19	21	7	5

policies shows that the foundations have in general become much more self-limiting over time. (Table 3.1 compares grantmaking restrictions at founding with those currently.)

One area where the performance in this early stage was most underdeveloped was in program evaluation and follow-up. Only a small number of foundations did any outcome assessment at all. In some cases the family told stories about well-intentioned but misguided grants that had become part of the foundation's ongoing mythology.

A donor was in the habit of responding immediately to perceived needs in his community. At one point while out on a drive he noticed a church needing roof repair. He contacted the cleric in charge and made a gratefully received contribution for the roof. Then, year after year, the same check was sent to the church. Finally after a decade the new minister came to call, saying that the roof had long since been repaired and they had not been soliciting contributions for many years.

THE LONG-TERM IMPACT OF FOUNDERS' EARLY DECISIONS

One of the most important and surprising characteristics of the Controlling Trustee stage of foundation development is how long it lasts—an average of twenty-seven years. In twenty-five cases the founder/donor led the foundation for more than a decade; in fifteen cases, for thirty years or more. This creates an extremely powerful imprint on the foundation.

The Controlling Trustee model can even extend well beyond the lifetime of the donor/founders. In five of the cases, a second-generation Controlling Trustee took over the foundation and ran it with nearly the same degree of personal autonomy as the founder. We discuss this style more fully in the next chapter in the section on Delayed Transition to a Collaborative Family Foundation.

Grantmakers versus Institution-Builders

The most prevalent story is very consistent across these cases. A successful business leader, sometimes with the input of his spouse, had been opportunistically charitable for many years. At the advice of a financial advisor, he created a foundation. There was no mission statement. If the donor's style was to be very businesslike and formal, with written rules and procedures, then the foundation was probably created in that style. If the donor was more of an entrepreneur, acting impulsively or at least spontaneously, then the foundation was run the same informal way.

For half of these donor/founders, the foundation was not seen as an organization with an agenda and needs of its own, it was only "a thing we do." The activity itself was the focus of their attention. The organizational setting was only a mechanical necessity. They didn't worry about governance, bylaws, or policies—they wanted to distribute charitable dollars. Some opted to do it alone, some wanted their spouses or children to be present, at least as observers if not "limited partners," and some went back and forth between wanting unfettered control and shared commitment. Either way, it was the actual dispersals that they cared about.

The other half had a more "organization-building" perspective. They liked the idea of the foundation as an institution. They wanted it to have an identity beyond themselves, so they paid more attention to structure, rules, and formal authority. They deliberated about whom to involve and on what terms. They had a dream about the organization's future, even if it was not well thought through or ever discussed with potential successors. They typically expected that some day responsibility for the foundation would be passed to one or a group of the offspring.

Sometimes they expected that the designated successor would be determined by primogeniture, or that the business leader would take on the foundation as part of the package. Sometimes they expected a compensating or balancing assignment, for a sibling not taking over the company. In a few cases there was a consideration of who seemed to be more personally philanthropic, or to have the time or inclination to run the foundation. But resolving these considerations into a specific succession plan was left for a later time.

What both the "grantmakers" and the "institution-builders" had in common was little interest in conceptualizing or discussing a *governance model:* a system for exercising control in the organization. That is, like most entrepreneurial organizations, very few of these

Controlling Trustee foundations thought about building an infra-structure that would be viable in the future. They attended to the legal requirements, and sometimes obsessed about procedures and rules, but in this stage their considerations were all focused on operational smoothness. They did not link organizational design and process to future unknowns: how the siblings will work together, the prerogatives of leadership, the mechanics of representation, the role of spouses, the entry of the next generation, the operational implications of their own estate plans, or the professional staffing needs of the future organization.

While providing clarity about who was in charge in the early years, this informal, personal process built an organizational culture that creates real challenges for continuity. The Controlling Trustee's discretion is very clear, which reduces conflict but also does nothing to develop a capacity for collaboration. In the language of our developmental model, these Controlling Trustees neglected to prepare their organizations and their successors for a transition to the next stage.

THE DEVELOPMENTAL CHALLENGE: WHO DEFINES THE ORGANIZATION?

The founders' initial stance on the distribution of authority and the exercise of control has a profound effect on foundation governance in later stages. Understanding this issue requires understanding the founder himself, and returning to the discussion of motivations for establishing a foundation.

What kind of person creates great personal wealth in the first place?[6] Hard working, entrepreneurial, intelligent, fortunate?

Having generated wealth, a person must make some choices about what to do with it. If the alternative of spending it all personally is not attractive, then there are three "streams of disbursement" to choose from. You can give it directly to heirs, and then it is up to them whether they will spend it or steward it and pass it on in turn to their own children. You can return significant portions of your wealth to the public through taxes. Or you can give it directly to others who have a need for it.

Taxes and philanthropy have similarities as ways to redistribute surplus wealth. Taxes, after all, are a form of public charity. They are contributions from personal holdings to a common fund, out of which a board of directors—in this case, elected officials—make programmatic expenditures.

The difference is that in private philanthropy the donor determines who the recipients will be, while in the public charity of taxation, the donors' control over the grantmaking program is so diluted as to be nonexistent. In fact, the grantees themselves (the public) control the process, since they elect the board (the legislatures).[7]

Many descendants describe their wealth-generating predecessors as hating taxes not because they were stingy, but because they resented not having any say in the use of their contributions. From a distance, the overall flow of resources in taxation and philanthropy is remarkably similar. The difference is *control*.

Therefore, of the three options available to a person of wealth for distributing surplus resources—bequests to heirs, taxes, or philanthropy—*charitable giving, and particularly establishing a foundation, is the one that offers the highest level of ongoing personal control by the donor.*[8] These philanthropic wealthy are motivated to do something useful and instrumental with their assets. They believe that they know what needs to be done. And they believe that they have a right to do it, because they earned the money.

If this view of founders' motivations is correct, it makes sense that they would be reluctant to create truly collaborative, authority-sharing governance systems at the start. The foundation gives them control over the implementation of their philanthropic agenda. For some, that is all that the foundation needs to do.

It is more complicated for those who want to personally control the grantmaking but also to involve the family in the process. Many of them believe that they can accomplish both goals by offering *access* without sharing *control*. Whether through coercion or generosity, a desire to model values or to demand them, a wish to be close or an unease with closeness, the typical outcome is the same: "This is what I → we → you are going to do with this resource."

The system colludes in supporting the right of donors to dictate. Technically, there is no obligation. By law the directors or trustees control the organization. Clearly the endowment is not the donor's; it is the foundation's (and, as we discuss below, the public's, at least for the percentage that would otherwise have gone to taxes). Why do foundations implicitly agree to let donors control grant-making?

Several hypotheses come to mind:

1. One impulse that causes trustees to let donors control comes from deep within the family hierarchy. Because the donor *could* have put the money elsewhere, or kept it, or spent it, many family members act as if he still has it. In particular, offspring who are self-consciously aware of their potential inheritance are extremely reluctant to voice any opinion that makes them appear greedy, overeager, or interested in prematurely separating their parents from their money or their control over it.

2. Focusing on the donor's prerogatives is easily described as a constraint, but it also can be a reassuring refuge. If you are simply continuing a dispersal pattern initiated by the founder, unless something outrageous happens you don't have to worry, "Is this money well spent? Are we getting the greatest return for our investment? Are these grantees the best providers of the service we care about? Is the public interest well served by this program?" However, that interpretation is increasingly being challenged, even in family businesses, as an abdication of governance responsibility. Contemporary organizational thought is not sympathetic toward boards of directors who declare, "Whatever the shareholders and management want to do is the right thing to do—our responsibility is only to enable."

3. Professionals in philanthropy rarely challenge the basic concept of donor control. They are concerned, perhaps rightly, that the incentive toward philanthropy depends upon the donors' expectation that they have the right to shape the organization's purpose, and that that right will be protected in perpetuity. They worry that if the norm shifts so that donors no longer have unilateral rights to govern their foundations, there would be little incentive to start one. However, that is an untested assumption. In fact, it may be that creating foundations dominated by donor control discourages and drives away more philanthropic impulse in families than it nurtures, particularly among later-generation potential donors.

Most of the study participants felt that concentration of control was not a problem while the donor was alive and active (or at least in the early tenure of the foundation). The problem is that this initial implicit agreement to let the donor be in control becomes a template for later phases. When the organization's governance system is not given responsibility and authority in the organization at the beginning, it is hard to start to do things "by the book" later. The game instead becomes "who inherits the donor's right to control?"—even though that right never actually existed. Battles are fought over who sits in The Chair, or who sits at the table, or who has a more direct understanding of "donor intent."

The echoes of this early deference are felt very strongly as the foundation matures, even long after the donor has departed and the foundation becomes endowed. Throughout their lifecycles some foundations struggle with their sense of "whose money is it?"

Those who focus on the donor's contribution, whether annual or in a lump sum, are emphasizing the ownership aspect of private property: that is, the donor owned resources and "put" them in a foundation as a place where they could be used. In their minds, some strand of ownership remains with that donor. The donor/founders amassed (or inherited) the money, it was theirs, this is what they voluntarily chose to do with it, and the moral (if not actual) right to determine its use remains with them forever. This perspective can be so strong that it even obscures the cases where there were multiple financial donors.

For these "donor-focused" individuals or families, the right of the donor to determine the activities of the foundation is active in perpetuity, and sometimes is a deeply felt emotional commitment. They do not just disagree, they are deeply offended by efforts of others to reshape or modify the donor's agenda.

In contrast, other individuals or families are "organizationally focused." For them, it is the foundation's money. The donor gave it to the foundation, and from the day those papers are signed it does not belong to him or her anymore. The economic as well as the ethical "thread of ownership" is terminated. The foundation has its own authority structure, and it is not only the organizational leaders' legal right to decide what to do with it, it is their moral right—and duty—as well.

With this perspective, it doesn't make any difference whether there was one donor or 100, or whether the donations happened at one time in the past or continue. The donors were (are) the sources of the funds, but their control ends at the moment they write the check to the foundation. Semantically, these donors do not "put" their money in the foundation, they "give" their money to the foundation, so that it is not theirs anymore. As current leaders and participants change, so may some aspects of the foundation, without regard to the originators.

One powerful and often overlooked fact in this dilemma between "donor-focused" and "organizationally focused" views is that there are always at least two donors in a foundation. When an individual donor creates a charitable foundation, he always has a partner: the general public. For every dollar contributed by a donor to an endowment, the public makes a codonor contribution in tax abatement (since 1917, at least). For those foundations begun at certain times in the middle 1900s, the public's contribution nearly matched the family's.

This point of view complicates the donor-focused perspective that it is "the donor's money, put to use." In fact, the most conservative view of donor intent, arguing that donors have the right to determine the uses of the foundation's disbursements in perpetuity, should also be the strongest defenders of the rights of the "public" codonor as well, demanding accountability and community representation as trustees and directors. It is the "organizationally focused" individuals who should make the argument that the foundation can set its own agenda without regard to any donor, private or public.

There is, of course, a middle ground between the donor-focused and organizationally focused views. In this case the donor is looked to for inspiration, not control. While change is embraced, the organization recognizes that reinventing itself with every change of leadership or every new member on the board of trustees is not feasible. A core mission and a legacy of purpose is not just honoring the past, it is a good operational strategy. In choosing among the unlimited array of possible self-definitions, these foundations look to the donor for guidance, and in about half the cases it is there to be found in some form. Then the key challenge becomes: What agenda can we find that encompasses the values and passion of both the founders and the current enactors?

So the primary risk that the initial donor control creates for continuity in the foundation is that it complicates the development of an empowered governance process. Those Controlling Trustees who treated the structure, the bylaws, and the board's oversight responsibility as pro forma and meaningless at the beginning made it harder for legitimate authority to arise later. As we will see in the discussion of the Collaborative Family Foundation in the next chapter, making the transition from individual control to collective authority needs to resolve these difficult issues.

CORE DILEMMA: FOUNDER'S PURPOSE VERSUS FAMILY DREAM

The central lesson from the Controlling Trustee stage of foundation history is that every founder or group of founders has to make a fundamental choice. They can establish a foundation that is primarily intended to achieve a particular consequence in the world, or one that is primarily intended to create a particular process in the family.

Founders of the first type say, "I have generated wealth beyond my needs, and I want to put it to charitable use. There are issues or needs that I care about, or obligations that I intend to fulfill, and the foundation will do that in the name of all of us. Follow me, and we will make a real difference."

Founders of the second type convey a somewhat different message: "I have generated wealth beyond my needs, and I want our family to use that as an opportunity to demonstrate shared values and work together. Few of us may be involved in business together, but all of us can participate in philanthropy, and it will be what keeps us connected in the future. Join this effort, and we will all shape its future together."

In the first case, the founder offers a legacy of impact; in the second, a legacy of opportunity. Either choice is completely defensible as an honorable effort and a responsible utilization of wealth. But the paths of institutional development are very different in the two cases.

When founders choose the former—a vehicle for the expression of their personal philanthropic agenda—they should focus on clarifying the mission, formalizing the structure, and seeking successors to continue the work after they are gone. They need to be honest about their intention to control the organizational purpose, and not use coercion or guilt to require participation by those who do not share their priorities. If they cannot find any takers to perpetuate that particular agenda, then they should spend out or turn the foundation into a fund and let others manage it. This is a fine and underutilized solution for donors who have a clear idea of the foundation's best purpose and worry about it being corrupted by future boards.

If, on the other hand, they have the second goal—to create an opportunity for their family of descendants to work together on an ongoing philanthropic task—then their efforts are better spent on building an infrastructure that makes possible broad participation by family members, an education program that focuses on helping each individual discover the potential and meaning of philanthropy in her or his own life, and a process that maximizes flexibility, diversity, and the continuous reinvention of the foundation. They may be dominant during the early years, but from the beginning they have to offer more than access—they have to share control, and allow potential successors to be partners in charting the foundation's course. That is a difficult stretch for most of these donor/founders.[9]

It is only through looking at the experiences of these foundations over time that the importance of this core dilemma becomes clear. This is a choice, and the cost of ignoring it can be high, especially beyond the second generation. When the founder unilaterally determined the purpose of the foundation but at the same time also assumed perpetuity, sooner or later there was typically a slide into passivity, obligatory participation, and a loss of vitality. In this sample, all of these foundations continued, and some found a path to satisfying collaboration on their own, but it would have made the road to success easier if the donors had been more clear on how they saw the foundation's future, and what they were offering to those who they hoped would take it there.

Finally, while this is a fundamental choice, it is not cast in stone. Many founders want both personal discretion and the enthusiastic involvement of other family members. They ask, "Why not control the foundation during my lifetime, set guidelines for the future, and allow some flexibility after I am gone?" There are families that make this work, but it requires sensitive and very honest planning.

It is difficult to mandate one process in the present, but promise a different one in the future. Trying to exert unilateral control but expect enthusiastic commitment underestimates two costs: the problem of the patterns and habits that result from years of powerlessness, and the problem of the "dead hand" of the past governing the future. Foundations where the offspring and extended family are not empowered for many years, and where mission is constrained by the traditions or rules of the founder, may struggle for generations to form an identity other than the founder's work.

Founders who want to have personal control during their lifetimes but do not expect to retain it after they are gone can do their followers a great service if they make that intention clear and help the system prepare to implement it. Founders and Controlling Trustees can be more open and precise about their own purpose, motivations and style, while offering explicit permission to "reinvent" the foundation when control passes from their personal hands into the collaborative family system.

The explicit permission is crucial; otherwise following generations will be trapped in endless arguments about interpreting donor intent. It requires courageous consideration of each policy and procedure in terms of whether it serves the Controlling Trustee agenda of the present, or the Collaborative Family agenda of the future. And it must include preparation for successors that is meaningful and respectful of their personal interests, even if those conflict with the founder's. Founders who engage the next generations in this way have the opportunity to "eat their cake and have it too," while enhancing the chances for foundation continuity.

NOTES

1. In this research we tried to maintain a distinction between "founders" and "donors." Interviewees sometimes used these terms interchangeably, but they are not the same. We use the term founder to designate the individuals who initiate the creation of the foundation as an organization. They cause the trust or the corporation to be designed and to begin operations. Donors contribute funds. Most often the word donor is used to describe the source of the original funds, but anyone who adds to the endowment of the foundation is a donor.

2. We would have preferred a racially diverse sample, but the population of foundations in non-Caucasian families that met the other criteria of age and continuity

was very small. Only one appeared in our pool at all, and they declined our invitation to participate.

3. When exploring the earliest period in the history of these foundations, we are relying for the most part on the memories or imagination of current participants about the behavior and thoughts of parents, grandparents, and beyond. (Our sample did include four founders who are still involved in their foundations. Their own reconstructions of the past may be more or less reliable than the observations of others.)

4. See also Nielsen (1985).

5. There were a few cases where the multiple donors were in fact partners from the beginning. These were predominately cases where donors were working in a family business together and created the foundation as a cross between family and corporate philanthropy. These examples will be discussed in chapter 4.

6. Andreoni (1998, 2001) has done some of the best empirical work on motivations, tax incentives, and control needs in wealthy individuals.

7. You can make the argument that one way to increase personal control over public funds is to use wealth to influence public policy, through lobbying and political contributions. It would be naïve to ignore these widespread practices, but that does not change the comparison between taxpaying and philanthropy. Creating a foundation, and taking advantage of tax deductions for wealth distributed through it, is one of the most significant means for maintaining personal discretion over funds that otherwise would pass into legislative control.

8. Within the "inheritance" option, the counterpart to donor-directed philanthropy is a trust. Trust law allows settlers to exercise remarkable control over inheritors. While it is outside the scope of this project, it would make a very interesting research to correlate the levels of restrictiveness of trust documents and foundation charters.

9. An example, stated humorously, of the ambivalence of this approach, not from this sample but from the well-known actor, Alan Alda. "From the beginning, we've been on an equal footing with [our children]. Everyone has an equal vote. Arlene and I as founders don't have any greater influence just because we gave the money in the first place. We don't even have any moral advantage in an argument. It's maddeningly democratic. One person, one damn vote" (Alda 1996).

4

THE COLLABORATIVE
FAMILY FOUNDATION

There is a classic dream of family philanthropy. It has two parts: the work, and the family relationships.

In this dream the foundation is a hub of meaningful, important work, with significant accomplishments beyond the capabilities of individual family members: saving a symphony that would have dissolved, building a hospital wing to care for thousands of community residents, starting an after-school program for twelve-year-olds who otherwise would hang out in malls or return to empty apartments. Not every need can be met, but the most worthy and creative community leaders receive the help they need to help others. The results are services or institutions that would not exist without the application of the family's wealth.

The relationships are an equally powerful part of the dream. In the foundation, relatives bring their best selves into a room to work together. They listen, express their opinions, make reasoned arguments and find compromises, honor their parents and provide extraordinary models for their children. The family dynamics that have been wounded by old battles are healed here by the very nature of the activity.

Family members do not overpower, manipulate, undermine, or exploit each other for personal gain. Brothers and sisters reconnect with each other, recovering the appreciation and laughter that had been eroded by petty grievances or geographic separation. Cousins get to know one another. Grandchildren and great-grandchildren hear about their ancestors and learn what their family stands for. And the community sees that this is a family of quality, not just wealthy but generous, and unified in fulfilling its responsibilities as citizens and neighbors.

In the traditional dream of family philanthropy, both parts are essential. The work enhances the family, giving it a purpose beyond the personal enjoyment of their time together. In return, the family enhances the work, as the familial relationships provide mutual support in fulfilling a challenging commitment. It is the dream of *working together on this particular task* that leads to the creation and perpetuation of the family foundation.

Of course, in the actual living foundation, experience does not often match the dream. Sometimes the dream is intact but not realized. Parts of the work go well and other efforts fail, either through habitual mediocrity or spectacular mistakes. Some meetings may be enjoyable, maximizing laughter and affection and a sense of shared accomplishment, while others are torture.

Sometimes the dream is not just unrealized, it is not even imagined. The activity of philanthropy exists, but not the overarching sense of collective family purpose. As we described in chapter 3, most founders begin with a task, but not a vision. They are effectively charitable, but sharing and continuity elude them. And sometimes the later generations falter at the same threshold.

We have come to believe that continuity may not require a collective dream, but the transition to the true Collaborative Family Foundation does. Grantmaking can succeed with good "mechanics" even in the absence of an overarching purpose and a guiding dream. Governance cannot. A viable dream does not need to be fully realized, but it does need to provide an "imagined possibility"[1] of a goal worth working for.

At this second stage of development, if the foundation is to thrive, the family must consciously explore, choose, and find appropriate ways to implement its philanthropic dream. In the earlier stage the founder carried the vision himself. It was his design and his responsibility. In return, he had the authority to act. Whether his style was authoritarian or inclusive, he was the leader and the others followed. At this transition the organization changes from serving the personal agenda of the founder(s) to the collective agenda of a group of relatives. If that change is to have a good chance to take hold, it must be grounded in the collective dream of all the stakeholders. They must consider and share some common vision of the family's and the foundation's philanthropic potential.

We use the transition model described in the Introduction as our template for these changes. The *developmental pressures* build during the Controlling Trustee period as both the system and the participants mature. The *trigger*, either an event in the lives of the family or in the environment of the foundation, puts in motion a reconsideration of the organization's structure and process. The senior leaders are motivated to *disengage* from the old system and to enter a transition to a form that will be viable for the following generation. Then, in the all-important *exploration* phase, all the stakeholders must consider the alternative designs for the new system, taking into account their own motivations for engagement and the realities of the resources and demands around them. When the exploration is complete and the common ground identified, the *choice* of the new structure and procedures is made, and the foundation moves on into its future. For nearly all the foundations in this study, this transition to the Collaborative Family Foundation was the critical moment in their history.

THE OSTROVE FAMILY FOUNDATION

When they established their foundation, Mark and Janet Ostrove decided to include their five children and their attorney on the board. For two decades the foundation operated smoothly. Everything was very businesslike, with meetings and votes, but in fact Mark made all the decisions. Then the parents died close together, and their son Jack took over the foundation (the four daughters weren't considered).

Jack started out very individualistically, like his father, but after a period of quiet, the meetings became mired in petty squabbles and unacknowledged tension. The four sisters became more passive-aggressive, failing to read materials and canceling attendance at meetings at the last minute.

At first, Jack responded in turn by becoming even more controlling and dismissive. But he soon realized that his behavior only made matters worse. Taking the advice of a friend who was an experienced philanthropist, he tried a different tack. He gradually became more collaborative with his sisters. He refused to make decisions that the bylaws (and the tradition of his father's style) entitled him to, and instead asked for input and insisted on consensus. Over the few years that followed, the sibling group began to work well, enjoying each other, beginning to feel more competent, and increasing their collaboration.

Jack remained the nominal director, but all of the sisters joined him by taking executive positions. Ten years later, the oldest of the third generation became involved at the invitation of her mother. She joined the board and eventually took over her aunt's role as vice president. Five years after that she replaced her uncle Jack as the executive director.

CHOOSING TO COLLABORATE

Not every family experiences as dramatic and visible a transformation as the Ostroves. We found, however, that the families who most explicitly addressed the tasks of transition came closest to realizing the dream. They recognized the tug toward inclusion and collaboration, explored the organizational alternatives, chose a system and style of governance, and committed to achieving it. Those who didn't accomplish these tasks were more likely to veer into disinterest or disappointment in later generations.

Establishing the Collaborative Form at the Outset

Only one foundation in our sample was designed to be collaborative from the outset:

Constance and David Callahan specifically established their family foundation to be governed by their children from its inception, during their lifetime. The pressure built as external forces made this successful business couple feel increasingly vulnerable. The trigger was a combination of political events, business growth, and tax law changes.

Said Constance: "David and I began to think seriously of setting aside a sum of money for the purpose of establishing a charitable association, to be administered by our children. David had a consultation with our family attorney, who was familiar with some of the legal problems involved. After hearing his advice we called a family meeting at which all of the children were present. All readily assented to our plan, and having obtained their consent, we took steps to secure a charter and organized a not-for-profit corporation. After that, we adopted bylaws and elected a board of directors."

The sons and sons-in-law of the founders became the initial board, and the foundation began monthly meetings. In their first year, they made grants to 129 different organizations. After a few years, the daughters were also invited to participate.

The Callahans represent the only example in the sample of an initial Collaborative Family Foundation with a well-articulated participative grantmaking process and a strategic, programmatic grantmaking system from the very start. This beginning set the tone for the decades since. This was the most self-reflective foundation in our sample, continually reconsidering its mission and the effectiveness of its grantmaking. The Callahans also have one of the most elaborate representation systems, and the highest level of community representation on the board.

In a second example that bypassed the Controlling Trustee form, the foundation was established as a bequest. The donor was gone before the foundation was funded, so the governance was put in the hands of a family group from the outset.

Virginia Laureston Ashton was not known as a philanthropist during her lifetime, but she was a strong political conservative who objected to all forms of taxation. She provided that the proceeds from the liquidation of her assets at her death would endow a foundation, to be governed by the second generation.

The clear trigger was the donor's death, but the absence of any preparation made it difficult for a sibling group to start off as collaborative grantmakers. In this case they organized themselves enough to hire an executive director and let him run the grantmaking. They bought themselves some time with significant discretionary funds so that each sibling could carry on individual "checkbook" philanthropy, and provided only minimal oversight of the foundation's operations.

With this breathing space, they could afford real exploration of their options. Over time, they are learning to work together, and the nonfamily executive has proven to be a sensitive and skilled guide. In particular, the third generation are eager to be more involved and to create a more strategic, collaborative process.

There is a third case that technically began as a simple Controlling Trustee system, with the founder/donor using it for his personal philanthropy. However, he very quickly changed his mind, and within two years he had asked his two offspring to join him. So they began working on their collaborative skills almost at the very beginning.

"Iron Mac" McInerney retired after the windfall of the sale of his trucking company. On the advice of his attorney he established a foundation with himself as the Controlling Trustee and his children as silent observers. But in only one year, the foundation moved rapidly through a transition to an exemplary Collaborative Family Foundation.

The second-generation spouses were added, and soon thereafter a development program was put in place for the next generation. They have worked together to sharpen their mission and program focus, reach an agreement on discretionary funds, and manage dramatic variation in priorities and politics.

A critical example: one branch wanted to use their discretionary fund for an organization whose mission and values were offensive to the other branch. They realized that even though they thought of themselves as using the discretionary grants as separate "minifoundations," they were still viewed by the outside world as one foundation and one family. This led to an agreement on a new policy that discouraged using discretionary funds for organizations that violated the core beliefs of other trustees or with which some trustees did not want the foundation's name associated. "The fact that we are willing to agree on this policy without rancor demonstrates that, in the end, family relationships come first."

On the other hand, the foundation is not a pure democracy. There is a hierarchy of "centrality"; Mac McInerney is still the strongest individual voice, the offspring who works as executive director has the most direct influence on the overall operation, and the spouses are active but slightly subordinated to the blood family. Nevertheless, their ability to discuss issues openly, the mutual respect between generations (Mac does not use his seniority to overpower others, and they defer to him on issues they do not consider critical) have led to a working collaboration.

In these cases, the transition to create a formal organization and to a system of family collaboration occurred together. The "exploration," "choice," and "commitment" tasks were addressed by the founder and the other stakeholders together (or in the founder's absence).

FROM CONTROL TO COLLABORATION: WINDOWS OF OPPORTUNITY

For the much larger group that began in the Controlling Trustee form, a new transition was necessary to move to a Collaborative Family Foundation. In these cases the developmental pressure for change built up within the foundation after it was already operating as a Controlling Trustee system. As we will see, this pressure was often a combination of aging, expansion, environmental change, and a growing dissatisfaction with the rewards of the Controlling Trustee model. In the most positive case, the Controlling Trustee and the other stakeholders invested in the tasks of exploration, choice, and commitment together.

Most of these transitions took place during certain "windows of opportunity" that each foundation either passes through or passes by:

1. The founder's "moment of realization"
2. The death of the founder
3. The delayed transition into the third or fourth generation

Finally, some of our cases passed by *all* the windows of transition. Either the shift to a Collaborative Family Foundation was delayed even further, or they moved to a different form and chose not to engage in a dream of collaborative family philanthropy at all.

The First Window: A Founder's "Moment of Realization"

This route to collaboration includes the majority of the sample. These founders acted as Controlling Trustees during the foundation's early years, but at some time they initiated increasing participation from their offspring. The next generation family members were invited to "watch and wait," and the developmental pressures built. This period may be as short as a few months, or as long as years. (In this sample one foundation stayed in this blended state of "readiness" for over forty years, as the founder maintained de facto control from age forty to eighty-five.)

Then things began to change, often stimulated by a developmental event: a milestone birthday, an important death in the family or of an associate, a change in the status of the business, or a crisis of conflict or frustration in the Controlling Trustee operation. The founder had a sudden moment of awareness of two realities: that he was not immortal and must prepare the foundation for a future without him, and that the foundation as it was operating was not fulfilling the family collaboration part of his personal philanthropic dream. This "trigger" opened the door to the transition. New options for governance, or meaningful timetables for transition, were discussed—often for the first time.

Beginning the transition did not mean that the seniors were ready to back off yet. Many founders would initiate new grantmaking rules, but not fully comply with them. Therefore the formal structure and the informal process diverged significantly. For example, a programmatic grantmaking procedure may have been adopted, but the founder made large multiyear commitments that left little discretionary funds for the new process to disperse. Or there might still be an "out of process" bypass procedure that the founder could use without oversight.

Nevertheless, founders who took advantage of this "window" instituted significant changes. In this sample, some very common marker activities indicated that the real transition had actually begun:

- Holding a retreat to consider strategy or mission
- Redrafting the governance rules
- Hiring a consultant
- Increasing the intensity of immersion in a regional or national philanthropy organization
- Hiring someone, family or nonfamily, into a managerial role

In ten of the cases the marker of real change was when one sibling took on more of the staff functions, either paid or volunteer, or when additional second- or third-generation trustees were added.

Kathryn and Arthur Antrim managed their informal foundation for thirty years before a health problem led them to buy a second home in Florida. That in turn initiated the transition. At first they talked in terms of passing some of the administrative responsibility to one son and his spouse. But once the door was opened, the second-generation couple began to transform the foundation into a more collaborative family activity.

The "exploration" phase of the transition was prolonged. The seniors backed away slowly, and incrementally. Over a period of several years the offspring professionalized the grantmaking, added their siblings and in-laws and began to involve the third generation. The transition did not actually reach conclusion for a full decade. However, by the time of the parents' death ten years later, ten trustees from all branches of the family were collaboratively managing the foundation. At that time they had their first board retreats, formulated a mission, and prepared to bring on professional staff.

Sometimes in these cases of gradually increasing participation of the second generation, the transition was a smooth one. The offspring had observed their parents' philanthropy and wanted to continue it.

Polly Calkins established a foundation with inherited, appreciated stock, and her husband Bill ran it as a Controlling Trustee. Their children were invited to join the board, but Bill made all the important decisions for twenty years. One of the daughters, Mia, was identified as a "successor in training" and devoted significant effort to supporting her father and learning the work. When Bill resigned, Mia took over, following his practices and policies to a "t." Polly and Bill stayed on the board along with Mia's siblings, and the grants continued in the same program areas. As the second generation have aged and withdrawn, third-generation offspring have gradually been added.

This extended apprenticeship model worked well in this case. Even though the daughters had little voice in the foundation for many years, Mia says their introduction to the foundation was close to ideal. "It's hard when one member of the younger generation comes on board alone. My sisters and I had the advantage of joining as a group, so it wasn't so intimidating. Also, both our parents were teachers who always encouraged our learning. We approached grantmaking as students, and tried to learn as much as we could."

The shadow of subordinated participation can be very long, however. In the eyes of some, including a nonfamily director, this foundation's biggest problem is its tame grantmaking. "The board has been reluctant to break away from the traditional giving patterns established by the founder." He is urging the board to take more risks.

As these Controlling Trustees tried to change their style and prepare the system for the next generation, many of them learned that wanting family collaboration does not necessarily mean having the skill to accomplish it. Entrepreneurs—hard-driving, demanding, creative, individualistic, and opinionated—typically approach philanthropy the same way they do everything else. They have some charitable goals that they want to accomplish, and the foundation is their chosen vehicle. But their agenda as parents may be different. They want to encourage certain values in their children (a mature attitude toward money, loyalty to the family, noncompetitive mutual respect among the siblings, and a pleasure in compromise and joint decision making), not fully realizing that throughout their lives they have demonstrated a different value set (determined self-reliance, confidence in one's own ideas even when others are discouraging, and sometimes, competitiveness and even arrogance). In other cases, the power of their parental personalities has led their children to be overly wary, timid, deferential, or counterdependent. So although they decide to modify the foundation's grantmaking processes to require collaboration, they are not skilled at designing a truly inclusive process or creating a collaborative capacity.

Larry Erlich, an entrepreneurial, successful businessman, and his wife Sue were personally very charitable, and decided to create a foundation. Original trustees included the Erlichs, and three nonfamily business associates. Their son (the heir to the family business) and their daughters were added as they reached their twenty-first birthdays. When the last one joined, Larry "retired" the nonfamily directors, thanking them and saying they were no longer needed.

That was the extent of successor development. "Once a year dad would get us together to tell us what he 'recommended' for the foundation. We would all nod and say, 'That sounds great,' and then mom would say, 'OK, let's have lunch.'"

On the death of the founder, the Erlich siblings took over control, but they were ill-prepared for governance. For twenty years the brother managed the foundation very informally, with minimal input from his sisters. Their fundamental disagreements were mutual irritations, but never pursued to the point of serious conflict. Family business and family office staff did the support.

It was only with the emergence of the third generation that the inadequate governance has become an issue. Members of the now-large family who were recruited for involvement in the foundation complained about long-winded and directionless meetings, impulsive grant-making, and relentless petty squabbles. Those who were not engaged in the foundation wondered why it was continuing, and advocated spending out. Those who were more deeply involved felt frustrated and discouraged. They have made several attempts to revitalize the system, but it is hard to sustain any of them and the leadership has not been skilled or charismatic enough to galvanize fundamental change.

Despite the vague attempts to include the children, the first real transition to a collaborative structure was initiated only at the founder's death. The next transition, to a collaborative process, will probably have to wait for the third generation to rise to control, if it happens at all.

In some cases, it was not family dynamics or the maturation of the second generation, but economic factors that triggered a shift toward collaboration. The sale of a family business or a new bequest from the estate of a deceased relative dramatically enlarged the foundation endowment, putting sudden pressure on grantmaking. The Controlling Trustee needed help.

Although involved for some time, these second-generation participants were initially passive observers to the work of the Controlling Trustee. After a leveraged buyout of the family's major asset, the younger generation members had to redeem their stock. Faced with huge capital gains taxes, they each contributed about $1 million to the fund, and their father added another $5 million of his stock, doubling the size of the trust and creating more pressure on the trustees to come up with projects to support. At this point, the founder said he had "run out of ideas" and urged the second-generation participants to become more active in coming up with proposals.

In this type of transition to a Collaborative Family Foundation, second-generation trustees can be added all at once, as they reach adulthood, or according to some other criterion of readiness and appropriateness. When parents involve their children for the first time, after years of exclusion, the process by which the first next generation members are invited is very important. Sometimes the parents are unaware of how closely their children will watch their actions at that moment. All the kids, or only some? All at once, or one at a time? In what order: age, gender, role in the family company, geography, personality? Will rules of equality and balance be applied, or will the invitations follow interest, ability, preparation, commitment, or convenience? The parents may approach the decision in an offhand way, or use some "objective" criteria for choosing. The offspring almost always experience it as a personal, emotional, and meaningful act.

This foundation was governed for twenty years as a business-focused community service organization. When the nonfamily trustee died, the couple decided to add one of their four children to fill the vacancy. Two of the offspring had moved away. One was working with the father in the company. The other son, a middle child, was between careers. The parents invited that son to join them on the foundation. They were unaware of how important a gesture it was to their sons. The chosen one decided his parents were "reaching out to a certain side of me, encouraging me, and the chance to be involved with Dad was so important." The other son, working closely with his father in the company, wondered why he was not chosen, but felt it would be wrong to ask.

In general, among the cases that moved from Controlling Trustee to the Collaborative Family Foundation in this way, the "glacial pressure" built over time, through the aging of the founders and their gradual realization that the next generation, if present, had a very limited sense of commitment or responsibility for the foundation.

The "trigger" was most often an event in the lives of the senior generation that gave them a sudden sense of limited time and an unfulfilled family continuity agenda. The "disengagement" most often entailed some specific changes in the makeup of the board and the grantmaking process, but it was typically compromised by the seniors' ambivalence about stepping away and the juniors' reluctance and unreadiness to take over too quickly.

The "exploration," when it was done well, included retreats, the hiring of consultants, the involvement of nonfamily staff, and a new level of deliberation throughout the entire family. Finally, the "choice" and "commitment" led to some form of collaborative process, often involving many new trustees and additional professional resources for grantmaking. We will look more closely at these cases later in this chapter.

The Second Window: The Sudden Withdrawal or Death of the Controlling Trustee

When a strong controlling parent dies relatively suddenly, without having initiated a governance transition, the remaining family are confronted with an entirely new world. The surviving spouse may have been involved in the past, but in a subordinate or peripheral way. In some cases, there is no surviving parent or anyone else from the senior generation to take over, and the responsibility for the foundation is very abruptly passed to an unprepared group of siblings. The captain has gone, the ship is adrift, they don't have a map, and they have spent their lives reading in their cabins or playing on the foredeck rather than apprenticing the craft of sailing.

The founder in this small foundation did all the grantmaking. Once a year he called everybody together and told them to whom the foundation was giving money that year. When he died very suddenly, his widow was persuaded to continue as president to continue his work—he had left one-third of his estate to the foundation. She wanted to honor her husband's legacy, but neither she nor any of the family members were prepared to manage a grantmaking operation. They engaged the first in a series of professional executive directors, who have guided the foundation for thirty years.

In another case, three siblings, who were not previously involved, inherited responsibility for a foundation at their father's death. Their mother was the titular head, but with little energy and failing health. The brother, most like the father, assumed leadership but did not have the skill, interest, or time to do it with much enthusiasm. His sisters, always mildly resentful of their father's assumption that they were not appropriate heirs to his career, began to voice increasing frustration with their brother's leadership. Finally one of them took over. They struggled as a group to find a procedure that could work. They decided that the foundation was not large enough to justify professional staff, but none of them had the time to do the grantmaking the way they thought it should be done. They tried reducing the pressure on collaborative grantmaking by putting most of the money into discretionary funds, but all of them had trouble making adequate grants. In the end they gritted their teeth and accepted the burden and the responsibility of running the foundation, each in his or her own world, all feeling incompetent and frustrated.

There are some cases when successors respond to the sudden and unanticipated departure of the Controlling Trustee by immediately engaging the broad family in sharing governance responsibility. In a few such cases, the transition was facilitated and sponsored by the surviving spouse.

When the Controlling Trustee died suddenly, 90 percent of his estate went to the foundation, immediately expanding its endowment and its grantmaking obligation several times. His widow told their offspring, already in their thirties and forties, "You're going to help me with this now." She rotated them through one-year appointments as president, to work with her. Within a few years, the second generation began telling their own children that they would attend meetings and be involved as they became adults (16, 18, or 21). The grandmother was the leader, and her children and grandchildren all joined together.

In a few other cases, it was the sibling group itself that moved quickly to the broadest possible democratic involvement of the entire family. Perhaps as a reaction to the Controlling Trustee's authoritarian style of leadership, these families designed systems with minimal authority in any individual. They attempted grantmaking by consensus, volunteering for tasks, and rotating responsibilities.

This foundation, founded at the death of a childless donor, began with a brief Controlling Trustee period, the tenure of the oldest nephew. After only a few years, a second nephew took over, who believed that the whole family needed to be involved. He began to act as a "first among equals," purposefully limiting his own discretion and actively inviting collaboration. Over the years and decades that followed, the circle of involvement and leadership got larger and larger, until today fifteen of the nineteen adults in the extended family have an active role in the foundation.

In contrast, some examples bridge the area between this "window" and the next, when the transition is delayed into the third generation or beyond.

This foundation was started for tax avoidance by a successful businessman, who ran it as a Controlling Trustee for ten years with an attorney friend. When he died, he left nearly all of his money to the foundation. He named his two nephews as cotrustees with his friend. The founder had no conversations with anyone about the foundation before his death. The three men continued his institutional giving to a few selected organizations for the rest of their lives, followed by the entry and succession of their younger sisters. The design of a collaborative system took the next twenty years. Under the guidance of the sisters the foundation gradually became more inclusive and more formalized. They adopted bylaws, discretionary funds, succession rules, and began to talk about grantmaking priorities.

One of the interesting findings across many different particular situations in the sample was a period of paralysis following the death or withdrawal of a Controlling Trustee founder. This was a common phenomenon even when the second generation was supposedly prepared for the transition, but it was especially powerful when the founder died suddenly.

There was rarely a power struggle for control of the foundation immediately after the founder's death. Most often the board tried to make as few changes as possible to the structure or process. Grant-making during that period continued traditional obligations—under pressure from longstanding grantees and to the reassurance of the community. There was not much change in makeup of trustees, professional staff, or advisors—asset managers, attorneys, accountants, and so forth. It is as if the shock of the loss of the founder had left the system teetering, and everyone involved responded by making every effort not to add to the trembling and to let it settle down.

The senior founding couple had made all the grantmaking decisions themselves during their lifetimes, and the widowed father continued for the six years after his wife's death. When he died, the foundation suddenly doubled in size and all the grantmaking responsibility fell to their four children. Their first reaction was to replicate the exact granting pattern of the last years of their parents' control, and to simply enlarge the amounts and add a few of their own special interests. After a few years, however, they found that this "avoidance" solution was not viable. Feeling very inadequate about designing a truly collaborative process, they found a nonfamily executive director and turned the responsibility completely over to him.

This "posttraumatic shock" does not mean that the grantmaking comes to a halt. The typical pattern is for a period of continuation of the parents' grants, followed by the development of some extensive discretionary process. That may be formal, with individuals or branches having unreviewed authority to give away percentages of the funds, or de facto, with a kind of quid pro quo process of "you don't question my grants, and I won't question yours." But either way the foundations avoid truly facing the vacuum created by the departed leader and doing the constructive work of creating a collaborative system.

This "transition paralysis" period typically lasted between one and five years, although in a few cases it seemed to drag on for another decade. Several triggers typically brought this drift to an end.

The endowment may grow to the point that the trustees cannot give away the money fast enough. Or, most commonly, the "automatic heir," who was chosen by birth order or gender or role in the family company, runs into trouble.

Especially in cases where the second generation were not well prepared to run a foundation, this assignment of a successor may initially have been reassuring. Over time, however, reassurance gives way to frustration. The successors often try to replicate the Controlling Trustee model. They are misled by the acquiescence of their brothers and sisters for the first years. They often do not see the signs of increasing confidence in their siblings, and instead interpret it as meddling or resistance. Ultimately, the siblings or cousins interrupt the routines of grantmaking to openly challenge the governance process.

Once the shell is broken, the paralysis period comes to an end, and a whole generation of unexpressed dynamics can bubble up. Leadership is challenged. Marginalized or excluded siblings and branches ask for admission. Complaints about the meetings come in an avalanche. It is as if the founder is finally gone psychologically as well as physically, and the successors are suddenly free to challenge the status quo. Although it may feel chaotic, it is with this burst of energy—sometimes laced with rancor—that the transition to the Collaborative Family Foundation actually begins.

In a few cases, the successor at this moment realized—like Jack Ostrove in the example that opened this chapter—that the models of the past would not work in the second generation. "First among equals" leadership in a sibling partnership is a delicate dance.[2] The "first" needs to balance taking charge with being a team player. The transition is not just from one generation to another, it is from one system of governance to another. Not all sibling leaders realize or accept that reality, but those that do stand a better chance of shepherding the transition to collaboration, learning with their relatives as they go along.

Sometimes the new leadership hangs on to the old model tenaciously, never "disengaging" from the old template. The meetings may get so uncomfortable that the family turns for the first time to outside help. Eighty percent of the foundations in this sample had their first retreat to reconsider strategy, organizational structure, or mission between one and three years after the death of the founder. Others decided to bring in a nonfamily staff person, who began to formalize the process and mediate the interactions. Or a family member from the periphery, often a spouse or grandchild, became first a communication hub and then a management force in the grantmaking.

Alan Oliver established the foundation and ran it for twenty years with no involvement of his children at all. He didn't have any confidence in his children, and had been minimally involved in their upbringing. In fact, he vacillated between endowing the foundation with his children as trustees, or passing his estate to a community foundation.

In the end he did create individual inheritances for his children (then aged 27–35), endowed the foundation, and named them all trustees. But they were totally unprepared for the task. Barbara, the eldest, had some experience with charities, but the rest knew nothing about grantmaking, had never volunteered in nonprofit organizations, and had not been successful in their education either. Making matters worse were raging sibling rivalries and the siblings' personal feelings of insecurity and inadequacy.

First Barbara, then her brother Rick tried their hands at running the foundation, but neither could control the family wrangling or escape the criticism of their siblings. Throughout the entire decade, the foundation was a "theater," housing and stimulating the family conflicts that had been unaddressed since childhood.

But they were gradually learning. With the firm guidance of a long-time family friend and advisor, they became more skilled at collaborative tasks. Now they review about fifty proposals per year. Reappointed as president, Barbara does site visits and prepares reports. She has toned down her authoritarian style: "I've changed. I'm more self-confident now and more sensitive to my brothers' and sisters' feelings. When I changed the way I acted with them, they changed how they reacted to me."

Together the siblings have designed a way to begin to invite the next generation to participate, instituted policies and bylaws, and made use of a generous discretionary giving program to buy them time while their collaborative skills slowly develop. It is possible that in running the foundation with the help of a caring nonfamily guide, the Oliver siblings will mature together and become the collaborative family that their parents were unable to create while they were alive.

In summary, in these cases the pressure may be building during the Controlling Trustee stage, but it is not sufficient to change the foundation during the founder's life. The departure of the founder is enough of a trigger in some of the cases; in others, the early post-founder years are spent in paralysis and a continuation of the old patterns. The trigger, when it comes, typically is accompanied by a period of conflict. The "exploration" work is often prolonged. It requires essentially redesigning the foundation from scratch, especially if the Controlling Trustee did little to prepare the successors for governance. However, if the system is fortunate to find a skilled leader, either from within the family or in the form of a staff member or consultant, the work may ultimately be successful. Easy or hard, quick or slow, the Collaborative Family Foundation that emerges from the transition can be the blueprint for continuity through future generations.

The Third Window: The Delayed Transition to a Collaborative Family Foundation

In some foundations, the transition from Controlling Trustee to Collaborative Family Foundation did not occur in the last phase of the Controlling Trustee period, or at the death of the founder(s). Instead, the tradition of one dominant voice continued, with limited or no participation from others. In five cases, a successor Controlling Trustee emerged in the second generation; in two cases, the pattern continued beyond the second generation to the third.

A strong businessman created a foundation and ran it personally for twelve years until his death. His son took over both the family company and the foundation and continued as an individual Controlling Trustee for forty more years. During that period he added his children as trustees but with no actual participation. He involved nonfamily trustees as informal advisors. Then, at age seventy-five, he was persuaded by an advisor of the need to plan for the future. The advisor arranged for a retreat with the third-generation offspring. The father organized the retreat, but decided not to attend, feeling that he didn't know how to work in a collaborative process and they would all be better off without him there. The retreat marked a dramatic turning point in governance. The third generation designed a branch representation system with a rotating chair, some new strategic initiatives for the program, and an adjunct board for the fourth generation. Following the death of their father two years later, they are beginning to address conflict resolution and to create a more collaborative style.

Another foundation was managed by a sequence of Controlling Trustees, fifteen years in the first generation, twenty years in the second, and an additional ten years in the third. The third leader finally admitted other family members into influence. Within a few years the foundation hired its first professional executive director, held its first retreat, and derived its first mission statement. But it may have been too late—all those years of noninvolvement and autocratic rule led to fragmentation. Most of the family's philanthropy now happens outside the foundation. Some family members are trying to generate enough participation to transition to a professionally run foundation with steady but minimal family oversight, but it is not clear whether there is enough family goodwill to sustain it.

In a third example, the founder/Controlling Trustee died after ten years and a nephew took over both the foundation and the family company. The nephew purposefully excluded his siblings from the foundation to eliminate the potential for family conflicts. They knocked on the door, and he said "no, not now"—which turned into "not ever." They did a little grumbling, but accepted it as his decision to make. The new Controlling Trustee created a "distinguished" board of outside directors, and continued to support university capital campaigns for twenty years.

A potential "trigger" emerged: explosive growth in the family business, which was funneling dividends into the foundation faster than the Controlling Trustee and the board could disperse them. However, collaboration was not the first response. The second-generation Controlling Trustee consulted with his directors, and they all agreed that the foundation needed more professional management: a director to establish a giving program and money managers to invest the dividends. He hired a strong nonfamily executive director, and gave him free reign to develop a mission "that would allow the foundation to move forward in time and yet not disturb the dead." Although he also invited some of his children (already in their thirties) to join the board in a limited role, he was not prepared to work with them in transitioning to a true Collaborative Family Foundation.

After fifteen years of staff control, a second "trigger" occurred: the executive director's failing health. This time it led to one daughter taking over as president. Relatively unprepared for philanthropic leadership, she continued the departed executive's policies, relying on his advisors and staff to bring her along. Her father is still a presence, and the fourth generation is still young, but the third-generation siblings are for the first time thinking about putting their mark on the foundation.

It would be a significant culture change—perhaps not possible to realize while the second-generation Controlling Trustee is on the board. And there is still much uncertainty about collaboration. The third generation remains strongly influenced by their father's conception. As one of them put it, "This foundation is run as an independent foundation, not as a family foundation. The family just happens to be running it but their interests aren't influential. My father did this intentionally because he wanted this to be a professional foundation. We're here to do good work. We're not here to bond." The next few years should determine whether they complete the transition to a Collaborative Family Foundation, bypass collaboration and move to a Family-Governed Staff-Managed Foundation, or spend out.

In three of the Controlling-Trustee-to-Controlling-Trustee successions, there was a slight variation. A single founder or founder and his son began the foundation and managed it without input from any other family until the father's death. At that time, the person who entered the governance system and became a coleader with the successor son was his wife. In none of these cases was the mother a force in the foundation, but in all three it is the contribution of the daughter-in-law that brought new energy and helped the system continue after the loss of the founder.

A father/son team managed this foundation for its first fifteen years, closely integrated with the family business that was the preoccupation of both (the third trustee was a silent business associate). When the senior founder died, no other family members became involved, but the son's wife was brought in as the third trustee. She was quite involved in philanthropic activities before this so in many ways it did not seem like a memorable or eventful transition.

The couple acted as a remarkable partnership in developing the foundation and steering it through growth and formalization of its procedures. They talked easily of their work together, their shaping of the mission, and their pride in the foundation's activities. The husband's interest in historical and community activities seemed complementary to his wife's strong interests in the arts and culture. They each had their pet projects and interests, but they seemed to cooperate on setting agendas and conducting the work of the Foundation.

In a few of the cases, the transition to a Collaborative Family Foundation was delayed past the second generation not by a cycle of Controlling Trustees, but by the longevity of the founder. The first-generation leader stayed in control for such a long time that the second generation was already moving past middle age when he withdrew.

In some cases this was fully supported by the second-generation siblings. As the parent aged and withdrew from active leadership in the business, the foundation provided a place where he could remain active and somewhat "out of the way." By the time of his death, the third generation had reached adulthood, and they were the ones to restructure the foundation into a collaboration.

In other cases the second generation wanted to be more involved but were not allowed to, and that led to some elements of backlash in the family. The second generation's frustration or resentment was expressed in a number of ways that threatened continuity, such as lack of confidence in new leadership, or a general withdrawal of enthusiasm for the foundation.

In the Quigley Foundation the founder, E. G. Quigley, remained the dominant voice into his nineties. When he died his sons, who had been working in supportive roles in the foundation but were now already in their sixties, felt that the foundation needed an executive director. One of the third-generation cousins convinced them to give her a chance at the job, even though "they weren't very enthusiastic about it and my uncle didn't think I could do it."

The decision proved to be a good one; both generations are very pleased with the work Sarah Quigley has done in her brief tenure. In an inspired choice, she devoted her first years to an elaborate process of determining one major gift to honor members of the first and second generation. It kept the focus on the seniors but also gave her a chance to reorganize the structure and invite broad participation while protected from intense pressure of a quarterly grant-making cycle.

Despite the success of that effort, the second generation are muted in their endorsement of Sarah as the cousin leader and equivocal about their commitment to continuing the foundation. As they move into their seventies, they emphasize that there are no term limits on their generation. One of the seniors said, "There were all kinds of options. We could sunset the foundation, split it, or continue. Maybe splitting is the best thing. My brothers and I don't want to see the foundation run by outside directors and have it be a family foundation in name only. After all, you can only do this for so long." In contrast, the third generation is enthusiastic about continuing, and they anticipate some difficult discussions ahead.

Passing All the Windows

In four of our cases the family chose not to, or found that it could not, form a collaborative family-operated foundation at all. In each of these cases, the second generation had dispersed geographically during the years when the founder tightly controlled the foundation. When the offspring were local, they were not involved. By the time a transition was possible, reconnecting in an intense way was extremely difficult.

In two of the cases the dissolution of the family business rendered the idea of collaboration even more peripheral to the lives of the siblings and cousins. The philanthropic opportunity was not enough of a lure to justify the logistical headaches of travel and the requirements to stay familiar with their former communities. In these cases, the family chose to evolve directly into a professionally managed foundation, with only a moderate level of family influence and a significant reliance on staff.

For the first thirty years of this foundation's operations, the founding couple were the only trustees, and the wife was active in name only. The foundation had no staff and operated as a tax umbrella for the founder's personal giving. By the time he invited his three oldest offspring to serve on the board, they had each established their own foundation. They rubber-stamped their father's wishes during the last ten years of his life.

After his death, they strove to honor his interests—interests they did not all share. A strong family culture of conflict avoidance, however, prevented them from having frank discussions about their differing priorities. Moreover, their "philanthropic dream" was invested in their individual foundations. They found a series of experienced executive directors to manage their parents' foundation, but the board—now joined by the third generation—continue to avoid addressing fundamental disagreements about mission and strategy.

DEVELOPMENTAL CHALLENGES FOR THE COLLABORATIVE FAMILY FOUNDATION

Because the development of family collaboration emerged as a critical theme of the study, we looked closely at the key challenges that families had to meet to achieve their desired form of collaboration. In the remainder of this chapter we will explore five of those challenges: leadership, formalization, strategies for inclusiveness, individual versus collective agendas, and the approaches of ownership versus stewardship. Of these, the single most helpful guide through the transition from a Controlling Trustee to a Collaborative Family Foundation is inspired, charismatic, process-sensitive leadership. Good leaders can create the conditions for families to navigate through all the other challenges of the transition.

Leadership

As the Controlling Trustee stage comes to an end and the bonds of individual control are loosened, the system may have to deal with an element of chaos. Many forces of individuality, personality, and priority are unleashed. It is the most challenging situation for leadership.

Too strong a hand, trying to perpetuate or re-create the centralized authority of the former Controlling Trustee, will anger and disengage many essential constituencies. Too loose a hand, trying only to placate without providing direction and clarity, will be equally frustrating. This is the moment in the foundation's history when, more than any other, the future is hanging in the balance.

LEADERSHIP FROM WITHIN THE FAMILY

We have discussed the variety of ways that authority is passed down in the family at the withdrawal of the Controlling Trustee. Overall, about one-third of these cases were able to form a successful sibling partnership fairly quickly. As the transition unfolded, a leadership solution emerged from within the second generation that brought a new level of organization to the foundation. Another third of the cases also have solved the problem, but it took them longer. They went through a series of unsuccessful arrangements before they found an authority solution—usually in the third generation. For the remaining third, the struggle with family leadership was more difficult, prolonged, and in some cases never satisfactorily resolved.

This may seem a poor performance, but it is characteristic of family enterprises in general. The demands on second-generation family leadership are formidable. In this way family foundations are quite similar to family companies. Like the Collaborative Family Foundation, the Sibling Partnership form of family business is the hardest to structure successfully.[3]

Collaborative governance among siblings has to tread a delicate line between autocracy and chaos. On one hand there is the strong pull to replicate the individual control and hub-and-spoke structures of the earlier stage of one-person rule. Countervailing that is the push toward democratic equality among offspring. For a Sibling Partnership to work the parties have to negotiate a middle ground of participation and hierarchy. They have to solve the dilemmas of authority, differentiation, respectful disagreement and conflict, and of simultaneously looking backward and looking forward. It is a daunting challenge. Only a minority of family businesses accomplish it.

The critical process issue in Sibling Partnership businesses is equity. Whatever the division of labor, talent, interest, and authority in the sibling group, most sibling-run organizations are constantly renegotiating the fair distribution of resources, responsibilities, and rewards.

In foundations, most often the expression of that issue is in representation on the board. Siblings may have very unequal reservoirs of passion for philanthropy, time to spend, familiarity with the traditional program areas or the geographic service area—but that does not alter the strong bias in favor of equal representation on the board.

Three siblings joined the board of the foundation as their parents became frail and withdrew. For several years, each simply did what she or he wanted with one-third of the grant money. One of the next-generation cousins recalls, "There was constant needling, bickering, and belittling of one another's agendas. My aunt acted like the heir-apparent. My uncle was very contentious. My mother rode it out on the back of a few extra Bloody Marys." The aunt added her husband to the board, which livened up the meetings even more and caused some concern about a "branch takeover." As a result, the board was enlarged to include oldest cousins, and then some younger ones, to re-achieve equity across the branches.

The family's financial dependence on the business helps support the stability of the Sibling Partnership to some degree. There are tremendous pressures in a family company toward seeking the most talented successors and assigning roles according to performance. Parents who want to demonstrate that they love and value their children equally may make them all inheritors of the wealth and ownership in the company, but they usually try to develop and choose leaders who they believe will be most successful.

This often leads to what is called a "First among Equals" structure, where one sibling is given more authority in the business system, but requires the support and concurrence of the others for important actions. While it is true that the initial selection of the leader in sibling partnerships may be based on nonrational criteria (gender and birth order are the primary ones), those arbitrary characteristics are almost always augmented by meaningful ones over time.

For example, the opportunity to enter the business and apprentice under the Controlling Owner is part of the development package for the successor-designates, no matter how they are initially chosen. By the time the sibling generation rises to control, the "first among equals" leader has a real advantage in stature, experience, and ability. The rest of the group are very reluctant to foment revolution and risk the company's financial performance just for the sake of retributional justice.

That is not to say that fear of disruption gives the appointed sibling leader a free ride. The family business literature is full of stories of Sibling Partnerships that dissolve into chaos. Once given the opportunity, the sibling leader must show great sensitivity to group process. Even in very hierarchical systems where the successors are anointed and protected, if they do not have the skill to make the company succeed, the other stakeholders will not tolerate their leadership indefinitely without resistance. The great test is results—all leaders look brilliant when the system does well, and incompetent when it does not.

However, in the foundation the requisite leadership skills are seen as more democratically distributed and more easily learned, and the consequences of mediocre performance seem less devastating. Defining successful operation is much more complicated. No one's dividends are dependent on excellent leadership and organizational profitability.

The family culture may induce siblings to work out their competitive frustrations passively or actively. In about half of the sample cases where significant dissatisfaction emerged among the second generation, the response was not revolt, but disengagement. That means that poor leadership is tolerated for a long time, especially if the family has other business interests and the foundation job was seen as a "consolation prize" for offspring less talented or more troubled than the ones chosen for the company.

Siblings may grumble or complain outside the meetings to each other, but overall they respond to poor foundation leadership with withdrawal rather than objection. There were several cases in the sample where the siblings kept their frustration under wraps until the next generation entered the process. Then the most outspoken members of the cousin group sometimes began to suggest that the emperor had no clothes.

In the other half of the cases, the sibling generation had the opposite response. The lack of objective performance measures in the foundation, compared to the business, made the siblings more willing to challenge "first among equals" leadership on equity grounds. This was more common when the same sibling was anointed as leader in the business and in the foundation, and when the others—excluded by birth order or gender—took the opportunity to object to the whole parental logic of authority. Especially in families with high-conflict interactions and unresolved disruptive family dynamics, the foundation can become the arena for finally voicing the core antagonisms about sibling competition, parental favoritism, and exclusion from authority.

This foundation represents a case of a delayed transition out of a Controlling Trustee stage. The father/son cofounders ran all grant-making themselves for the first twenty years. As in all of the father/son cofounders, at the death of the father the son continued on his own, delaying the transition to a Collaborative Family Foundation for a generation. Twice a year he would call his sister, his co-trustee on paper, and say "It's time to give away some money." When he received a request for a grant, he would send back a check in the same envelope. He would occasionally do his own site visits and was very fiscally responsible, but most of his donations were spur-of-the-moment personal impulses in response to direct requests.

Although he discussed the value of philanthropy with his family often, he did not invite any of his offspring to join him in the foundation. All six of his children, ranging in age from thirty-six to fifty-two, joined the board at his death, but none was prepared to lead a foundation. Among the older group, only one was not currently involved with the family company, so the siblings decided to "give the foundation to her." It did not work at all. She reacted to her lack of experience and knowledge by attempting to replicate her impression of her father's style: autocratic, private, and disdainful of input or criticism. After a year she resigned in anger, the rest of the siblings hired a nonfamily executive director and another sister took over as chair.

The same resistances that delay the transition to the Collaborative Family Foundation as a governance model until late in the era of the second generation or beyond may also delay the emerging leadership of a sibling in managing the grantmaking. There is evidence in this sample that it is easier for families to accept a professionalizing leader from within the family if she or he comes from the third generation rather than from the second.

Actually, this confirms a general conclusion from work with family businesses: second generations are the prime holders of griev-ances, and third-generation cousins are more inclined to forget them. If siblings can avoid making it a matter of loyalty to perpetuate old grudges, their offspring are typically motivated to bury them and seek collaboration across the entire generation. In this sample there are eight cases of generally positive experiences of a cousin or the spouse of a cousin gradually working into a coordinating role in the foun-dation. Often at first it is a volunteer role, without a title. Then the role is defined a little more formally. Finally, a full title with a salary (usually very small at the start) is approved by the board.

LEADERSHIP FROM OUTSIDE THE FAMILY

For many of these foundations, the leadership that pulled them through the transition came from outside the family. An inspired nonfamily executive has many advantages in trying to manage this pivotal moment. She or he can be free of family history and culture, unaligned with one branch or another, and able to rely on a more general, conceptual or experiential expertise in philanthropy. Families are less willing to behave badly in front of a respected outsider. For those families who are determined or lucky enough to find the right executive, it can make all the difference.

Three of the foundations had a guide who had been close to the Controlling Trustee and who was also able to build relationships of trust with the second generation. These gifted and dedicated indi-viduals are truly treasures. If they can make the psychological transi-tion from personal loyalty to the founder toward a generalized com-mitment to the succeeding family as a whole, they are in an excellent position to help the foundation move from the past to the future.

This attorney and lifetime friend of the founder was an original trustee of the foundation, but always in a facilitative role in relation to the founder. When the founder died, he intensified his role as legal and family counselor to the second generation. As the founder's lawyer, his primary relationship had been with the father. He did not know the children intimately and, as a result, he initially recommended governance policies that required more maturity and cooperation than the siblings were capable of. He stayed closely involved, however, and began to coach and teach the siblings about collaboration. His policy was to gently nudge the board in the right direction, letting them handle as much as they could on their own. He stepped in only when emotions got out of hand, or when serious problems arose, but on those occasions he was willing to take a firm hand and act decisively to implement the majority will. "My goal is to come up with solutions that reduce family tensions and increase flexibility," he said. "I try to help them balance competing interests and avoid strife." The biggest source of anxiety in the sibling group now is how they will manage without him in the future.

In another case, when the second-generation Controlling Trustee reached seventy-five years of age after managing the foundation for forty years, he recruited the first nonfamily executive. The new executive faced the typical challenges of preparing for a generational transition: redesigning the governance system, deciding on a strategic focus for grantmaking, anticipating and smoothing out potential family rifts. He was successful on all fronts. A rotating system of leadership was designed and agreed upon, and an adjunct board was created for the next generation. With the help of an outside consultant, the family used a retreat to chart a better-articulated program focus and grantmaking process. The nonfamily executive is realistic about his pivotal role, but also aware that in this family he needs to be careful not to raise his own profile too much or appear to be taking control away from the family trustees. He seems to be a perfect fit for this system.

Still another foundation began as the charitable arm of the family business, run by the company's vice president of advertising. When the company was sold, the founder brought in a highly qualified professional grantmaker. He has been managing the foundation for the past fourteen years. One third-generation family member observed,

"The executive director and the trustees were a good match; they wanted to learn and he wanted to teach."

He designed a program to gradually wean the hundreds of small agencies that had grown accustomed to unreviewed annual continuation grants from the foundation, and asked the board to approve an organizational development mission. Once the board targeted the program areas they wanted to fund, he educated them about each area, writing concept papers, bringing in experts to talk to the board, and arranging roundtable discussions about the key issues in each area and how they were addressed by other foundations.

He also dramatically increased the staff (from three FTE to thirteen), formalized all their governance procedures, and in general oversaw the professionalization of the foundation. Within only a few years, a foundation that had operated informally for fifty years had been dramatically transformed into a Family-Governed Staff-Managed Foundation, with an active, knowledgeable family board providing governance and strategic oversight.

In many more (24) cases, it is the second or third generation that decides to bring in the first nonfamily executive. In a few cases this was immediate, but more often it followed the "paralysis" period and the first attempt at maintaining the old structure, as described above. These first new executives were successes in about two-thirds of the cases. In the other third, the board had one or more false starts before they found someone who was compatible with the group. Once they found the right person, however, it was a great reassurance to the family and a stimulus for a more general reconsideration of the fundamental structure and process of the foundation going forward.

When the oldest sibling was unable to make things work by replicating her father's highly controlling authoritarian style, the sibling group decided to find outside help. In a short period, they added a nonfamily executive director, turned management of the endowment portfolio over to professional managers, and hired a consultant to guide them through program design and strategy and to plan for including the next generation. "There's no doubt about it. Those choices were the key to our success."

While an increasing role for nonfamily staff is often the consequence of growth, it doesn't always happen that way. Some foundations find nonfamily professional staff while they are still quite small. In some small families, there is no available family member to actually run the grantmaking, although the family is very capable and interested in setting program goals and overseeing the priorities.

Following the sudden death of the founder, the siblings and parent who made up the board felt that it would be helpful for the founder's widow to take over the presidency as a way to preoccupy and distract her from her grief. After a few years, the death of two of the four family trustees enlarged the foundation endowment—what had begun twenty years earlier with $100,000 was now responsible for dispersing $1 million per year in grants. Even with the foundation's local and specific program, the president was clearly not able to handle the new volume of grantmaking. The key stimulus was the Reform Act of 1969, with new compliance regulations. On the recommendation of a close advisor, the family hired its first part-time executive director.

FAMILIES STILL SEARCHING FOR A LEADER

Finally, in a small number of the cases strong leadership did not emerge from anywhere to facilitate the transition. (These included the four foundations that were rated "very low" or "low" on grantmaking vitality and "very low" on positive family dynamics.) They could find neither a strong successor nor a commitment to broad democratic participation.

In the world of foundations in general, some spend out at this point, or the funds pass over to another foundation with or without ongoing family involvement. Since all of the foundations in this sample have survived, it means that they found some way to continue operating. Things have gone well enough to maintain existing programs and to meet legal requirements, but the vitality of the foundation is gradually draining away.

This foundation has passed through a long Controlling Trustee stage and a passive, low-energy sibling partnership. As the third generation has taken control, leadership has fallen to the oldest cousin. Family members range in their private opinions from gratitude that any family member is willing to accept the role, to those who characterize him as "incompetent" and only filling the chair. In public, they all say nothing. The nonfamily staff director tries to organize the program but finds little enthusiasm in the trustees. A few fourth-generation cousins eagerly await their opportunity to join, but most are indifferent. The system is drifting forward, waiting for either more dynamic leadership or dissolution.

Formalization

The second core dynamic in the Collaborative Family Foundation stage is formalization. Here it is important for us to differentiate two interrelated but separate trends in the development of these foundations. The first is the involvement and relative authority of nonfamily professional staff. Over time nearly all of these multigenerational foundations came to rely in part on nonfamily human resources. In some cases this assistance has been minimal and in support roles. Other foundations have become essentially staff-run, as will be discussed in the next chapter. This involvement of nonfamily professionals is an important theme in this sample, but it is not the topic of the current discussion.

The second trend, which we are calling *formalization,* refers to the changes in procedure, policy, governance structures and processes, community awareness, quality control, asset management, and staffing that marked the development of these foundations from instruments of the founders' personal giving to free-standing philanthropic organizations. Formalization as we mean it may or may not include the use of nonfamily professional resources, but it includes much more than that. It is a way of doing the work.

This foundation has never hired a program officer. The family is committed to keeping operating expenses to a minimum and, more important, the family believes it is their responsibility to do the grant-making by themselves. One of the siblings said that she likes not having staff because from what she has seen of other foundations, staff either have their own motivations or follow the guidelines too strictly. "Family members feel more ownership and can act more spontaneously when different situations arise." But their level of professional grantmaking is very high by the standards of this sample. Their materials and preparatory work are comparable to many of the staffed foundations.

This distinction between *professional* staff and *formalization* is important because in past decades there has been a pervasive and destructive undertone of deprecation between family members and nonfamily professionals. Both sides have been unfairly stereotyped. The skills, experience, judgment, and commitment of nonfamily staff are often undervalued and underpraised by many family members.

At the same time, the exact same qualities of many family philanthropic leaders—skill, experience, judgment, and commitment (in our word, professionalism)—are sometimes dismissed by nonfamily professionals. In this sample we saw many examples of highly professional behavior by both family members and nonfamily staff. We saw glaring examples of unprofessional behavior by both as well. Since it is obvious that no category has a special claim on excellence, it has proven more useful for us to look at the formalization of the organization, not by who is doing the work, but by how it is being done.

We found that adding staff was an important marker of the transition from the Controlling Trustee Foundation to the Collaborative Family Foundation, but not in a majority of the cases. Only thirteen of the thirty cases designated their first staff person within five years of the transition out of the Controlling Trustee stage. After that there was a dramatic gap. The remaining staffed foundations added their first staff person on average twenty-three years later, stimulated by the third generation.

However, there were other typical indicators of formalization during the transition to the Collaborative Family Foundation, and in the years that followed as the collaborative governance form took shape. They included:

- Reviewing and revising bylaws
- Refining the mission
- Clarifying program priorities and information for potential grantees

- Training on restrictions on self-dealing and constraints on disqualified persons
- Upgrading facilities and clerical support
- Hiring outside asset managers
- Improving communication both inside the family and between the foundation and the community
- Stepping up (even modestly) site visits and follow-up activities.

The process of formalization was varied in this sample, but there was evidence of at least one or more of these changes in all of the thirty cases at some time during the Collaborative Family Foundation stage.

FORMALIZATION IN STAFFING AND OPERATIONS

Three of our sample foundations had a designated staff director during the early years of the Controlling Trustee period. Nearly all of the rest found that, over time, they needed someone to take on staff functions—the actual logistical and managerial work of grantmaking. Sometimes only family members have held managerial positions. Sometimes a family member was the first executive director or program officer, and nonfamily staff were hired later. In other cases, staff positions were filled by nonfamily from the beginning.

It is very important not to characterize formalization as an "all or nothing" choice. As Judith Healey, a leading advisor to family foundations, has pointed out, most families professionalize gradually, or in discrete steps. First, as the workload increases, the family volunteers begin to feel unable to stay on top of the grantmaking. A first step is often to use a consultant, and that may continue for years. Or they may hire nonfamily staff to take over specific functions, and as the foundation grows and their confidence in the process of supervision increases, the staff take on more and more responsibility.

Sometimes the first step was for one of the family members to start spending more time on foundation work. In six of the cases there was a formal designation of that person as executive director, or a comparable title. Almost always the position begins as part-time, with a low salary or no salary at all. It is a milestone in the formalization process when the volunteer asks to be compensated for her work.

"When my brother retired from the business and lost his secretary, we agreed that we should hire someone. Up to that point, the letters and administrative tasks had just been done out of his office and grant-making was rather informal. My niece said she wanted to do it, but she wanted to get paid. That was a shock, but we decided it made sense. In my experience, being a volunteer was noble and I had always been told that I shouldn't work because I would take a job away from a man. Times had changed." The staffing needs also coincided with some new program interests among the second and third generation that would require much more research and legwork in the community. As the senior leader describes it, "We brought my niece onto the board and paid her to be executive director. She's great, visits places, and sends us a whole stack of things to read."

For the first ten years the salary was very small and the assumption was that it was a part-time effort. Then one day, she said she needed a raise. "We told her to make a proposal. She researched what executive directors were paid and came back with a proposal which we approved. She considers it a full-time job and works nights and weekends." She instituted annual reports and the whole range of professional grantmaking procedures. One of the trustees added, "This has made her! It's given her so much self-confidence and pride, it's wonderful what it has done for her." The board consensus is that when she gets tired of this they would now be ready to hire an outside person, "though a family member would be given priority."

Another family has developed two subgroups, wide apart on philosophy and grantmaking priorities. They manage the balance well, but it puts pressure on the full-time family member executive director, the eldest cousin in one of the branches. For thirty years the foundation operated without any paid staff, and this family member has been its only staff for the past twenty. Now the family is moving to bring on a nonfamily professional, first as a program officer and eventually to be the successor executive director. With the person-by-person generational transition of family directors and a gradual adoption of a more strategic and focused grantmaking program, the foundation is professionalizing itself.

In other cases the inclusion of staff has been more "lurching," usually because of a persistent resistance or ambivalence in the family. Sometimes some members or branches are ready to move to a more staff-managed and family-oversight process while others prefer to maintain more of a hands-on family approach. The differences of opinion may be by individual, branch, or generation. In some cases they may represent the buildup of pressure for a transition to a new form of organization.

The decision to hire staff in this foundation was a complicated one, and each choice about adding staff requires a long process of negotiation in the board. The younger generation leaders feel that the executive director has brought the foundation to a more professional level and made it a national leader. But the remaining senior generation director has never accepted the authority of the nonfamily leader, and is "always wondering if she is acting according to the family's will or taking the foundation away from them." She acknowledges the contribution that the staff have made, but goes on to argue that they "sometimes push things the way they want instead of what the family wants. That is when the family has to be firm and make it clear whose foundation it is and what it should be doing."

The family may be unaware of the stress that this ambivalence creates for the executive director. She feels that no matter how hard she works or how much more smoothly the grantmaking now proceeds, the family does not appreciate her contribution and is grudging in its approval. She also thinks the family denies its own internal strains and is oblivious to how much effort and sensitivity she needs to devote to protecting the weaker family members while not irritating the more domineering ones. All together she wonders if it is worth it.

Sixteen of our sample foundations did not hire staff until after the second generation had established themselves—sometimes long after. In fact, in these cases it was often the third generation that raised the issues of evolution of the foundation. The second generation assumed that their obligation was to continue on the founder's path. Their most important innovation was to broaden the span of authority from the personal autonomy of the Controlling Trustee to the collaborative sibling partnership.

But second generations are traditionally conservative (in the classic sense of the term) in all forms of family enterprise. They are heavily influenced by, and often captive to, the original concept of the organization as determined by their parents. Most often that is the underlying source of organizational conflict with the third generation. That is, the second generation has more difficulty imagining a way to honor the legacy while dramatically restructuring operations. The third generation, on the other hand, with a more tenuous connection to the models of the founder and a different set of demands on their current lives, are freer to seek different organizational solutions.

Inclusion versus Selection

The third dilemma in the transition to a Collaborative Family Foundation is the tension between *maximum inclusion* and *criterion-based selection*. Should the foundation be seen as an opportunity for collective family action, or as a demanding task-based organization in which only the most skilled and appropriate family members should be allowed to participate? This is in part a dilemma of ability, and in part about the inevitable increase in diversity as the family grows across generations.

Foundations that tend toward the "inclusive" pole use a variety of techniques to recruit the broadest possible interest in the foundation. They let branches decide their own criteria for involvement, they invite observers and informal participation in meetings, they work hard on communicating both the outcomes and the content of discussions, and they make sure everyone's voice is respectfully heard. They may do a lot of work in committees with broad membership. They seek to be the "home" for everyone's philanthropy, however expressed, and they keep extending their flexibility so that no one is excluded.

Foundations that tend toward the "selective" pole focus on quality and consistency in their grantmaking. They want to do the work efficiently and to meet high standards. They tend to minimize branch discretion by establishing common criteria and taking parents out of the role of selectors. They prefer to exploit the accumulated learning of experience by keeping leaders in place for long terms. They accept that the foundation is not going to be the right place for all family members, or even for all active philanthropists in the family.

The dilemma about inclusion versus selection was most often confronted in these foundations when the families were deciding how to handle diversity in four characteristics: competence, gender, family role (blood descendants or in-laws), and geographic dispersal.

INCLUSION AND PERCEIVED COMPETENCE

One theme in the transition to the Collaborative Family Foundation that about half of the families described—but only a few admitted to—is that some of the individuals or branches were perceived as less competent, sensible, rational, collaborative, or dedicated than others.

It is hard for family leaders to acknowledge their concerns about giving equal access to all members of a category of relatives. When the founder generation make choices they are often reluctant to be open about their reasons. They avoid formal policies for as long as they can, to keep their hands from being tied about differentiating among potential successors. They stretch for rationales for including some individuals while excluding others.

Sometimes geography can be used, or age. Sometimes the limits on branch representation are set so that a potentially problematic individual can be avoided. In other cases none of these straightforward criteria quite fit the situation, so more subjective reasons are invoked: "We invited 'X' and not 'Y' because she was closer to her grandparents." "'Z' is so busy with her own career and her children right now that she doesn't have time for the foundation."

INCLUSION AND GENDER

Gender was a second special factor in the inclusion/selection dilemma in these foundations. Ten of these foundations began by including only the men on the board; another six included the primary donor's wife in name only.

Some founders clearly considered the foundation to be an extension of the family business, and the province of men. If the daughters felt resentment about their exclusion, for the most part they kept it to themselves, but they may have expressed it more easily in the foundation than in the company. There are several stories of daughters raising the question with their fathers, usually late in his life. There are even more stories of daughters and granddaughters raising the issue with their brothers.

The founder didn't encourage his daughters to pursue careers in the business or the foundation. This still rankles his oldest daughter in particular. She feels that her younger brother is now carrying on their father's patriarchal attitude. They have not found a comfortable way to discuss this issue directly. She is usually the voice of objection to his discretion as president; he reports that she needs to "enhance her leadership skills."

In those cases that continued a "men only" policy into the second and third generation or beyond, there was often a high price to pay in family collaboration.

After two generations of male Controlling Trustees, the eldest male grandchild was brought in as president. His leadership was characterized by resistance to formalization; he was nostalgic for a time when there was "more sentiment, less logic, more fun" in their philanthropy. When he stepped down his son took over. The seniors describe the transition as relatively smooth, but the female cousins are bitter that it was a "behind closed doors" decision and they were not even considered.

The history of bypassing the women in each generation is very much on the minds of the current cousins. Several of the senior male respondents referred to the women in the family as having "more passion and a deeper level of caring—you know, the female side of things." At the same time, they are referred to as "paranoid and obsessed with women's issues." The current cousins feel that they will need to design policies that reflect a more egalitarian invitation to leadership, and overcome the restrictive culture built by their parents.

The transition from Controlling Trustee structures to Collaborative Family Foundations very often was the opportunity for the first inclusion of women. Some families simply ran out of males and needed to turn to the women. In others, the sons were preoccupied with other interests and it was a daughter or daughter-in-law who became the founder's ally and successor. Whatever the reasons, the shift was dramatic. The first-generation leaders were 90 percent male. Currently the boards of these foundations are split almost exactly 50–50 between men and women, and the staffs are more than half female (including the senior executives). This is a much more dramatic change than is evident in the family companies.[4]

The inclusion of women seems to have a significant impact on the grantmaking process, especially if a woman is in the leadership position. This is a controversial topic and it is important to avoid stereotyping, but the patterns are too widespread across this sample to be ignored. It is not necessarily just gender at work. In some cases the male leaders of the foundation are also the leaders of the family's business, and they see the foundation as an extension of that enterprise. They use their business staff and colleagues for support, which reinforces the hierarchical tone carried over from the company. They also may be emulating the personal style of their entrepreneurial fathers: decisive, fast-acting, opinionated, efficient, and sometimes domineering.

The women of these generations were not so used to positions of unilateral authority in organizations. They looked for support from the group. They were more accommodating and better able to tolerate multiple agendas. They may also have been more in touch with different branches of the family, and more inclined to inclusion across branches and generations.

The first-generation Controlling Trustee was the husband of the donor. Following him, all the leaders have been women—daughters and sisters. Whether because of generational differences or gender, the process has been increasingly collaborative, diversified, friendly, and free of conflict as the daughters and granddaughters have taken control.

That is not to say they are passive or there is no sibling tension. Several of them commented that the sisters are very different—if it weren't for the foundation, they would have little contact. However, the family culture in the group of sisters allows interpersonal solutions to all conflicts, and a very ad hoc approach to procedure. As observed by one nonfamily trustee, "Watching this family work together, I've become a believer in what foundations can do to bring families closer."

That is not to say that the women who assume leadership in these foundations are weak or reluctant. In fact, it was remarkable how eagerly these women immersed themselves in the president and executive director roles. One reason could be that many of them were not invited into the family companies at earlier ages. When they have authority, they certainly use it.

The two brothers in the second generation took over from their father and ran the company and the foundation together for twenty years. When the older brother withdrew, his wife took his place on the foundation's board and immediately made an impact. "She has a strong personality and is really a force to be reckoned with. People are hesitant to challenge her at board meetings." The move toward strong female leadership was furthered when the first president chosen from the third generation was also a woman. A skilled leader, she also had a more accommodating and inviting manner, which worked well in the cousin group.

For some women in the sample, the opportunity to lead in the foundation was a life-altering experience.

In one daughter's words, her mother became "much more of a liberated woman after the children had left home." The men were preoccupied with guiding the business through a difficult period, so she quietly began to take an active role for the first time in the foundation.

She started going to Council on Foundations meetings and began learning about foundations. "She heard what was going on and came back with ideas about how we should change. We got tired of writing all the letters and not knowing what we were doing. So we cut out the local giving and the little donations. She tried to stress picking a focus right off the bat."

Her brother remained as president, but she took on the executive director role and loved it. Her daughter was so impressed with the change in her mother that, in her mid-twenties, she joined her in working on philanthropy, and eventually took over as executive director. The daughter's pride is very evident: "These leadership experiences within the foundation were powerful for both of us. And it's an exciting time in the field because so many directors are women."

INCLUSION AND IN-LAWS

A third special issue in the inclusion/selection dilemma is the role of blood descendants and in-laws.[5] The transition from the Controlling Trustee to the Collaborative Family Foundation is an opportunity to revisit the policy about the inclusion of spouses.

At the death of the founder, the three siblings in the second generation took over the foundation. They decided not to include their spouses, and they still remain adamant about this decision. They give their reason as primarily that the spouses "are very strong characters. . . . We're peacemakers. They would have fought, they didn't know what my father wanted, we wouldn't have spoken out, and they would have taken over." The siblings have tried to placate their spouses. "They give us some opinions about where they would like the dollars to go, we listen, but we do what we want. But frankly, they're still all bothered a little by this."

Another foundation defines its "foundation family" as blood descendants of the founder, because they want to keep the philanthropy as "their thing." In-laws are also excluded because of the family's concern that if the meetings get too big, little will be accomplished. The trustees feel that their spouses do not resent the exclusion and, if they are interested in securing grants for certain organizations, they can do it through their husbands or wives.

"In-laws are a sticky issue. Our parents think it would be too complicated because you would need to invite all of them to participate, and some of them are just not qualified to sit on the board. Most of them are not interested anyway."

It is possible that the policies about spouses differ depending on whether the family is focused on sons-in-law or daughters-in-law. It appears that first-generation founders may be more open to admitting their sons' wives to participation in the foundation than their daughters' husbands. This idea is supported by the fact that in five of the cases, a daughter-in-law became the first family staff person, while only one of the cases had a son-in-law in that role.

A key influence over the past decade has been the founders' only son's wife, who is the foundation's sole staff member. As Director of Grant Services, a part-time, unpaid position, she runs the foundation out of her husband's law office. She has brought a degree of organization and professionalism to the foundation, and, with her husband and sister-in-law, has facilitated a new focus in the city where they live, far from the original location. Although she maintains a kind of bemused tolerance of her father-in-law's eccentricities, she has on a couple of occasions threatened to quit after run-ins with him. The rest of her generation suggest that none of the founder's direct offspring would have been anywhere near as successful in managing him and creating enough space for the needed changes.

One interesting twist is that several foundations became more restrictive on direct descendants rather than more inclusive. That is, although the first generation often included the participation of both spouses, and the second generation may have included in-laws as well, the family agreed in the third and later generations to invite only direct descendants of the founders.

There was rarely an open discussion of the policy; rather, it was assumed and not challenged. When asked, the reason given was usually that the numbers were too large, or that the spouses had never expressed any interest. In the interviews, however, the issue of "too much diversity" was often raised. As divergent as the cousins themselves were seen to be, their spouses were perceived as truly "different"—and, by implication, unmanageable.

In this sample, thirteen of the thirty cases have bylaws which permit the inclusion of spouses as trustees or directors, although only seven actually have an in-law currently serving. Those foundations that exclude in-laws almost always voice the same rationales:

Openly and officially:

- The pool will be too large.
- The donor's preference would be to limit the foundation to descendants.
- The in-laws are too busy and would not be interested.

Privately and confidentially:

- The spouses are strong characters, who will forcefully argue their positions.
- If somebody gets divorced it would be uncomfortable.
- Some of the spouses are not popular in the family.
- It is embarrassing for the spouses to see how poorly the family works together.
- Things are going well; why ask for trouble?

We estimate that half of the families who specifically or traditionally exclude in-laws do so out of inertia—that is the way it has been, and nobody is clamoring to change it. In another quarter, it is a positive valuing of the particular interaction among siblings, and the desire to protect that process. And in the final quarter, it is because of negative feelings toward one in-law (or more than one), so that the family leaders would rather exclude the whole category than have to deal with the rejection of an individual.

INCLUSION AND GEOGRAPHY

Geographic dispersal is the one nearly universal challenge that these foundations face, typically when trying to make the transition from the second generation to the third.[6] Eighteen of the foundations had geographic restrictions on their grantmaking in the Controlling Trustee stage, and nineteen maintain some restrictions currently—although the geographic areas may have changed or expanded over the years.

The siblings in the second generation all once lived near each other in the founding city. As members of the principal branches have moved away from that area, the foundation has supported projects in the different areas where they live. The pressure to spend more funds outside the original home is creating the central tension within the family and the foundation.

On the one hand, the families living in other cities think contributing to projects in their area will help to get their children interested in the foundation. On the other hand, there is the feeling that the family's wealth was created in the home county and that's where the founders would have liked it to remain. Social service agencies there sense that the foundation may be packing up and going elsewhere. The three outsiders on the board staunchly resist the trend; they are the most unambivalently committed to the original geographic limitations.

As the family disperses and tries to form a policy for inclusion, they have limited choices regarding geography:

1. Maintain a focus on the original geographic service area, and limit family involvement to those members who still live in the area and can be actively involved.
2. Maintain a focus on the original geographic service area and allow family members from all over to serve, but minimize the requirements for community knowledge and site visits so they can stay involved.
3. Maintain some focus on the original geographic service area, but also divert some percentage of the funding to areas where family now live (often via discretionary funds).
4. Eliminate any focus on geographic service areas.

Solution #1 is the most "backward looking," traditional approach (only two foundations in the sample operated this way). It emphasizes donor control and the link between the present philanthropy and the past wealth creation. It generally requires a large, nonmobile family or the willingness to let control pass to nonfamily directors. Otherwise it creates a "foundation insider subfamily."

Solution #2 is a combination of a traditional mission with what typically becomes a highly professionalized, staff-driven process (seven cases in this sample). If the family is comfortable with this evolution, the foundation is on the path toward the third type, the Family-Governed Staff-Managed Foundation. However, those foundations that try this approach without investing in adequate staff resources find themselves unable to do much program monitoring, and therefore tend to be the least adventurous or strategic grantmakers. They also may find it very difficult to maintain trustee enthusiasm and involvement, especially for more than one generation.

Solution #3 is the most popular (nine cases) but it is often dealt with as a policy issue without adequate consideration of the procedural and governance implications. This model requires high effort on the part of both trustees and staff. The limited availability of staff to service grantees and applicants from other areas almost always means the grants in those areas come from a discretionary fund, rather than the collaborative docket. While designed as a way to keep family integrated, it can in fact become a force for disintegration if it is not managed very actively.[7]

Only one foundation has adopted Solution #4, to eliminate geographic considerations completely (11 never had a geographic restriction). They have developed a very well-articulated programmatic focus and support programs on a national scale.

SUMMARY OF INCLUSIVE VERSUS SELECTIVE APPROACHES

In moderation either style can lead to continuity. Inclusive solutions work well in small families with easygoing styles and good interpersonal relationships. It helps if the range of diversity is not so great that it creates a collection of very different individuals all trying to play on the same team.

Inclusive foundations have to be careful to not let broad acceptance slide into mediocrity or worse. The great danger of the most inclusive policies is that they can compromise quality to the point that no one is proud of the foundation. Even if the "welcome" mat is always out, a shabby home is not an attractive refuge.

The selective solutions lead to less concern about maintaining quality. On the other hand, they risk becoming more trouble than they are worth for potential successors. If high standards and a focus on quality become excuses for people in power to self-righteously pick and choose participants, there is little chance for long-term continuity.

The evidence from this sample suggests that high quality performance is extremely important in fostering enthusiasm and positive emotional experiences for family participants. If clear rules and expectations are combined with flexibility and a truly welcoming atmosphere, then the likelihood for both collaboration and continuity are maximized. The relationship between organizational policy and successor development is discussed further in chapters 8 and 9.

Collective versus Individual Philanthropy in the Foundation

Is the family dream a collection of individual aspirations, or is it truly a collective vision? To understand this aspect of the transition to a Collaborative Family Foundation, it is necessary to consider the developmental dynamics of the family itself. In every family, as each generation rises to adulthood and independence, there are two opposing forces at work.

On one hand is the centrifugal force of *individuation*. As offspring move through adolescence and into adulthood, they begin to find their individual identity. Strong or weak, smooth or lurching, each young adult must move at least somewhat away from the center of the family, represented by the parent(s). Entire theories of psychology and family dynamics are based on this concept of individuation. It is everyone's lifetime task of discovering what is unique and different about oneself, and then finding a place in the world to be that person as authentically as possible.

At the same time, there is an opposing, centripetal force of *connection*, which is the tether that binds the individual to the family. It is made up of the strands of affection, obligation, history, authority, and identification that are woven into the ropes that hold a family together. The family network, tied together by all these interpersonal tethers between individuals and generations, makes collective action possible in the family foundation.

Since all families must face the dilemma of fostering both individuation and connection in their members, all family organizations— including the foundation—must do the same. When family members get together to do collaborative work, one of the most powerful underlying dynamics is the pull of individual agendas versus the push of the collective task.

If a lot is at stake and a single course of action must be found, as is common in the board of a family business, there is strong bias toward the connection side of the dynamic. Individuals who want to change the core business to fit their particular interests, or who have points of view on ethics or management or marketing that are idiosyncratic, have to contend with reality in pushing their personal views. It is assumed that the overall best interest of the system, not self-expression, will lead to the most prudent course.

But in the foundation the process can be very different, because its purpose as an organization is so different. Earlier we discussed how family companies must succeed in the marketplace to survive. Their performance is measurable by quantifiable metrics (sales, profit, market share, stock price). But the foundation sets its own criteria. "What I want to do" and "What we can do" are the same as long as the legal requirements are fulfilled. This provides enormous encouragement for the "centrifugal" side of the force field in the foundation. Each individual can see the foundation as potentially the enabler of her or his self-image and social agenda—a chance to use large resources to demonstrate "who I am."[8]

For example, a disagreement in a foundation board that appears to be about program priorities may in fact be about personal identity. One trustee may see the foundation as a defender—in some cases, the last, best hope—of our most traditional cultural establishment. She observes the pulling back of the public's ability (or willingness) to support core cultural institutions, and she fears that our basic cultural legacy is in danger.

Another trustee takes exactly the opposite tack. She sees the foundation as an opportunity to be the spearhead of social change. She argues that the foundation is the best opportunity for bold, creative, groundbreaking leadership.

One person sees herself as a patron of the arts: the foundation is not just a funding source, it is the enabler of a social role that means a lot to her. The other feels the same way about the opportunity to be a revolutionary social engineer. There are an infinite number of other identities. Some people want to use wealth to be flamboyant leaders. Some want to be invisible. Some want to be deeply spiritual, or even pious, while others want to immerse themselves in the neediest segments of their very real worlds. The potential for self-definition, in turn, generates enormous potential for individual conflict, as each participant fights for the ability to realize her or his own goals.

The problem is not that there are different individual priorities. All groups must deal with differences of opinion and preference. The problem here is that there is no objective standard or process by which to choose whose point of view to follow. All of them are worthwhile. All of them have willing "customers." All of them are logistically possible. This makes individual expression very strong. But if the foundation aspires to achieve collaborative philanthropy, it must find common ground.

Another factor in the powerful centrifugal force that threatens to fragment family foundations is the individual rewards that can come from large-scale philanthropy. Without denying the altruism and generosity that is the essential bedrock of charitable behavior, there are also very attractive benefits for participants. Grantmakers may receive the gratitude of their communities, have access to powerful and glamorous leaders, and be given the opportunity to designate how some aspects of community or organizational life will be designed.

Especially for later generations, who do not receive much credit for starting or growing the family enterprises, philanthropy can be their best opportunity for recognition. There is nothing inherently negative about enjoying being appreciated. But "the foundation" cannot stand on the platform, or receive the proclamation, or shake the hand of the mayor, or be hugged by the students, patients, beneficiaries, and contest winners—only individuals can. Choosing which individuals, and which platforms, is one of the dilemmas that emphasize the "me" and challenge the "we" identity of the foundation.

How can the foundation possibly counteract this potential? The centripetal, collaborative side of the equation, bereft of external support, has to rely on historical and normative controls: Legacy, tradition, cooperative spirit, family identity, and sometimes donor intent. The work of maintaining a "we" mentality in the face of such pressure favoring "me" agendas is never-ending. Even if one generation finds a resolution that works, through authority, quid pro quo arrangements, pruning the tree, discretionary funds, rotating leadership, or passing the baton to professional staff and consultants, the entry of each new generation reinitiates the struggle.

Ownership versus Stewardship

Few foundations ever fully resolve the ongoing challenge of simultaneously honoring tradition while operating in the present.[9] In the transition from Controlling Trustee to Collaborative Family Foundation, the issue is sometimes framed in terms of *ownership* versus *stewardship*.

One of the most interesting aspects of family foundations is the way they illuminate the issue of ownership. In a capitalist economy, individuals can own things if they provide the capital that leads to possessing them. You buy an object by paying for it, and then it belongs to you. For an enterprise, you buy it by exchanging your capital for the buildings, materials, and inventory, and you own the products by exchanging your capital for the labor required to create them.

Given that simple definition, can you own a foundation? If a donor provides the capital that creates the product (the grants) and that capital is used to pay for the labor that does the work (the staff and costs of grantmaking), does the donor own the foundation itself? The quick answer is "no," but why? Because the donor does not buy the foundation; he does not even invest in it. He gives away what is his, and the foundation is the recipient. All organized philanthropy, where foundations give away resources to grantees, begins with this original gift—from the donor(s) to the foundation itself.

As we discussed in chapter 3, there has been increasing debate in recent years about "Whose money is it?" Some point out that the family members often act as if it is still theirs, while others counter that it is now "the public's" money. Clearly, by law and by logic, neither of those is correct. Private bank accounts are personal money. Taxes are the public's money. The endowment of the foundation is specifically *the foundation's* money. The law clearly gives the authority and responsibility for those assets to one group—the board of directors or trustees of the foundation. They are the governing body. Everyone else is a stakeholder, but that is not the same thing as being a stockholder.

But then what of the descendants' feelings that the money could have been theirs? Does that lead to feelings of resentment and guilt?

If the family continues to generate wealth, and the family stays as rich as the foundation, this response is less likely. But if the business is gone, and some branches of the family are poor, then the sense of having been an involuntary donor can be very strong.

At the transition from the Controlling Trustee to the Collaborative Family Foundation, some families begin to struggle more directly with the dilemma of ownership versus stewardship. Sometimes it arises as a specific discussion about discretionary versus program-focused funding, or about adding community representatives to the board. It may also be stimulated by research and discussion on the question of the public's interest in private philanthropy.

This foundation, run by a Controlling Trustee during its first phase and a disjointed sibling partnership during its second, is for the first time struggling to form a collaborative identity.

Members of the third generation, with the support of the non-family staff leader, are beginning to actively voice the view that "inheritors of wealth that has accumulated tax-free have an obligation to use it for the benefit of society." Another cousin made the suggestion that the family should only have control over the funds for five or ten years, and then the fund should evolve into an independent foundation, professionally run with little or no family control, or be dissolved. "The work of foundations can produce arrogance and intellectual corruption. We all have to be aware of that."

The issue is on the back burner while the board is still dominated by second-generation members, but it will undoubtedly arise again when they depart.

As we have seen, some trustees—who define themselves as *stewards* of a legacy—are very focused on understanding and connecting to their interpretation of the philanthropic agenda of the founders. They do not get much help, since most of the founders were not very concerned with mission. In addition, those who had a deep personal agenda rarely articulated it for the foundation. Of those six foundations where the founder was specific in stating a mission, none of them are among the group with the most specific and focused strategy-driven grantmaking programs today. In contrast, the group of foundations with very highly focused current missions are predominantly those where the founder stated no mission at all.

A big issue in this foundation is who speaks for the founders. This is a common situation when donors don't put any foundation mission in writing. In this case, a mission was crafted on the basis of the founder's record of giving during his lifetime and the second-generation's reading of the founders' values and interests.

This manufactured mission is at various times regarded as strict donor intent by the board. At other times it is bent to fit their individual agendas. For example, the donor's pattern of supporting universities was modified to justify responding to the interests of several current trustees in public elementary school education. On the other hand, when traditional granting in another area is challenged, the same trustees will bring forward the donor's intent as sacrosanct.

Participants on the more evolutionary side see themselves as the current *"owners"* of authority and responsibility. They speak of ownership not in the legal/economic sense but in terms of psychological and emotional commitment. They argue that the success of the foundation is not in its adherence or its faithfulness to the legacy, but rather in the quality of its performance.

Foundations are not only expressions of family values, they are organizations with work to do. Their ability to do that work well will depend more on the personalities, histories, talents, rewards, and motivations of the current players than on the clarity of the legacy from the past.

Of course, the legacy and connection to ancestors can be a motivator—a current force in the day-to-day decisions made by current participants on whether to read a proposal, to attend a site visit, to take advantage of a matching fund or discretionary program, and so forth. But it is the decisions and the actions themselves—not the motivations—that determine a foundation's current success and viability for the future.

Foundations that take an evolutionary approach tend to negotiate constantly between programmatic choices and the core identity and intent of the foundation. They believe they are honoring the priorities of earlier generations without abdicating their own ownership (governance) responsibilities.

The newest trustee in this third- and fourth-generation foundation said, "I knew in the past that my dad and my aunts and uncles had put a focus on private schools because their kids were in that phase. So when I came on board there was still a lot going to private schools. But gradually we became more focused on impacting a lot more people. We still do some private school giving, but as our generation graduated, it didn't become such a tight focus. We saw a great need in the public sector, so we fund programs mostly in public education now." When asked about the founder's intent, she repeated that she didn't see the problem. "This is our way of doing our giving—bringing family members together for a cause outside of themselves." She did not know her grandfather. She thought it was the right focus now.

Ownership versus stewardship is not a dilemma for resolution, it is a theme for ongoing reexamination. As some families reconsider it from generation to generation, their debates may figure among the early signs of a transition to the next type of foundation, the Family-Governed Staff-Managed Foundation.

CORE DILEMMA: TRUE COLLABORATION VERSUS COEXISTENCE

There may be nothing more difficult to create than true collaboration. It requires such a delicate balance in so many areas: authority, discretion, competence, respect, differentiation and identification, leadership and followership, and priorities. It also requires procedures and policies which can protect that delicate balance and turn intentions into actions. But more than anything else, it requires a viable collective dream.

We have detailed the process through which each of these families evolved from their initial Controlling Trustee form into something else. There was ample evidence that nearly all of them followed the transition steps of triggered change, disengagement from the past, exploration of options, and eventually a commitment to a new way of governing their philanthropy. They needed to find a new system that was broader, more diverse, and more complex, because families inevitably become all of those things as they move from generation to generation.

The fundamental choice that these families faced at this moment is essentially the same as the one that the founders confronted a generation or more before. At that time it was "founder's purpose versus family dream." At this time, with multiple individuals and families involved, it is between "true collaboration" and "coexistence."

Some of these families chose to follow a path of coexistence. They did not try to, or were not able to, find unitary leadership that integrated all their parts. For some, the foundation was not a high enough priority to compel the work of negotiation that such integration would have required. For others, they were simply too different, and the potential or reality of conflict was too high. The best implementation of the coexistence choice is a process of mutually respectful, individualized grantmaking—either through discretionary systems or procedural understandings among the current participants.

Other families took a different path, and pursued true collaboration. They found someone from the family or from outside who could guide them through the sensitive construction process. They found a common approach to inclusion and a comfortable level of formalization. More than anything, they discovered—sometimes in the second generation, and sometimes not until the third generation or beyond—that they could construct a common dream. For this group, and for many reasons, the sense of passion, commitment, and joy that the participants feel about their philanthropy is best served by a collective effort.

Obviously, powerful grantmaking can be done in either way. Family foundations can also survive with either model. But to be true to our experience with these foundations we must comment that the most dramatic cases of real joy in the work were among the truly collaborative families. It went beyond satisfaction with their accomplishments. They had found a level of fulfillment and pleasure that was unmatched in either the Controlling Trustee or the Staff-Managed foundations. The common dream that we described at the beginning of this chapter found realization in these cases, and they would not trade their experience for anything.

NOTES

1. This concept is from Levinson's description of the "Dream" that guides our adult development. See Levinson (1978, 1996). The "Dream" is discussed in more detail in chapter 6.

2. See Gersick et al. (1997) and Lansberg (1999) for a discussion of the different models of sibling leadership in family companies.

3. For further discussion of Sibling Partnerships, Controlling Owners, and other stages of family business development, see Gersick et al. (1997).

4. Our sample fits well with the industry norms. The *Foundation Management Series,* 11th edition (Council on Foundations, 2004b) reports that, among the 1,392 trustees from family foundations responding to that survey, 782 (56.2 percent) of family foundation trustees were male and 610 (43.8) were female. Interestingly, this was by far the highest percentage of female trustees for any foundation type: among all foundations responding to the Council on Foundations survey, females made up just 35.0 percent of community foundation boards; 29.9 percent of independent foundation boards; and 35.2 percent of public foundation boards. An even more striking statistic comes from the *2003 Grantmakers Salary and Benefits Report* (Council on Foundations, 2004a), which reports that, among the 862 staff from family foundations responding to that survey, 622 (72.2 percent) were female and 240 (27.8 percent) were male.

5. For additional information on this topic, see Stone (2004).

6. One of the best discussions of this challenge is in Stone, *Grantmaking with a Compass: The Challenges of Geography* (1999).

7. See Born (2001) and Goldberg (2002).

8. Ylvisaker (1990) has some thoughtful words on this point.

9. Some of the most thoughtful work in the field has been on this topic. For example, C. Hamilton's excellent compilation *Living the Legacy* (2001).

5

THE FAMILY-GOVERNED STAFF-MANAGED FOUNDATION

W hat happens when the operational needs of the foundation exceed the resources of the family? Some of the families in this sample were confronted with this dilemma in two ways. Either the work got too large, or the family got too small—or both.

Grantmaking done well is very labor intensive. Many grants require hours of proposal review, making contact with the applicant, deliberation, budgeting, site visits, administration, and follow-up. Add to that the demands of endowment management, record keeping, compliance with all laws and regulations, public relations, learning about new program areas, and general administration, and the requirements are significant.

Even the most dedicated families have limited time to spend on philanthropy. In many cases in this sample, it was not only the expansion of the work that strained the limits of the foundation's infrastructure, but the decrease in availability of family resources. Small families or branches that die out, other philanthropic vehicles, disinterest, reductions in personal wealth, and particularly geographic dispersal in the successor generations can leave them feeling unable to meet the management demands of excellent grantmaking. As a result, they may consider a different model of family philanthropy that permits, or requires, outside professional help.

Nine of the cases we studied have evolved into what we are defining as the third type of family foundation: a Family-Governed Staff-Managed Foundation. In essence, this form places the responsibility for *grantmaking* activities in the hands of nonfamily professional staff, while the *governance* responsibilities remain with family directors or trustees. The characteristics of this category include:

- A senior nonfamily staff executive
- Family directors or trustees responsible for general oversight and final approval, policy, mission, and strategy
- Nonfamily staff responsible for proposal review, report generating, docket creation, grantee relations, site visits, and program evaluation
- Endowment management by nonfamily professionals
- Some level of staff hierarchy, with senior executives supervising line staff and responsible to the board

Families choose this form for several reasons. Sometimes they want to bring new and different resources to their philanthropic dream. Sometimes they are overwhelmed by the demands of mandated dispersals. Sometimes the family's aspirations for research, comprehensive knowledge about program areas, and follow-up are simply beyond their capacity. They may come to believe that turning these tasks over to nonfamily staff will provide relief from the relentless day-to-day work of quality grantmaking, while retaining the commitment and satisfaction of supporting worthy endeavors.

There is certainly evidence that a seasoned and sensitive professional management team can help a family learn to improve its skills in both grantmaking and governance. This is especially true in situations where the successors lack adequate preparation for their roles. As they get better at the work, they take more pleasure in their philanthropy.

But this choice does not appear equally attractive to all individuals and families. Some families take such pleasure from the nuts-and-bolts practice of philanthropy that they have no interest in hiring others to do it for them. Others have more than enough family resources to cover the work of a foundation that has remained small or medium sized. Finally, some of the families in this sample were not motivated to take on ambitious, strategic, program-driven grantmaking. They had confidence in their traditional patterns of giving, kept the process very simple even as the mandated dispersals increased, and felt able to be both conscientious and collaborative without hiring nonfamily managers.

On the other hand, a few families were struggling to keep up with their foundations' work, and although they admitted enjoying it less, they still did not want to consider a significant investment in staff. For them, a Family-Governed Staff-Managed Foundation raised the negative image of unsupportable cost increases coupled with a loss of control over the direction of the foundation. In these cases, any suggestion of expanding the role of staff met with resistance and resentment. Sometimes these families were able to maintain high quality grantmaking by raising their own efforts, and sometimes they were not.

The families who successfully explored evolving into the staff-managed form were able to put aside stereotypes and assumptions and deal with the realities of their collective dream and their resources. For about a third of our sample, in that moment of self-reflection they discovered that what they really wanted was not only to add nonfamily employees, but to change the role of the family in the foundation. As we have seen in the two previous chapters, as the pressures on the current structure build, meaningful continuity seems to lie in the family's ability to complete the tasks of transition: articulating a new model, letting go of the old one, and then choosing and implementing appropriate new structures, systems, and processes.

As we saw with Collaborative Family Foundations, some of these choices must be renegotiated with each new generation. Because of the special nature of some Family-Governed Staff-Managed Foundations, the choices may also have to be renegotiated—or at least restated—with each change of professional leadership. Even more than the transition from the Controlling Trustee Foundation to the Collaborative Family Foundation, the adoption of the Staff-Managed form is not a developmental progression, it is an organizational choice. In fact, there were several examples in the sample of foundations that moved back and forth between the two forms, depending on the particular resources available at different points in their history.

THE PORTER FAMILY FOUNDATION

Jeff and Leslie Porter, a successful entrepreneur and his wife, started a foundation to coordinate their personal giving. After ten years, when the grants exceeded $100,000, the couple hired an executive director and turned everything over to him. One third-generation cousin recalls, "Grandfather was so busy with the business that he was glad to have someone to organize and run the foundation. The staff did the research and made funding decisions. Four times a year they asked for a meeting and, in a couple of hours, the staff would describe what they were doing and the family would apply the rubber stamp."

This continued during the twenty-six-year tenure of the first executive director, and accelerated during the twelve-year reign of his successor. Especially during the second regime, the family had no effective role, either in management or in governance.

Then the third generation staged what is generally described as a revolution. The executive director and the senior family leader were both invited to retire. The foundation entered a decade of redesign, negotiation, and soul-searching. The fact that this was the family's first experience with open discussion of mission, areas of focus, values, and governance was complicated by the size, complexity, and precedents in the grantmaking process.

There have been many wrong turns. The successor executive director did not work out, nor did the second try. Many talented family members declined the opportunity to join the board because of the intensely demanding workload. The staff, largest in this sample, have a powerful momentum of their own. The third-generation leaders of the family's re-emergence in the foundation are burned out and exhausted.

Today, the Porter Family Foundation is a powerful and extremely professional organization that is trying to define the optimal role for the family in the future. It is beginning to have the conversations that are necessary to see what family "dream" can emerge for the future, and how it can be implemented. So far, the quality of the staff and the professional procedures built over its first fifty years have allowed it to continue excellent grantmaking while it addresses these governance issues for the first time. There is a window of opportunity, since the oldest of the next generation are still teenagers.

THE INCREASING PRESENCE OF NONFAMILY STAFF

The Porters may be an extreme case, but they are hardly alone in their experience. As we discussed in the previous chapter, nearly all family foundations turn to nonfamily resources to augment their capacity at some point. In most of our cases, the first outside hires did not occur until many years after the founding. Although two of the cases had paid staff positions from the beginning, and another four hired their own staff during the Controlling Trustee stage (many more "borrowed" staff from the family business or family office), the average time span from the founding until the first dedicated staff person was hired was twenty-seven years (with a range of 0–50 years).

The thirty cases in our sample have gone down widely divergent paths from those beginnings. Currently, two of the foundations have no staff roles, either volunteer or paid. The trustees manage the grant-making. In one they share the work approximately evenly; in the other the chairperson takes on most of the responsibility, and the role rotates. One of these is the smallest foundation in the sample, and the other is moderate sized.

Another four foundations have given a staff title to a family-member volunteer. They work pretty much the same as the unstaffed foundations. They represent only 13 percent of this sample, but the vast majority of the family foundations in North America.

Seven more foundations have a paid executive director, sometimes with a part-time secretary, but no other staff. Five of these seven employ a paid family member in the role (two full-time, three part-time). These foundations have crossed a line that differentiates them from the unstaffed or volunteer-staffed cases—they have decided that grantmaking is a professional activity, and that some of the foundation's resources should go toward supporting its capacity. It is a significant psychological change, and the decision to pay a salary for staff services was an important moment in the history of all of the foundations who have taken that step. In this sample at least, that step was easiest to take with a family member in the first salaried management position.

The remaining seventeen foundations have at least two staff. The range in this sample is from two to twenty-four FTE; the average among those who have any professional staff is about five FTE. Two of the foundations in this latter group have a family member as an executive director or comparable role. One has a small staff serving under the family leader, and the other has a very large one. The other fifteen have a nonfamily executive director, or president, or other executive title. The nine cases we identified as Family-Governed Staff-Managed Foundations all came from this group.

A nonfamily executive director by itself does not put a foundation in the Staff-Managed category. Among the seventeen foundations with nonfamily senior staff, we categorized eight as Collaborative Family Foundations, because the professional staff in those foundations work as implementers of a grantmaking program with significant family "hands-on" participation.

One could argue that the discrimination is artificial. Conceptually, collaboration and professionalization are separate and independent processes. As we discussed in the previous chapter, you can imagine a foundation that is both collaborative and professional, or neither, or any combination of levels of each. And many foundations sit on the boundary or are in transition, with some characteristics of each type.

However, in this sample and in practice, there is a meaningful distinction between the two types of foundations:

1. In Collaborative Family Foundations, the *governance* (policy, strategy, mission, and ultimate funding decisions) and the *grantmaking* (creation of descriptive materials, proposal screening and review, grantee relations, site visits, follow-up, compliance with regulations, and financial administration) are both handled primarily by the family (with or without staff support); and
2. In Family-Governed Staff-Managed Foundations, the *governance* is the family's responsibility and the *grantmaking* operation is managed and carried out by the professional staff.

The family's image of the best design for their work is what differentiates the two groups, rather than any arbitrary criteria of size or program. For example, our sample includes four foundations that are similar in size, all with nonfamily executive directors and small staffs. The first two, described below, are good examples of the Family-Governed Staff-Managed Foundation, and the next two are Collaborative Family Foundations.

The third-generation leader of the Plaistow Family Foundation came to the conclusion and convinced his siblings and cousins that the foundation had "become a business that required professional management." They had to struggle to move beyond individual influence and branch representation, but their children now look at the nonfamily executive director as "the leader, the one with all the knowledge and information."

In the transition to staff management over ten years they have adopted term limits, brought on nonfamily directors and instituted "at large" elections, formalized the grantmaking process, and begun a discretionary grant program to "reward the trustees for their voluntary service and take the pressure off every discussion."

The executive director looks at all the proposals and makes a recommendation on each. She declines many on her own judgment and does site visits. Trustees receive all of the information at each meeting about all proposals received, declined, and recommended. Their discussions are engaging, although they do not tend to challenge the executive director's judgment.

This foundation began changing from a dysfunctional Collaborative Family Foundation to a Staff-Managed Foundation when the third generation hired the first nonfamily executive director. Before, meetings had been chaotic as the family struggled to meet the dispersal demands of a growing endowment. The family members were committed to the general legacy of philanthropy, but none was willing or able to devote much time to foundation management.

Over several years the new leader guided the family through discussions to sharpen mission and program priorities that reduced the number of proposals under review by two-thirds. As the family became more reassured of the director's competence and respect, they increasingly withdrew from grantmaking. Now each recommended proposal has a brief description prepared by the staff, with a recommended amount for the grant. In very brief biannual meetings, trustees go through the list and decide to accept it as recommended, to accept it but to change the amount, or to reject it (which has only happened once in ten years). Staff do all site visits and follow-ups.

In contrast, in the two similar-sized foundations we have categorized as Collaborative, the families rely significantly on their staff leaders for operational management, but still retain an active involvement in grantmaking. It appears that they are on a trajectory of increasing autonomy for staff, but have not yet transferred full responsibility to nonfamily professionals.

From the outset, Norm Greenberg's secretary did all the support work for the grantmaking of his Five Hills family foundation. When she retired, Norm decided it would be important to increase the staff to a professional level. With the help of a head-hunting firm specializing in nonprofit organization executive recruitment, he developed a job description and a profile for an executive director and hired Phyllis Byrd.

Over the years since, which included the founder's death, Phyllis has gradually professionalized the operation and family governance has gradually separated from day-to-day operations. As executive director, Phyllis does the initial analysis of all proposals. After she has made sure that the projects comply with the guidelines, she presents them to the family committees depending on what category they fall into. She has the first right of refusal and only presents the proposals that she knows meet the foundation's criteria and have a chance of being accepted by the board. But the committees discuss each recommendation and they actively present their suggestions to the full board.

Decisions to hire new staff are made by the family directors after the executive director makes a recommendation. Supervision is the executive director's responsibility, although directors do have some direct contact with staff members.

The family is very appreciative of the change that the professional staff have made in the foundation. All of the family directors reported that the executive director had been "a godsend," that she has professionalized their organization, helped them focus their grantmaking and go beyond their family and personality difficulties.

However, the family periodically reasserts its intention to stay involved beyond general policy. The ranking member of the senior generation is clear in her assessment. "Without Phyllis, we wouldn't have a foundation anymore. She has a strong personality and sometimes pushes things the way she wants as opposed to where the family wants, but this is when the family has to be firm and clear—and she always gets the message and acts on it."

This family may move to the Staff-Managed type in the near future. The executive director is now stretched to the limit and is hiring new staff. The family members are becoming more and more comfortable turning over their remaining role in the day-to-day operation of the foundation. If they make that transition, it will happen when the senior generation are gone and the third generation reassesses their availability and priorities.

John Thomas, the longtime executive director in the Lawton Family Foundation, reports to the family chairman, but he is pretty much left alone to run the day-to-day operations and represent the foundation in the community. He has never had a formal performance review in twenty-seven years. He hires and supervises staff. He organizes the docket and facilitates the grantmaking meetings. He has also played a key role in managing family involvement. He is the contact person who keeps everyone informed about foundation activities.

John also does a lot of listening to family members' complaints and ideas. Everyone credits him with shaping the foundation, understanding the families' desires, and bringing in some of the best proposals. He was also the one who raised the issue of the preparation of the next generation. On many issues, the executive director was the one who thought strategically about the foundation while the senior family members concentrated only on grants.

But the Lawton family was not interested in giving authority over the grantmaking to the staff. Most of the funding went to trustee-initiated proposals. The family members made their own arguments, and often did whatever site visits and follow-up they had time for.

John Thomas was valued for his behind-the-scenes preparation and maintenance work on the family relationships, but the senior generation family members maintained control. It was not a staff-managed foundation yet. Whether it becomes one will depend on how the fourth generation interprets its role as the seniors withdraw, and what kind of individual they bring in to follow this supportive, facilitative leader.

In some of the cases, the governance–grantmaking relationship is more strained or ambiguous. The balance of authority and responsibility remains unclear, and often is a source of tension.

The executive director is a dynamic, bright, and competent staff person, whose confidence and work satisfaction are slowly being eroded by some of the family dynamics and design problems concerning her role. "We are really understaffed for the size of our foundation, and in all honesty the trustees don't really listen to me. A few times I've had to resort to threatening to leave to get the point across that what I have to work with doesn't match what they expect from me." She is sure there's a job description for the executive director, "but I've never seen anything in writing." The chair of the board supervises the executive director and staff.

The executive director has not received permission to publish guidelines regarding their mission. The board sometimes adheres to its stated program priorities, and often does not. Directors sometimes take the lead and make commitments, and then inform staff. Neither board nor staff does any follow-up evaluation on grants and whether programs are effective. The executive director says that the staff is "working on that right now," but they are too stretched to get very far and the family is not pressing it.

There are no standing board committees, but there have been ad hoc groups to study specific grantmaking areas. There are no term limits on board service.

The foundation has accomplished some excellent grantmaking, but has also suffered some very rocky family dynamics. Staff are somewhat demoralized. Most family members appreciate the contribution that the staff are making ("The program staff are gems—they should only stay!"). But turnover continues to be a problem.

In another foundation, the dilemma is that the staff have taken over the grantmaking process but the family has not been able to address pressing governance issues. The entry of the next generation is much discussed but without conclusion or action. Term limits are on the books but ignored. The work of the foundation is going on extremely well because the family has invested adequate resources in a full staff, well trained and supervised by the executive director. But continuity is threatened by their extreme conflict-avoidance and their inability to wrestle with the remaining governance policy issues.

Table 5.1 summarizes the similarities and differences we found in the Collaborative Family and Staff-Managed stages of foundation develop-

Table 5.1.   Collaborative and Staff-Managed Governance Roles

Collaborative Family Foundations with Staff Support (20 cases)	Staff-Managed Family-Governed Foundations (9 cases)
Frequent board meetings	Annual or semiannual board meetings
Family active in grantee relations	Staff manage grantee relations (site visits and
Detailed board or committee review	follow-up)
of proposals	Summarized board review of grantmaking
Average one FTE staff per $1.5	"slates"
million annual giving	Average one FTE per $1 million annual giving
Family supervises and evaluates staff	Staff leader supervises and evaluates staff

ments. As we noted in the Introduction, families may also move back and forth across these categories. Two of our sample foundations (including the Porters) spent some number of years with staff in control of grantmaking. The family performed some of the governance tasks but were not involved in the day-to-day operations. Then at the time of a generational change, the family reassumed management of the grantmaking operations. Today they are in a middle ground. The staff still retain significant responsibility for the program, but the family are increasingly directly involved. In both of these cases, the era of a very strong and autonomous staff director has given way to family control.

FOUNDATION SIZE AND STAFFING REQUIREMENTS

To some extent the impetus to adopt this form of foundation governance is a matter of size. The median asset base for the staff-managed foundations in this sample is $100 million, compared with $54 million for the sample as a whole.

It is an axiom of business families that families grow faster than businesses. That is, across generations, the number of individuals in the family as a whole expands faster than the assets or revenues of the business. That is very relevant for the degree of financial dependence on the business that a family can sustain over generations. The growth, profitability, and available dividends from an operating company get divided into more and more slices as the generations continue, and in almost all cases (at least beyond the second generation) that means that each slice gets smaller and smaller.

While the number of family "consumers" of the business success increases, the percentage of each generation that is involved in company management or governance usually gets smaller and smaller. The collaborative work of being a shareholder is minimal. Family business leaders operate the company on behalf of all the family, and augment their own resources with many nonfamily employees.

In these foundations, some of the dynamics are the same as in business and some are different. In many of the cases the assets expanded in leaps, and the available family resources increased more slowly. In a few cases the family stayed relatively small, while the assets of the foundation (and the resulting requirements of grantmaking) expanded exponentially. Instead of too many consumers of steadily growing profits, the family generated too few providers of suddenly exploding work.

This small family funded their foundation from the proceeds of a very successful family business. Over the course of five decades, while the number of family members doubled, the foundation grew from an initial $100,000 to almost $200 million in assets. Halfway through this process, the family hired its first nonfamily executive director. Over the following thirty years, a series of nonfamily executive directors and program directors has guided the growth of the foundation. The next generation of family trustees has reached adulthood and gradually assumed leadership on the board, but they have not reasserted direct control of the grantmaking process.

In another case, two sons took over both the family business and the foundation at the death of their father. They were completely preoccupied with the company, and happy to turn the foundation over to a small group of financial professionals who have run it for the past decade. The enthusiastic staff organize the requests, do the investigations, and prepare a recommended docket. The small family board meets quarterly for a couple of hours to endorse the program.

The system may be beginning to fray around the edges, particularly due to the family's slow ramp up of their attention to governance and funding issues. The staff has been challenged recently by the rapid growth of the endowment, and they have tried to nudge the family toward a more strategic approach. Also, the nonfamily executive director is the one thinking about preparing the next generation of cousins to someday become trustees. At present, however, the brothers are very content to support the foundation wholeheartedly (including financially—the company continues to make large annual contributions to the endowment), but to let the professional staff manage its affairs.

Although size is clearly the most significant predictor of staff control, it does not tell the entire story. There are smaller foundations that are completely staff-run, and larger ones where the family have retained a much more active role in grantmaking—attending every site visit, conducting the first review of proposals, and, in another arena, directly overseeing the investment portfolio. So, while correlated with size, professional staff-managed grantmaking is also a matter of style.

The trustees in the Simonton Family Foundation are seasoned grantmakers. They have sat on many nonprofit boards, including various family foundations. As a result, they have firsthand knowledge of many social service organizations and private schools in their funding area. However, in this foundation, they do not initiate grant proposals, or go on site visits. Rather, they rely on the program officers' research and recommendations.

The foundation awards many small grants (under $20,000) in addition to the larger grants. The program officers identify and screen applicants and do the site visits. Before presenting their recommendations to the board, the program officers meet with the executive director, who acts as devil's advocate, presenting arguments in favor of proposals the officers recommend rejecting and against the ones they like. The executive director's job is to keep in mind which proposals will most appeal to trustees.

The project officers try to have follow-up contact with grantees, but given the number of grantees it's hard for them to stay in touch with all of them. One program officer who covers the arts estimates that she is out approximately 100 evenings a year, attending performances and exhibits and staying on top of developments in the arts community. Extensive dockets are prepared for each quarterly meeting: Each proposal is presented with a detailed written review, which may exceed 100 pages.

The board rarely rejects staff recommendations, but sometimes it asks for more from the staff. Recently they have pushed for more accountability in the foundation's grantmaking. The board asked staff to periodically prepare brief summaries of a random number of grantees. Usually the staff reports only on the successes. One director encouraged them to report about the failures as well so that the board and staff might learn from them.

In contrast, the Goldfarb Family Foundation—one of the largest and oldest in the sample—has remained firmly in the Collaborative Family Foundation category. They have had nonfamily heads of staff for fifty years, and each one "understood that their role was to carry out the wishes of the family." Grantmaking is managed by large, overlapping committees of family members covering multiple geographic areas and program priorities. The committees make recommendations to the trustees at semiannual meetings. In addition, there are funds allocated for individual contributions. At any one time there might be seventy to seventy-five people working on foundation activities, all direct descendents of the founders.

As the family begins to incorporate the fourth generation, there is some indication that the collaborative model is under strain. Some family members feel the time has come to respond to the sheer size and complexity of the family and turn more grantmaking responsibility over to nonfamily professionals. Others worry that "if you make it terribly professional, it takes the life force out of it—the heart and soul slips away. I don't see it as a business."

The new staff leaders are caught in the family's ambivalence. The executive director described his role as "a cross between a community organizer and an executive secretary." Until now it has been clear that the staff are definitely not to be public spokespersons for the foundation. Now some family members want more productivity and accountability from staff. The executive director has proposed formalizing management, including staff job descriptions and evaluations, but the family's response has been lukewarm. There may be a transition in this family's future, but moving toward it will be a complicated process.

THE SUCCESSFUL TRANSITION TO A FAMILY-GOVERNED STAFF-MANAGED FOUNDATION

The Importance of a Skilled Nonfamily Executive

Not surprisingly, the one essential ingredient that makes the Family-Governed Staff-Managed Foundation work is the highly skilled and self-aware executive director. All nine of these foundations had found such a person at least once in their history. The descriptions are remarkably similar across cases:

Sandra Brigham, speaking of the former executive director who dramatically changed her family's foundation during his fifteen years of service, said, "He was a champion, and he really opened our eyes. The family was getting very large, very diverse, somewhat disinterested. He showed us that the philanthropy work was serious business, worthwhile, important, but that we had to do it well, with authenticity. We needed to know our communities, to know firsthand the people we were helping."

During his service there was no question that he was the driving force behind the foundation, and the prime shaper of both its strategy and its procedures. Since other executive directors have succeeded him, the foundation has returned to a Collaborative Family Foundation format, with family members managing the operation directly. "He helped us create the foundation that we have now, and then we took responsibility for it back in our own hands."

The most sensitive and intelligent leaders are able to negotiate the family dynamics as well as the foundation's internal works. Such leadership is common to all of the cases that are satisfied and comfortable in this category.

This executive director hires, supervises, and evaluates the performance of this large staff. Program officers praise her for her fairness, tactfulness, accessibility, and helpfulness. She is also a master of diplomacy in dealing with trustees. After fifteen years on the job, she knows intimately the family members, their quirks, and the family's dynamics, and they respect and trust her. When trustees have concerns, they speak individually with her rather than discuss these matters with the full board. She seems to encourage this practice, perhaps wishing to contain emotions brewing below the surface. She makes a point of never taking sides and never repeating to one what another has told her in private.

Triangulation and Control

The cases where the executive director has this kind of intimate, interpersonal influence are, of course, complicated. Triangulation—the intervention of a third party as a mediator, facilitator, interpreter, or defuser—into the conflict between two family members is a well-studied phenomenon in the family dynamics literature.[1] Early theorists saw triangles as essentially destructive to family process. By "shunting" around conflict they reduce the family's ability and motivation to resolve it directly. However, contemporary theorists are more mixed. They see triangles as sometimes an efficient coping mechanism. They can lead to solutions while keeping chronic, unresolvable conflict from destroying the family's overall ability to get work done.

In these cases of effective triangulated intervention by the executive director, the family has to balance the benefits and risks. A staff leader who knows the personalities and quirks of family members well enough to steer the discussion around the rocks can make the difference between hostile or interminable meetings and effective, light-hearted ones. But even a well-meaning executive director who is committed to furthering the agenda of the family will find it hard to be effective without sometimes being manipulative, in the service of "what's best for the family."

That is where the risk comes in. If the family uses the staff facilitator to avoid essential negotiations and arguments, or allows him to tilt the balance of influence toward one individual or branch and away from another, or to manipulate the overall priorities and process of the grantmaking, then the "effectiveness" of the director has obviously gone too far. The staff leadership is there every day, dealing with program officers, grantees, and family members in private conversations. A power-hungry executive will have more than ample opportunity to bend the system, out of the view of the occasional participation of distant family trustees.

Sometimes the problem goes beyond occasional discomfort with style. There were a number of cases in the study where the nonfamily manager did not read the family intentions well, either accidentally or by design. Sometimes the fit was poor. While the data are not clear on this point in many cases, we estimate that fully half of the foundations in the sample who ever employed a nonfamily executive director had at least one bad experience that led to a resignation or a dismissal.

From "Rescuer" to Renegade

While the fear of losing control to renegade staff is voiced in various ways by many individuals, in our sample it had some reality in only two of the cases. In each of these situations the staff first entered as rescuers. They formed a bridge from a Controlling Trustee to an unprepared younger generation, or they brought a higher level of organizational or grantmaking expertise to a foundation that was in danger of disintegrating. The foundation then began to adapt to their agendas, and the executive director came to be a more visible representation of the organization than the family. (In both cases, the family use almost identical stories to describe the warning sign of the director beginning to refer to the organization in public as "my foundation.")

These problematic individuals are different from their counterparts who carefully self-monitor and maintain a clear distinction between the trustee and staff roles. They became carried away with their own philanthropic mission. But in each case they did so with the approval of the senior authority in the family. The family dynamic that kept them in control was the conscious or unconscious endorsement of the senior generation, and the reluctance of the younger generations to challenge it. In turn, the end of this phase of staff dominance was typically initiated by the accumulating objections of the younger generation. At some point an individual successor leader emerged in the family, and a transition back to family control began.

Milton Greene, the second-generation leader (and cofounder) of this foundation brought in a visionary and impressive executive director when the dispersal demands of a growing endowment were more than he could handle on his own. The executive took the foundation in a dramatic new direction. She made extensive use of highly technical advisors to focus the foundation on funding advanced research in its field. This provided status for the foundation but very little connection between the family trustees and the work.

Gradually the executive director became the primary voice for the foundation. She operated as the senior trustee's proxy, which eventually became intolerable to the rising generation. They prevailed upon their father, who was also beginning to worry about the shift in control. When new information emerged about the executive's mismanagement of the investment portfolio and potential conflict of interest, it moved the father to action—although out of loyalty and a reluctance to reframe his earlier decisions as mistakes, he continued to defend the executive's performance and attribute her problems to minor facets of her style. "She is a smart woman and a valuable friend but an autocratic leader. She was getting too independent, and some directors thought she was giving too much money to projects in her own field." The executive was helped to retire and a member of the third generation became the new president.

In this foundation, the childless founder was the strong, individual Controlling Trustee during his lifetime, but it has been a nonfamily employee who has taken on the role of his "voice" in the decade since his death. He has no vote on the board but likes to remind the trustees that they should be grateful to their uncle for what he left them (the business that made them quite wealthy besides the foundation). He also reminds them that the foundation money is not their money so they should "behave." He has an accounting and tax background and has never worked elsewhere. His father also worked for the founder.

This administrator, who says that he defines himself as a family member, has very strong opinions about governance, such as: (1) It is a bad idea to have nonfamily trustees on the board, because they bring conflict of interests, by being on boards of other organizations, and it is too difficult for family members to disagree with them; (2) Too much information is not good for trustees. A summary of recommended grants and a few words about each grantee is enough preparation for the board's grantmaking meetings. They rarely invite individuals or organizations to present their proposals to the grant committee, because they talk for too long, confuse the trustees and don't add much to the decision process; (3) It is stupid to publish a mission statement, because "that pins you down and makes it more impossible to deny that you said something if you change your mind later."

The family is very dependent on his ongoing efforts and staff work, but they are beginning to realize that their values are not always reflected in his actions. This tension is likely to continue to build. It has taken the trustee group, all second-generation members and not direct descendants of the founder, a decade to begin to feel empowered and responsible for the foundation. They are now beginning to prepare for the eventual entry and transition to their offspring. The executive, with increasing fervor and isolation, is hanging on by championing the founder's style and ideas. A next transition in leadership is imminent.

CHOOSING THE STAFF-MANAGED FORM

What starts a family down the path of withdrawing from the grantmaking tasks (proposal screening and review, grantee relations, site visits and follow-up) and focusing on governance (policy, strategy, mission, oversight of investment performance, and ultimate funding decisions)? The first answer, in some cases, is, surprisingly, legacy. As we briefly discussed in chapter 3, while most of the donor/founder Controlling Trustees were very hands-on grantmakers, not all of them were. Eighty percent of the Controlling Trustees relied on family business employees and financial or legal advisors to support the grantmaking process, and at least half of them turned over significant tasks to these staff. Half of the original boards had nonfamily members, typically from the same category of business subordinates or service professionals. (These percentages hold true for the sample as a whole and for the Controlling Trustee subsample.)

Even when the Controlling Trustee was unilaterally in control of the foundation's philanthropic agenda, in many cases the actual grantmaking was managed by others from the very beginning. Their tasks included fielding requests from prospective grantees, accumulating proposals, conveying responses, and in some cases even recommending funding levels or matching available funds with the levels of requests. Managers were not employees of the foundation, but in all other respects they operated as nonfamily professional staff.

As we discussed in chapters 3 and 4, these individuals were very personally connected to the founders. When the founders retired, so did many of them, and their functions had to be covered by others. The transition to the collaborative stage, as described in chapter 4, is frequently marked by a reassertion of family control at both the board and operational levels. As we noted, the first dedicated staff were not hired on average until twenty-seven years after the foundation was founded, and in about one-third of the cases the first position was filled by a family member. However, the percentage of non-family grantmaking staff continued to rise as decades passed. It is not a surprising trend. But it is a source of ambivalence and concern in many of these families.

The Common Worries: Cost and Control

Two constraints tend to inhibit families from following this developmental tendency into a transition from a Collaborative Family Foundation to a Family-Governed Staff-Managed Foundation. The first is cost. Most families do not know the appropriate level of expenditure on operations, but they assume that less is better. The theoretical goal is no expenditures at all. The concern with administrative spending grows out of the first part of the philanthropic dream, to do good work. Every dollar spent on system maintenance is seen as a dollar taken away from grantees. The issue of expenditures on infrastructure will be discussed more fully in chapter 6.

The second reason that families resist extensive use of non-family staff is the fear that the family will lose control. This grows from the second part of the dream, to enhance family dynamics and integration. If the foundation provides a collaborative venue for the expression of the family legacy, the fear is that it will be lost if the foundation is "turned over to outsiders."

In fact, the results from our sample provide extremely strong reassurance in response to both fears. Foundations that have successfully accomplished this transition have done so without compromising either cost-effective performance or family control. Quite the contrary: It is the resistance to this transition in the face of enormous evolutionary pressure that threatens continuity in some of these foundations.

Trying to maintain a bare-bones, family-only structure in a large-scale foundation overstresses both procedures and people. The best talent get burned out. Grantees become neglected and frustrated. Procedures are short-circuited due to lack of time, which undermines credibility. New program development slows or ceases altogether.

Most importantly, the pressure of giving away mandated funds becomes a burden rather than an opportunity. The smaller families may recruit participation by younger family members just to get the work done. That drives away those who are ambivalent or at stages of their lives with maximum other demands, and makes those who say "yes" feel resentful at being exploited.

Some families turn to nonfamily staff because the family resources are simply not enough. However, the successful cases of foundations that decide to turn significant responsibilities over to nonfamily staff are those who think carefully about how this will create *different* resources, not just *more* resources.

The role differentiation does permit a kind of specialization between family and staff that has worked extremely well in most of the cases of this type. As they become more comfortable with nonfamily staff, they begin to evolve in two directions. The family gets better at governance, and the staff get more skilled at grantmaking.

This family would probably describe itself as a Collaborative Family Foundation, which is a testament to the savvy and subtlety of the nonfamily executive director. In the ten years since he joined the foundation he has guided it into a professional level of operation without raising the defensiveness of the quiet, polite family. The staff plays the major role in managing the family involvement, identifying programs to support, setting priorities, and organizing the trustees.

Although the family trustees are not very proactive in developing strategy or programs, they are conscientious in examining and evaluating grant proposals and shaping guidelines for grants. The executive director is skilled in knowing how family members will respond to particular proposals and is always respectful of their wishes. At the same time, he does his best to educate them in ways to professionalize the foundation, focus programs, and develop the next generation.

In a similar case, the trustees do not interfere in, or closely monitor, the executive director's management of the staff. For the most part he also is skilled in managing relationships with the family. He knows how the board thinks and what it values. He communicates that to the staff so that they keep the board's interests in mind when they present their recommendations to the board.

The staff attends to grantmaking alone; it has no role in family matters. The executive director has never discussed succession planning with the board members nor have they raised the topic with him. Other than dining together at a nice restaurant the night before board meetings, the board and staff do not socialize. The one "sticky patch," ongoing bickering between the executive director and one of the senior trustees, is considered minor by the board; overall they consider him an invaluable asset to the foundation.

Specifically regarding the fear of loss of family control and cohesiveness, the most important conclusion from this project concerning professional staffing is an ironic reversal. Most professionals and practitioners in this field assume that good grantmaking grows out of good family processes. That is, they believe that families who manage their relationships well, contain conflict, and have affection and respect for each other will be able to generate good grantmaking procedures and effective operations.

We found that it works in the opposite direction. That is not to say that a family doesn't need a threshold of good process—a basic ability to work together, to have meetings, to talk about the task. But good performance in the foundation's work creates good emotional experiences and commitment, more often than the reverse.

It shouldn't be a surprise. Business works that way too. A failing, parochial, totally family-focused business can destroy a family, rather than sustaining it. On the other hand, by treating the work seriously, relatives end up treating each other seriously as well.

"I'm very proud of what we have accomplished. We've done a lot. We know internally that it's worthwhile. It's fun and beneficial. I guess what I mean is, knowing that it's beneficial is a big part of what makes it fun."

We return to this theme in the discussion of family dynamics in chapter 7.

Links between the Family-Governed Staff-Managed Foundation and the Overall Family Enterprise

The change to a Family-Governed Staff-Managed Foundation often accompanies a parallel evolution of the other parts of the family's enterprise: the family business, a family office, or other interdependent financial arrangements. Five of the families who run these highly professionalized foundations still have an operating family business; four do not. That is a slightly higher percentage than for the foundations in the Collaborative Family Foundation group, where only nine of twenty-one have a currently operating family business. In both groups, however, the distinction between the foundation and the business has increased over time. Organizationally the two systems have become very independent by this stage. In fact, several of the businesses had developed their own corporate philanthropy capacity, replacing the role that the foundation played in its early years.[2] The roles of family members in the various parts of their enterprise evolve over time. In the second generation in particular, individuals begin to specialize within the family governance structures. Within a sibling group, some would be in the family company, some on various boards, some in a family office or family council, some trained as professionals providing services to family members, and some in the foundation. These assignments are usually some combination of personal preference and parental encouragement.

This entrepreneurial father had a grand scheme for dividing up the family empire among his five children. The eldest was given the grandparents' family trust to manage, which provides generous annual disbursements to all family beneficiaries. The second son runs the family business, and his younger brother sits on the board. The oldest daughter is the successor president of the foundation. Her younger sister was offered the position of copresident, but turned it down. She does fill one of the trustee seats, and may increase her involvement at a later time.

Everyone in this family assumed that the third-generation business leader would take over the foundation when his father retired, but his sister, a younger daughter of the senior, was chosen instead. The brother admitted, "My sister and I are very competitive, and since I was taking over the company and also had young children at home, my father and I decided that my sister should become president." In fact, the official plan is for the presidency to rotate through the sibling group of the brother and three sisters, but most of them assume that the first chosen sister will stay in the role as long as she wants.

Third-generation families often perpetuate the role specialization that the second-generation siblings began. It is quite common in these families to see more family business executives coming from one branch than another. The foundation, however, is still much more likely to be governed by an equity model of representation.

This sometimes creates a dynamic of imbalance. Some branches which are not represented in the operating business would prefer not to have to share foundation governance with branches that are in both. They view the foundation as their "territory," a compensation for being excluded from the company.

In some families, those in the business were happy to agree. Encouraging other branches to focus on the foundation took the pressure off of them to also invite their siblings or nephews and nieces into the company. But in other families, those in the business still fought for equal representation in the foundation. They felt it was more of a family entitlement, a way of remaining close with parents, and an opportunity to have a public face that the business did not provide. It is an issue the families often find difficult to address directly. If there is tension about branch rights and representation, the resulting avoidance may interfere with good planning about succession and successor development.

Another factor adds to the give and take of the family's human resources across all its collaborative efforts. In most of the Staff-Managed cases where the family business still exists, the family's role in that business has undergone a dramatic change. Family members have withdrawn from executive roles in the company, and the presence of family members at all levels of management is greatly decreased. The family is transitioning from "owner-managers" to "owner-investors" in the companies that generated the family's wealth. In the eyes of the displaced executives, the foundation can appear as a suddenly more attractive activity. There is some evidence of increased tension between individuals and branches as a result of these changes, which in several of the cases has occurred only in the last several years.

Furthermore, in most of the cases in the broad sample where the family no longer has a business, the family's withdrawal from an operating business was voluntary and strategic. In five of the cases, however, the businesses that provided the initial resources to establish the foundation subsequently failed, or are currently in trouble. The reasons are varied. Most commonly no one in the current family blames the leadership for the downturn. These businesses ran into industry problems and could not maintain their competitive edge.

In a few cases, however, there is either an explicit or implicit conception that poor management was responsible for the failure. Either way, the role of the foundation changed dramatically when the business disappeared. Displaced executives sometimes looked for an increased role in the foundation. The internal hierarchy of family branches was altered, as the "wealth generating" branch lost its basis for status. If the lingering explanations and recriminations about the closing of the family business are underlying dynamics in foundation governance, they need to be identified and resolved before they compromise continuity planning.

Nonfamily Board Members in the Family-Governed Staff-Managed Foundation

There is an important distinction between two types of nonfamily board members. The first subgroup includes family friends, personal advisors, business associates, and service professionals such as attorneys and accountants. Over half of these foundations began with at least one nonfamily director on the original board. These individuals were more like staff than trustees. The Controlling Trustee maintained the authority and discretion to make decisions on behalf of the foundation. The nonfamily board members in this category shared the founder's values or at least were committed to implementing them.

When nonfamily trustees are added later in the life of a foundation, especially if they are part of the transition to a staff-managed foundation, their role is very different. They are asked to provide an outside perspective in the governance and grantmaking processes. Eight of the foundations had at least one of this kind of nonfamily trustee on the current board. Sometimes the expectation is explicit that they represent constituencies served by grantee programs. Sometimes the "community" representation is more general, referring more to the geographic area. In a few cases they do not represent grantee constituencies, but rather skills and experience, such as investment oversight or nonprofit management.

The families also mentioned other important benefits of adding nonfamily board members to the foundation:

- They tend to be "control rods" that temper the emotion of family dynamics. This is partly because they don't share the same family history or carry the same memories, and partly because no matter how close they are to the family, relatives don't want to embarrass themselves by behaving badly in front of outsiders.
- They encourage family members to prepare more conscientiously for meetings. Again, the family does not want to be embarrassed. In our sample, professional staff were asked to provide better and more complete board books when the board included nonfamily directors. And more of the board members will have read them.
- They are sources of informal information about current and prospective grantees.
- They force a reconsideration of what level of commitment and service it is reasonable to ask of all trustees, and what rewards the trustees have a right to expect in return.
- When they ask the family, "What do you want us to do?" they encourage the family to ask itself, "What do we all want to do together?"

In addition to these benefits, we observed several other characteristics of nonfamily board members that were more problematic:

- Nonfamily board members are not particularly focused on continuity planning or involving the next generation. They tend to concentrate on the "here and now." They spend effort getting to know the current family trustees and building trust with them, so they are not motivated to encourage turnover. They also may be supportive of the concept of the legacy of philanthropic values from generation to generation, but diverting time and resources for long-term training and socialization is not their first priority.

- Nonfamily board members tend to be very conservative on geographic concentration of projects. Those nonfamily trustees who were chosen specifically to represent the interests of the local community quite naturally resist efforts by trustees who live elsewhere to diversify the granting regions. "Too much money is going outside the county now. That wasn't [the founder's] intent. He made his money here and he was committed to these people." This is a particularly difficult, and surprisingly unforeseen, dilemma in the foundations at this stage, since the family's evolution to a governance rather than management role, the inclusion of community-based directors, and the geographic dispersal of next-generation family members often happen at exactly the same time.
- Once involved, nonfamily board members are difficult to change. Family members are more polite with their nonfamily trustees than they are with each other. In some cases, the family report being somewhat intimidated by their community trustees.

The solution is not complicated. Most of the foundations with outside directors say that they could not do their work without them. But they don't take their contributions for granted. Foundations that exploit the benefits of outside directors and avoid the pitfalls do so by attending to good governance practices in general. When the role of the board or trustee group in setting strategic direction is clear; when the criteria for all directors are specific, written, known by all members and actually adhered to; when terms are set and when reviews for renomination are meaningful for all directors; and when policies such as geographic focus and programmatic flexibility are fully discussed by the entire group, then the outside directors can add a unique and valuable dimension. On the other hand, when they are added impulsively or at the recommendation of one individual without full debate, and when they are treated like either strangers or guests, then they can become a factor that the family "deals with" instead of one it benefits from.

CORE DILEMMA: FAMILY GOVERNANCE
VERSUS FAMILY MANAGEMENT

The distinction between governance and management is one of the most important and complex issues in family enterprise. It is probably second only to succession planning as a topic in the family business literature. In business the distinction is becoming clearer. Managers provide leadership for the operations, supervise tasks and staff, oversee expenditures, and are responsible for the actual work of the company. The governance structure, primarily the board of directors, is responsible for establishing the overall strategy, setting ethical and performance standards, guarding the financial health of the company, overseeing the performance of key executives, and in general representing the interests of owners. In small companies, the circles can overlap, as entrepreneurs and leaders act as "owner-managers," fulfilling the responsibilities of both. As companies grow the roles become differentiated.

In a foundation, the grantmaking operation is much like the production or service part of a company, but not exactly. The trustees are sort of like a corporate board of directors, but only in part. As we have pointed out, management is different because the "market" for the organization's work is different. Philanthropy is a business where the provider pays the customers instead of the other way around. And the board role is different because the trustees or directors are not actually owners of the foundation.

The complication this creates is that families have to work hard to differentiate the roles and responsibilities of governance from those of management. In the confusion, it is usually governance that gets forgotten. For decades the focus of foundation conferences and publications has been overwhelmingly on grantmaking. There have been great strides in determining "best practices" for public information, programmatic research, proposal review, program evaluation, grantee relations, and efficiencies of grantmaking.[3] Not surprisingly, that is what most people identify as the essential work of the foundation—and by extension, the essential work of the family in a family foundation.

But that can undervalue the essential work of organization development and governance. There are also tasks of mission review, successor development, long-term strategy, policies and procedures, and program prioritization at the level of values (not specific proposals) that enrich the life of the foundation.[4]

To be sure, the distinction between governance and management is not always apparent. The values, the strategy, and the particular funding choices of a foundation are all interrelated, and the dividing lines can blur. But there is still a difference. And it is easy to see examples, in this study and in the field in general, of foundations that do one type of work well and dramatically neglect the other.

There is a fear in some of these foundations of an inherent conflict between family governance and staff management—a battle for control. However, the most successful and satisfied foundations realized that that assumption is false. At every point in their development, these foundations used formalization to strengthen, rather than undermine, family control.

Some founders depended strongly on the services of an efficient, knowledgeable business colleague or employee. Many of the families would not have succeeded in creating a collaborative family governance system without the supportive—and often guiding—hand of one or more nonfamily professionals. A significant subgroup of the thirty cases point specifically to a time in their history when the professional staff or consultants saved the foundation from disaster or decay. In only one case does the family feel that they relied too much on nonfamily staff and could not find a way out.

Most of the foundations that consider evolving to a Family-Governed Staff-Managed Foundation are brought to that option by growth. The work is too demanding for the family to do it all itself. Once they make that decision to hire nonfamily staff, they face the challenge of rethinking the family's role. Some use staff resources to help them do everything; others differentiate the family's role from the staff's, and find sufficient meaning in oversight instead of frontline grantmaking.

Either way, it is very important to realize that staff-managed grantmaking does not in any way diminish the demands of governance. In those families who have turned over operational tasks to professional staff, the ones who are the least ambivalent or threatened are the ones who have *redefined* the leadership role, not abandoned it.

In every case in this sample where executive directors seemed to be going beyond the boundaries of responsibility that the family intended, they were in fact moving into a power vacuum. The family leadership had abdicated, or at least withdrawn from, exercising appropriate governance control. They had not continually debated and clarified mission and priorities. They had not honestly resolved representation, term limits, and expectations for directors. They had pulled too far back from a general knowledge of the grantee community and the new developments in the high-priority program areas. They lacked a solid understanding of program evaluation that could guide the staff's performance reviews.

If the staff were inappropriately running the foundation, it was because the trustees inappropriately were not. At this stage, like all the others, the first task of the family is to choose who it wants to be and what it wants to do, and then, of course, to do it with passion and to the best of its ability.

NOTES

1. The classic work is Bowen (1978); see also Kerr and Bowen (1988), and Stone (1997).

2. See Levy (1999) for an interesting exploration of corporate philanthropy. Also see Porter and Kramer (2002).

3. Peter Karoff explores some of the dangers of overvaluing "impact-driven" philanthropy in Karoff (2004). See also Sievers (2004), in the same volume.

4. J. Hughes, who has long been one of the most thoughtful leaders from the legal profession in thinking conceptually about philanthropy and wealth management, offers some suggestions about how families can approach quality governance in *Family Wealth: Keeping It in the Family* (1997).

III

LESSONS ON GOVERNANCE
AND CONTINUITY

What does all this mean? Are there lessons, suggestions, and warnings that these experienced foundations can convey to today's philanthropy?

This study has brought us to a new view of family foundations that survive over time. We see them as evolving task-focused organizations, shaping and reshaping their designs and the way they go about their work. We have been impressed with how much the vitality of these foundations and the positive experience of these families depend not only on the quality of their grantmaking, but also on the attention they pay to organizational governance.

In our ongoing work with family foundations, we have identified four central themes that are linked to continuity: mission, family dynamics, organizational structure, and successor development. The organizational mission, built on the collective dream of the participants, is the source of energy that makes the foundation viable. The family dynamics can either facilitate or frustrate those dreams. Organizational structures and processes determine whether the foundation can do its work, and developing human resources in the next generations determines whether that work has a future. In chapters 6 through 9 we summarize the key conclusions and implications of the research regarding those four themes.

Finally, in chapter 10, we offer some overall conclusions and implications from the study.

6

MISSION AND DREAM:
INVENTING AND REINVENTING
THE FOUNDATION

A family foundation, like any organization, is a place where people work. Reduced to its most basic core, the foundation only exists as long as individuals are willing to engage in its purpose, and act within its structure and routines. Why do people choose to make that commitment? What is it that motivates them to spend their time and energy in one organization instead of another?

More specifically, what goes through the mind of cousin Amy, a thirty-five-year-old mother of three, a teacher or a real estate broker in San Diego or Buffalo, when she has to prepare for a quarterly board meeting of the foundation her grandparents established in Missouri or Texas? Why does she take four of her precious weekends per year away from her husband and children, not to mention the evenings reading the board books and the phone calls and conversations about programs and grantees? Why does she care about a community she has never lived in, full of people she has never met? What if every meeting is dominated by talkative Aunt Jenny or grumpy cousin Max? What gets her on the plane?

This is the basic continuity challenge for the foundation. Consciously or unconsciously, every participant—in this case in particular, every family member—must confront two fundamental questions:

Why are *we* doing this? and
Why am *I* participating?

The answer to the first question is the foundation's mission. The mission is the reason that the organization exists. It is the purpose that

181

the foundation sets for itself, the goal toward which it applies all of its capital, financial and human. The mission declares to its constituency, the family and the others who are listening, "This is work worth doing. Join us and contribute to accomplishing it."

The answer to the second question can only come from the internal deliberations of each individual. Responding to this question requires a person to be self-reflective about his or her "Dream"—both the general dream for life, and the special philanthropic dream. We have used this term in its generic sense throughout this book. The Dream is actually a specific concept defined by Daniel Levinson in his pioneering work on adult development. In his research on normal men and women across their life span, Professor Levinson discovered that as they entered early adulthood most individuals began to form an unconscious image of what they wanted their life to be about.

> The Dream is a vague sense of self-in-adult-world. It has the quality of a vision, an imagined possibility that generates excitement and vitality. At the start it is poorly articulated and only tenuously connected to reality, although it may contain concrete images such as winning the Nobel Prize or making the all-star team. It may take dramatic form as in the myth of the hero: the great artist, business tycoon, athletic or intellectual superstar performing magnificent feats and receiving special honors. Or it may take mundane forms that are yet inspiring and sustaining: the excellent craftsman, the husband-father in a certain kind of family, the highly respected member of one's community. (Levinson 1978, 91)[1]

The Dreams of individuals are the guiding beacons of their evolving lives—sometimes clear and definitive, more often obscure and dimly perceived. They are activated when a person is faced with an important choice: this job or that one, yes or no to this relationship, another child, a move across country, a year off after college to travel? But they are also just beneath the surface at the point of other smaller, more subtle choices. Do I visit my parents? Do I stay in contact with my sister? Do I become active politically? Really learn to play the piano this time? Start going to church regularly again? And, most relevant here, do I care about this foundation? Should I participate?

The viability of an organization like a foundation is dependent on its connection to the Dreams of its participants. It may survive without that connection, but it cannot thrive. To reach that critical mass, the individual Dreams of enough participants must overlap and be woven into a collective family Dream for the family in the foundation.

Ivan Lansberg has done the most compelling work on the process of integrating individual Dreams into a Shared Dream that can sustain continuity in a family enterprise.

> The Shared Dream is a collective vision of the future that inspires family members to engage in the hard work of planning and to do whatever is necessary to maintain their collaboration and achieve their goals. . . . In family companies, Shared Dreams are highly personal and must grow from within, often over a period of years. The Shared Dream emerges from the family's fundamental values and aspirations. It defines who they are, who they want to be, what kind of enterprise they wish to build, and how they wish to be perceived by the world. . . . Above all, the Shared Dream endows the family enterprise with *meaning*—it conveys a profound explanation for why continuing the business is important to the family.
>
> Such a vision is not easy to create. It is forged through an ongoing conversation in which each of the members links his or her individual Dreams with some larger vision worthy of the family's best efforts. It may take years for family members to articulate their individual Dreams. For many it takes considerable effort to share their Dreams openly with other family members, which is the first step toward a consensus on a vision of the future. Whatever time it takes will usually be worth the effort. For a success or failure in passing on the business and continuing it as a viable enterprise depends on the family's ability to create such a common vision. (Lansberg 1999, 75–76)

The parts of the Dreams that connect to the foundation may be straightforward or subtle. It is easy to see how specific philanthropic goals are connected. The importance of religion and spirituality, the sense of obligation to a community, or the desire to be exemplary as a family are all parts of a Dream that can find easy application to a foundation.

Other parts of a Dream may connect more obliquely. Individuals may be primarily motivated by a dream of nurturance, of being a caretaker and a healer. That Dream may take them into a career in medicine or nursing, but it also can sustain a strong commitment to the foundation if the mission includes health care and eliminating disease, or providing shelter and food to the most needy. Another individual may dream of becoming an explorer or a great scientist. That could propel her or him into graduate school in biology, or on an arduous trek into the equatorial jungle. But it could also sustain their passion for the foundation if the mission covers scientific discovery and a global mandate.

The point is that these considerations go far beyond "interests." They are the link between a person's deepest aspirations and the foundation as a place where those aspirations can be lived out. It is not so much "What do I want to support?" as "Who am I? Who do I hope to become? What work can help me on that path?" In the foundations that are the most vital, exciting, and satisfying, the collective Dream is built on the common ground where the answers to those questions for all the participants overlap, and the organizational mission enacts that collective Dream.

THE WOUTERS FAMILY FOUNDATION

The Wouters Foundation's early grantmaking consisted mostly of ceremonial grants to a few large institutional grantees, making the foundation a leader in this very specific interest of the founders, Frank and Carmen Wouters. However, both the endowment and the Wouters family grew over the next several decades. The family branches became widely dispersed, both geographically and philosophically.

For several years, the branch still living in the same location maintained the foundation. But over time, the grantees changed also. A few ran into organizational difficulty and could no longer make use of the increasingly large bequests. Efforts to find new recipients within the same narrow funding category were frustrating. Money ended up getting "parked" in neutral academic and community support institutions. The now-elderly second-generation trustees had less and less energy for the maintenance work, and less interest in the social status and ceremonial invitations that running the foundation generated.

After more than two decades, a third-generation niece has emerged as a successor executive director, and she has organized and professionalized the grantmaking functions. She is a talented facilitator and an enthusiastic supporter of the foundation, but she is confounded by two challenges: how to keep the escaping diaspora of the family connected to the foundation, and how to develop a consensus for new funding areas to absorb the increasing mandated dispersals.

Every effort to expand the foundation's scope beyond the founders' original objective initially met with strong opposition from one family branch or another. Her first priority was to keep the peace and not drive any relatives away. She has persisted for five years with a gradual opening of discussion about individual priorities and common goals. Progress has been slow, but a core of enthusiastic cousins is emerging. The next year or two will determine whether a sufficient collective Dream can be found.

FROM DONOR INTENT TO CLEAR CURRENT MISSION

In the majority of our cases, current trustees cannot rely too much on donor intent, even if they want to. There is remarkably little specificity in the original mission statements of these foundations—only six say anything detailed enough to guide current grantmaking. It is likely that these Controlling Trustee founders saw no need to specify what the foundation would be about. They knew what they intended, and what would be the point of tying their own hands?

The lack of specific guidance from founders puts the long-standing discussion of "donor intent" in a different light. We found that the current interpretation of donor intent was at least as likely to have been created by the descendants as by the ancestors—that is, a post hoc construction of what the donor would probably have done with the funds if he or she were still around. These constructions are a stew of hints from early documents, memories of the donors' actual actions, fantasies and myths about their inclinations, and projections of the passions of current family members onto the deceased ancestors. Nevertheless, the process of arguing about this derived "donor intent" can be emotional, as it is used alternately by one or another subgroup as justification for an amazing range of proposals.

Whether the donor was specific or not, the key challenge for current trustees and directors is to take responsibility for the mission of the foundation and to make it their own. We concluded chapter 3 with the core dilemma for founders: whether to choose a specific purpose in perpetuity or to encourage self-determined collaborative family philanthropy. When the founders choose the specific purpose, the task for successors is to decide whether that agenda interests them, and then to apply the ongoing mission into a viable program under current circumstances. If the founders' purpose was brilliant, and forward-looking, and flexible, and compelling enough to be sufficient in its original form, the current leaders can quickly move on to implementation. But the vast majority of our cases found it necessary to reinterpret—or at least clarify—the mission over time.

When the founder's choice is for an ongoing collaborative opportunity, then the demands on current successors are even more far-reaching. Successors in those cases understand that their present and future collaboration must be built on personal passion for an emerging and common dream. They accept both the right and the responsibility to reinvent the mission, but that is only the first step. How do you sustain collaboration in a family that has become many times more diverse than the founder could have imagined? Do current leaders have sufficient leverage to restructure and change the organization? Is family harmony inherently incompatible with tough choices?

The family foundations that thrive through later generations find answers to these questions in their ongoing reflection, negotiations, and planning. In the terms of the transition model, they monitor the buildup of pressures by noticing how far apart board members are on funding priorities, and how long it takes to reach decisions. They watch carefully to see how many new ideas and initiatives are brought to the table and what kind of response they receive. They pay attention to members whose ideas are the most challenging and the most frequently denied, and note whether the dissidents maintain their enthusiasm or fall silent.

In particular, they attend carefully to transitions in membership and leadership: departures and additions to the board (especially the first representatives of any generation to either come or leave); turnover in chairpersons, executive directors, and program officers; and significant changes in the endowment or the demands from the environment.

When the transitional pressures have accumulated, these families watch for the trigger and recognize it for what it is—a call to break routine. Rather than coping with the crisis and forging ahead, they make the space and the time to reconsider the "big picture" of the foundation's work.

This is when the mission becomes the focus. It is brought down from the engraved plaque or out from the drawer, placed at the center of the table, and reconsidered thoughtfully and in detail. Through the review of the mission, all of the other pressures find their way into the discussion—logistics, resources, procedures, performance, and the overlap of philanthropic dreams.

Out of this process emerges the blueprint for the future: the collaborative family Dream. Most often, it is partly a reconfirmation of tradition, and partly a new interpretation or a new direction. When the mission is well articulated *and* accompanied by a strong family Dream, the family knows which mountain to climb and can concentrate on climbing it well.

The change over time in the clarity of mission in this sample of multigenerational foundations is remarkable. (Table 6.1 compares mission clarity at founding with those currently.)

The evidence suggests that clarifying the mission pays off not only in survival, but in performance. The researchers coded missions in two ways: whether or not there is any specific written mission statement ("Mission Statement"), and the overall clarity of mission in documents and in the reports of the current trustees and directors ("Mission Clarity"). We found that both measures were consistently and significantly correlated with other high ratings of organizational performance: Clarity of the program, grantmaking vitality, quality control, efficient organizational structure, and successor development (see table D.1 in appendix D). A clear current mission is the single best predictor of most of the other performance variables as rated by the research team.

The fact that a clear mission is helpful in grantmaking and quality control is encouraging but expected. It was much more surprising

Table 6.1.   Mission Statements

	None	General/Implicit	Specific
At Founding	18	6	6
Current	5	8	17

that the clarity of the mission also was correlated with positive family process variables. The more clear and thoughtful the mission, the higher the ratings on family collaboration, enthusiasm, positive dynamics, and the foundation's likelihood of continuity (see table D.2 in appendix D).

It would be hard to find a stronger endorsement of the importance of a clear, relevant, fully discussed, and high-commitment mission for continuity.[2] The common thread for the foundations that are successful in dealing with this issue is a focused, protected, and intensive periodic reconsideration of mission combined with a recommitment to the dream.

Nearly all of them had the watershed moment of redesign, most typically as the "exploration" task of the transition from Controlling Trustee to Collaborative Family Foundation—whenever that occurred. Since then they have continued a "maintenance" level of attention to mission, setting aside some time at least once per year for an overview discussion separate from grantmaking.

A few have had a second major reconsideration and redesign, also at a generational transition. These data carry the clear message that over time, the maturation of the foundation's structure—from Controlling Trustee to Collaborative Family Foundation and, in some cases, to a Family-Governed Staff-Managed Foundation— requires a corresponding evolution of the mission and the family dream.

That does not necessarily mean change, but rather elaboration, clarification, interpretation and, very often, reinterpretation. The starting point was just that: a starting point of a journey of inquiry and recommitment. But family systems cannot be static, because families are inevitably in flux. Added to aging are the normal turns of family history: marriage and divorce, birth of children and death, adoption, remarriage, estrangement and reconciliation. As the human resources of the family change, so do the passions and priorities of its current members. There needs to be a process that adapts the mission and dream into the present, in touch with the resources and realities of the current foundation, rather than looking for reassurance and instructions from an immutable past.

This is completely consistent with the pattern of "punctuated equilibrium" system change we discussed earlier. Periods of stability are interspersed with moments of transition, when the system is open to reassessment and fundamental change. To reassess less frequently risks stagnation; to do so continually would certainly lead to exhaustion and diminished productivity.

Most of the foundations in this sample that engaged in this kind of fundamental review used specially designated retreats to do so. It was important to protect these discussions from the press of grant-making decisions. About two-thirds (18 out of 30) used an outside professional facilitator for these retreats, and the reviews were predominately positive.[3]

While the deliberations within the current board were important, an additional effort helped maximize the continuity-enhancing benefits of a reconsideration of the mission. For that purpose it was also necessary to reach family members not currently involved, to give them a chance to articulate their philanthropic Dreams. Family members as young as teenagers were included, as were individuals from branches or locations that had less direct access to the current board. Surveys, interviews, or discussions on the foundation and philanthropy in general at an annual family assembly were used by a few of these families, with great success.

One key was the facilitators' insistence on "two way" communication in a meeting with the whole family, so that the session does not reduce itself to information from the board to the family about current programs and grantmaking successes. (Both the National Center for Family Philanthropy and the Council on Foundations have numerous publications about the mechanics of family retreats and foundation mission.)

In summary, the foundations that were the most successful in creating a compelling mission:

- Acknowledged that the donor/founders were not primarily mission focused, and relied on the first generation more for inspiration and encouragement of philanthropy in general than for specific programmatic constraints.
- Paid particular attention to defining or redefining the mission at the point of transition from the Controlling Trustee to the Collaborative Family Foundation, and again (in some cases) at the transition to Family-Governed Staff-Managed Foundation.

NOTES

1. See also Levinson (1996).

2. One interesting finding has to do with the mechanisms for accomplishing the work of mission reinvention. We expected that the primary vehicle that families would use to discuss mission would be annual retreats or meetings designated for strategy and mission discussion. The data does not support that idea. Nine of the foundations report having such regularly scheduled meetings, but they are no different on the performance or family process variables (or any other measures) from the sample as a whole. It could be a matter of interpretation or measurement, but more likely these events work best when they occur at the moment of need rather than by the calendar (see C. Gersick, 1994).

3. Families that want to organize their own retreats or prepare themselves for the involvement of a facilitator may get some guidance from K. Gersick et al. (2000).

7

FAMILY DYNAMICS

In the most impressive family enterprises, you can feel the bonds of affection and mutual nurturing that connect the participants in all of their collaborative actions. At the same time, all that emotion also means that vulnerabilities are high and the potential is always present for anger, hurt feelings, conflict, and pain. The deep emotional connections that are the strengths of family foundations can also be their weaknesses.

The lessons about family dynamics are the most difficult to generalize. It is safe to say that the majority of the thousands of interview hours in this research project were spent hearing stories of family relationships. When asked in the right way, people love to talk about their relatives. But how do all these stories fit together? What is the common thread among thirty families and the hundreds of husbands and wives, brothers and sisters, parents and children, and beyond?

We found three overarching issues that helped organize the lessons about family dynamics from these cases: family culture, conflict management and avoidance, and leadership. Following an exploration of those themes, we offer our observations on the bottom line of family collaboration—the impact of family dynamics on the operation of the foundation, and the foundation's impact on the family.

FAMILY CULTURE AND COLLABORATION

The dynamics of families are partly determined by individual personalities, but also in important ways by the family environment—its culture. Families have powerful cultures that dictate a style of interaction. It would be very unlikely for a family to interact around the dinner table very differently from the way they interact around the board table.

Some of the characteristics are obvious. Always fighting? Often quiet? Never silent? Joking and laughing (either in genuine pleasure or nervous deflection of serious conversation)? Grave and solemn?

Some characteristics are more subtle, and take a careful eye. Do the seniors always talk and the juniors always listen? Do the men do all the talking? The women? Are the most eccentric or flamboyant individuals just dramatic personalities, or are they demonstrating something of the family style?

Family cultures can not only highlight philanthropy, they can define how a family thinks about itself as a social citizen.

During the 1950s, while her husband was focused on building a viable manufacturing company, Polly Calkins was very devoted to charity. She would see a cause or a need and simply send a check—paying a milk bill for a school, sending money to a family that had a fire, supporting any fund-raising drive. When she and her husband started the foundation, she simply continued exactly the same automatic and opportunistic giving. Philanthropy was the core of her personality, and therefore central and taken for granted in the family.

Later in her life, on birthdays and holidays, she would write checks to charity and send her grandchildren cards telling them what causes and groups had received $50 in their name. Those grandchildren, now adults and leaders in the foundation, describe their disappointment about not receiving a baseball glove, but are also appreciative of the lesson learned. As one put it, "I have always seen grandma as eccentric, but wonderful."

As a family develops across generations, its culture becomes more diverse and complex.[1] The differences that emerge as individuals reach adulthood, form new families of their own, and move away from the family of origin are the primary challenge to forming the Collaborative Family Foundation. Branch identity, geography, and family culture interacted powerfully in many of the families we studied. In five of the cases there were clearly defined camps which had migrated to different parts of the country.

The Michaels Family Foundation directors are roughly divided into an "east coast caucus" and a "west coast caucus," and the two are as far apart in their politics, religious outlook, and vision for the foundation as possible. Arisa Michaels and her family hold conservative Republican, Christian fundamentalist views. The Clement Michaels branch consists of liberal Democrats, with a "new age" fringe even further out.

Both sides are intelligent and articulate, and in the interviews were quite candid in assessing each other and their polarized views. Some differences are resolvable with an informal "quid pro quo," and everyone keeps a rough internal scorecard to maintain balance.

When Clement and his offspring wanted to get away from individual giving and put funds into program areas such as youth violence and community development, the other went along "for the sake of family unity," even though they described the idea as "another move by the wooly-headed liberals." In return, the ability to continue to give significant funds to private schools was protected, and the limits raised.

The families that experienced these deep ideological splits, but who wanted to stay together, tended to respond in one of two ways. If they had strong central leadership and valued a high level of interpersonal interaction, they developed balancing techniques that recognized the split and honored it, while still working toward agreements of consensus. They thought a lot about equity. They frequently talked about "balance," "fairness," and "turns." They looked for common ground but also found a way to respect each other's agenda without giving up the right to criticize it. That is, they demonstrated tolerance not just for the different program proposals and ideological objections, but for a fairly high level of joking, teasing, name-calling, and subtle ridicule.

Other families wanted to stay together, but were more disengaged in their overall culture and had less need to act as a unit. By chance or design, these families did not invest a moderator (either a family member or a nonfamily executive) with enough legitimacy and credibility to pull off such a delicate balance. As a result they tended to withdraw from each other. They established and respected firm internal boundaries. The developed "live and let live" structures with high degrees of discretionary funding and minimal collaborative grantmaking. They became associates under one banner but operated as independently as possible.

In both cases, the most significant challenges came at the moments of preparation for generational transitions. Whatever balancing process the siblings were able to work out, it was put at risk by the entry of the cousin generation. Most families felt their anxiety rise in anticipation of some of the cousins reaching adulthood before others, or when they realized that the differences in the size of the branches or their geographic proximity to the foundation home base would mean that one "side" would gradually have more voices, and more power, in the system. As we shall see in chapter 9, it is just the fear of this "unbalancing" that causes some families to avoid thinking about continuity until it is too late.

However, in this sample there were some strong examples of families who faced the culture splits directly.

The Southwick Foundation, one of the smaller foundations with a dramatic "east-west" split on style and priorities, was lucky enough to have just two siblings, each with just two offspring, all of about the same age. They could accomplish expansion without threatening the balance. They decided to create a "Next Generation Fund" which all the cousins from all branches would join at age twenty-one. The parent board funded and oversaw the youth group. Cousins could move to the main board only to fill a vacancy, maintaining the political detente there. It is seen as an imperfect solution, and will probably be temporary, but it took some pressure off the larger group.

Nevertheless, the issue arises periodically about whether it would be simpler to "divide up the pie," splitting the endowment into parts and letting each branch go its separate way. So far, there has not been much enthusiasm for that. For the present, the pleasure of working together has outweighed the frustration of the disagreements. And the founder's presence still hovers over the system. Shelley Southwick, the oldest member of the third generation and the one who knew the founder the best, said, "My grandfather's wishes are regularly verbalized at the meetings. When we get together, there's lots of chatter. In some ways we have a lot in common. The foundation has kept the family together. In that sense, his hope was fulfilled.

This case highlights a dynamic that has come up in our general work in family philanthropy. By definition, all thirty families in our sample have stayed together, although ten of the families have at least one other foundation in the extended family. In the broader field, some families decide to split up the foundation into parts, or to spend out, for family dynamics reasons. They experience too much destructive conflict, or they have to deal with one or more unpleasant personalities, or they cannot find enough common ground. Some feel they have to end the foundation in order to maintain the family.

It is undeniable that some families should not try to accomplish collaborative grantmaking. Later in this chapter we will discuss some of the lessons about how a dysfunctional foundation can complicate the lives of a troubled family, and when it is time to call it quits.

However, for other families, it is equally important not to pull the plug prematurely. As the Southwicks demonstrate, families can often work through conflict. In difficult times, relatives may underestimate the rewards they are getting from the collaborative effort, even if flawed, and as a result also underestimate the costs of splitting up. The current pain of antagonism is clear to everyone. The future losses if the foundation did not continue—particularly the informal, personal conversations that happen around the edges of the work and maintain intimacy, or at least familiarity, with otherwise distant relatives—are much harder to appreciate. It is important to weigh those costs along with the benefits and potential relief when a troubled family foundation considers splitting up.

FOUR DIMENSIONS OF FAMILY CULTURE

In our work with families, we have found that some core tendencies in family dynamics and culture always influence the process of family enterprise, whether a company or a foundation. In particular, we have found four characteristics of families that help to explain how the family process affects the organizational performance (figure 7.1). Our sample included a range of family cultures, from those that were extreme on each dimension to others that were balanced, showing characteristics of each pole.

The families who were most hierarchical are also most likely to have stayed in the Controlling Trustee mode for the longest time, and to have the clearest initial missions and programs, but less likely to do aggressive succession planning and to adopt term limits or other constraints on discretion. The families with more democratic cultures

HIERARCHICAL ◄───────────────► DEMOCRATIC	
Strong on efficiency, clarity of authority, respect for seniors	Strong on participation, feeling of empowerment
Problems with resentment by subordinates, underutilization of the talents of the less powerful	Problems with low efficiency, slow speed of decision making, frustration with "veto" power of disruptive individuals
VERTICAL ◄───────────────► HORIZONTAL	
Strong on branch identification and loyalty across generations	Strong on generational identification and loyalty across branches
Problems with creating a sense of the whole extended family, healing sibling grievances	Problems with maintaining a legacy, admitting younger generations to authority without revolution
ENMESHED ◄───────────────► DISENGAGED	
Strong on intimacy, creating a sense of belonging and mutual support	Strong on self-reliance, adventurousness, independence
Problems with independence, privacy, and separation	Problems with loneliness, sense of disconnection
AFFECTIVE/EXPRESSIVE ◄───────────────► COGNITIVE/RESERVED	
Strong on recognizing, expressing, and using emotions	Strong on decision making, avoiding conflict
Problems with impulse control, overreliance on "intuition," long recovery time from conflict	Problems with unexpressed feelings, experiencing the pleasure of accomplishments

Figure 7.1.   Dimensions of Family Culture

were quicker to involve second and later generation members in the grantmaking, and met more often for longer hours, seeking consensus on all grantmaking.

The vertically oriented families are much more likely to hold to strict branch-based representation rules for trustee selection, and to worry about block equity. Their typical response to culture divisions is to favor discretionary funds. The horizontally oriented families are more likely to set up separate next generation programs, to hold off the entry of each generation but then to admit them in bunches.

The enmeshed families are the least likely to bring in nonfamily directors and in-laws, and when they hire nonfamily professional staff it is most often as implementers rather than as independent executives. They spend a great deal of time thinking about mission, seeing it as an important and visible representation of the family's core identity. Most multi-generational family businesses are owned by families that have at least some characteristics of enmeshment in their cultures. Disengaged families, on the other hand, feel much more comfortable with a "live and let live" individuality in their collective activities. They have an easier time with multiple program areas, strong staff, and learning from the experience of other families.

Finally, the affective/expressive families relish the bonding emotionality of working together. Their grantmaking is sometimes volatile but rarely boring. They are the least likely to fall into the trap of passive withdrawal, but the most worried about conflict management. The cognitive/reserved families, on the other hand, are the great policymakers. They get the most out of their staffs and try to keep their grantmaking based on good decisions and grantee performance. They understand the value of formalization and can provide exemplary models. But they may experience philanthropy more like work, less like fun. Obviously most families have mixed cultures. On each of the four dimensions, there are often champions of both styles, and the behavior at any one time reflects who is in the room and what the current task is. The lesson for continuity and leadership is to recognize the dominant culture, exploit its strengths, and compensate for its weaknesses. Vertical families need to pay attention to the dangers of overemphasis on branch, and create integrating policies and activities. Affective/expressive families may need to agree to a more formal "code of conduct" to give a sense of security to the less assertive new members. Enmeshed families may need to consider whether allowing spouses to participate would bring in new talents and open their eyes to new ways of thinking. All of these cultures can be successful if they are based on moderation, self-awareness, and openness to change over time.

FAMILY DYNAMICS AND CONFLICT MANAGEMENT

Tension is part of the human condition. To varying degrees, every family deals with incidents of sibling rivalry, personality clashes, jealousies, and philosophical disagreements. Some families have developed ways for managing conflict, whether by talking through their differences or simply taking time out until tempers cool down. Other families are dragged down by conflict because they try to ignore it, overreact to it, or have never learned techniques for responding appropriately to it.

The topic of conflict and family harmony came up in every one of the thirty cases. Some families were proud of their peaceful style, some were disgusted by hostility and insults, some were worried about communication in the future. The participants described conflict between generations, among siblings, between branches, and between one particular individual and another. It was often the first issue raised when the interviews became more personal and open. It is clearly on everyone's mind.

But the basic lesson of these foundations is not what the individual sources would have expected. Of course, some of them do have disruptive conflict. There are wounds in some families that affect every meeting and the time in between, and in some cases have taken generations to heal or are still tender. But for the most part, it is not the conflict itself that has hampered grantmaking or threatened continuity in these foundations. It is the lengths to which they go to avoid conflict. The preoccupation with family harmony at any cost is the single most dangerous impact of family dynamics on these organizations. It has seriously hampered and impaired more than half of them, and threatens most of the others.

The eldest sister in the second generation of this family was at odds with her siblings from earliest childhood. Her two brothers and two sisters were quiet, compliant children of strong, charismatic parents. She was always an individual. She was the only one to leave the family's home city, moving away for college and never returning.

The family culture prized civility, mutual caretaking, and agreement. Each of the four younger siblings married spouses who supported the same style, and raised their children accordingly. In contrast, the eldest married a brash and flamboyant attorney, and their household was a circus of strongly held opinions argued—affectionately—to the limit.

By the time the founding parents were ready to pass on leadership in the family foundation to the second generation, the offspring were in their forties and fifties. They all wanted to honor their parents, who expressly hoped that they could work together on the foundation. But they couldn't agree on anything about the grantmaking, and more importantly they couldn't agree on how to disagree. The eldest sister's voicing her lack of interest in the parents' priorities was always met with polite smiles, placation, and a commitment to "think about that idea." Gradually the branches drifted into extremely conservative complacency and withdrawal.

Avoidance of conflict can, over the long run, sap the commitment out of a family foundation. If the underlying causes of frustration are not allowed some open expression, the natural response, eventually, is withdrawal. The action may appear impulsive or sudden, but in fact the buildup may have been very gradual.

This family has a long history of hiding conflict, with everyone holding on tight to their perceived view of the universe, and then ultimately splitting up. When the split happens, the subgroup in power seems surprised, confused, and upset about what happened. They do not understand why even when the reasons are explained. At the same time, the group leaving is very frustrated and clear about the reasons, but does not feel able to express themselves directly, until they finally give up. The remainder of the family, the group in-between, seems aware of the developing dynamic but powerless to change the course of the conflict.

Conflict avoidance does not always lead to dramatic explosions or separations. There were several families in the sample that simply do not argue. Their value of respect and civility is deep and broad. It is a judgment call in these cases whether there is a negative consequence of such a style.

"Our family cannot bear conflict. None of us like it, but it is especially painful for my mother. It would upset her terribly if we argued over grants." Only once did this family report a serious disagreement, and that was over a proposal to fund an alternative medical treatment. One sibling favored it because his children had benefited directly. His sibling labeled it "unscientific and quackery."

Very uncharacteristically, both held their ground. When they couldn't reach agreement, the person who opposed abstained and the board gave a small grant. But all parties were shaken by the disagreement and exchanged a flurry of e-mails "to process what had happened" and reassure each other that they were OK with the outcome.

One of the siblings didn't know what the impact would be on future meetings. "I know it's important to bring different perspectives to the discussions. Sometimes I think we're too congenial. Maybe we need some new input, and some different views expressed."

This case includes an interesting historical "myth" that was repeated by several directors. Under the guidance of a former chairman, the family adopted a "Code of Conduct" which encouraged mutual respect and polite behavior. Compliance with these values was enthusiastically endorsed by all participants. The result was that directors were afraid to debate foundation strategy because arguing violated the spirit of the Code.

When the board couldn't reach quick consensus, often no action was taken. The former chair said she "wrote the Code to create a more humanitarian atmosphere, but I think it spawned a dysfunctional culture." More likely the Code reflected, rather than created, excessive conflict avoidance, but it did give it procedural legitimacy.

This second-generation son began his leadership tenure as a copy of his father's warm but authoritarian style. Over a brief time, however, he modified his behavior to be much more inviting, collaborative, and supportive of leadership behavior in others. While he has remained the president for over forty years, his leadership style has been greatly appreciated.

All family members talk about how well they all work together. Everyone agrees that they make decisions easily, enjoy each other's company, and see the foundation as a way of getting closer with each other. "We are all very cooperative, we all get along very well. There is not much conflict. We are very respectful of each other, compromising; we'll listen to how the others feel. If the foundation hadn't existed, I wouldn't be as close to my brother and sister—we would have been friendly, but not close."

The only dilemma in this case is that part of their strategy for avoiding conflict is keeping the group very small and homogeneous. The broader family does not feel very connected to the foundation, and they have avoided steps toward continuity planning. There is the possibility that they are trading viability in the future for peace today.

FAMILY DYNAMICS AND LEADERSHIP STYLE

One of the most important factors in whether a foundation managed or mismanaged conflict was the level of interpersonal skills in its leaders. Like all organizations, these foundations struggle to find inspired, facilitative, high-performance leadership. We have discussed the functional abilities of leaders at several points in the developmental histories of these foundations. However, in addition, the nurturant, parental aspects of leadership also need discussion.

The particular interpersonal skills of good leaders were most critical as these foundations entered the complicated transitions from Controlling Trustee forms to Collaborative Family Foundations. For all the reasons we have explored in earlier sections, this transition is challenging and emotionally demanding. Some of the foundations were fortunate enough to have leadership in the family at that moment who could ease the anxiety and facilitate the work.

The Albert family went through two generations of Controlling Trustees, including a twenty-year presidential term of Katherine, the oldest daughter of the founder. She was a compelling personality, revered by her family, but not an effective manager. She and her sisters and brother made grants to traditional organizations without much coordination or program planning. When she decided to retire at eighty-five, her daughter Michele, the logical successor, faced a number of challenges. The sequential deaths of her aunts and uncles had significantly increased the foundation endowment. The cousin generation was widely dispersed and unprepared for collaborative grantmaking. Katherine's withdrawal triggered a transition that was marked by several cousins suggesting that the foundation split up or spend out.

Michele, a professional social worker, invited the rest of the family to explore other alternatives. In contrast to her mother, she had a very low-key, supportive, affectionate style, and she implemented a two-pronged approach. First she started calling her cousins on a regular schedule, to talk about the foundation but also to become more current about events in their lives. Her son, a computer programmer, designed a family website and e-mail network. At the same time, Michele hired a part-time program officer and asked for everyone's help with one specific project that was of interest to all the branches, and that could be accomplished in just a few months. The pleasure of their first truly collaborative grantmaking effort was a very positive surprise to the entire family.

Over Michele's first year a reservoir of untapped family involvement was discovered. The family had its first reunion in forty years, and one of the fourth generation started a biography of the founder. Frank Albert, Michele's youngest cousin, said, "There's something about her way of doing things. She never pushes, but she offers something appealing. Fighting seems silly when Michele is in the room. She makes us all feel that we have something to contribute, she reminds us that we basically like each other, and that this is actually fun. I don't exactly know how, but she reminded us of the good things about being a family."

Other foundations were not so lucky. Many did not explicitly consider interpersonal skill in choosing leaders, but focused on demographics (branch, birth order, and gender) or on prior level of effort in the foundation. That meant that some leaders may have been knowledgeable about philanthropy, but not very good at creating a positive emotional environment. There is no reason to expect that individuals who have negative styles and personalities as parents, siblings, spouses, or offspring would somehow be completely different in the context of the foundation. Their intentions may be faultless, but that is not enough.

Each member of this family has his or her own theory of the source of the chronic, dispiriting conflict that engulfs the foundation's activities. One daughter remembers her father as always having a lot of anger, which she believes derives from his disappointment over his lack of success in his career. Other siblings ascribe the conflict in this family to "ancient battles over lifestyle, conservative versus liberal values, and habitual ways of responding that get everyone's backs up."

Another daughter says of her father: "He engages people through negative statements, through criticisms or complaints, and you have to respond. . . . It just irks the hell out of me when my mother and father question whether [one of my] proposals is worthy. They haven't reviewed the proposal; they haven't gone on the site visit. They'll ask a question like, 'How many people is this going to help?' The way they ask the question has a negative edge; it isn't just casual. I'll say, 'Well, read the proposal,' but it's hard to enjoy a meeting after that."

The chair's leadership style has been problematic for the twenty years he has been running the meetings, but a much more serious problem in recent years. Always autocratic and detail focused, he has become a minidictator and obsessive as he aged. Whereas his incredible memory, analytical skills, hard work, and devotion to the foundation were assets when people were younger, as the foundation grew and his style deteriorated the problems intensified. Complaints included long meetings, absolute control of agenda and discussion, exclusion of grants, and yelling at members in the meetings. In the words of one niece, "the meetings were absolute torture!"

Just as no resource is more powerful in increasing the likelihood of continuity than sensitive, empathic leadership, nothing threatens it more than arrogance and blind exercise of authority. It is hard to get around a destructive leader. Nearly all of the thirty cases had some moment in their history when they had to cope with distracted, ineffective, or nasty leadership. It always sidetracked their operations and threatened their continuity. The foundations that were disrupted the least were the ones that recognized the problem and acted most decisively to correct it.

In the terms of our transition model, the developmental pressure that resulted from these episodes built steadily but at different speeds in different cases. In some foundations it was truly glacial in its pace, tolerating poor leader performance for years or even decades, responding with increasing frustration and resentment but only reaching the trigger point when some outrageous event occurred or the leader departed. In other cases the reaction was more concentrated.

Either way, once triggered, the transition typically included a disengagement from the old assumptions about leadership criteria. This was especially true if the source of those old criteria was only general assumptions and family culture (primogeniture, gender preference, extreme avioidance of conflict) that had proven inadequate to generate competence and skills in the designated individual. A key part of the exploration and choice phases of the transition in those cases was not just selecting new leaders, but a new definition of leadership from that point on.

THE IMPACT OF THE FOUNDATION ON THE FAMILY

We have focused on the impact of family dynamics on the foundation and its performance. We also need to remember that a significant number of the founders of these foundations hoped that the work of philanthropy would have benefits for their present and future families. In this vein, it is worthwhile to look at the opposite effect—the impact of the foundation on the family.

Can a Dysfunctional Foundation Damage a Struggling Family?

Apparently so, but not in the way you might expect. We did not see many cases of open conflict and hostility, stimulated by disagreements about philanthropy, spilling over from the foundation and threatening family harmony. What we saw instead, in a handful of the cases, was the burden of the philanthropy, in the absence of a shared mission or a collaborative dream, becoming one more reminder of the divisions, grievances, differences, and inequities in some families.

When the typical rewards of having a foundation are low priority to most family members, and the work itself is overwhelming, the foundation can become a dreaded obligation. If that is accompanied by a feeling of guilt at abandoning the agenda or disappointing the dreams of parents and ancestors, it can take even more of an emotional toll.

This second-generation foundation is in trouble, as one sibling put it, because "the foundation reflects the splintering of the family, where each sibling has gone his own way, not in a very happy way." She described how their father was the center of the family. When he was sick, they would all align to make sure they were helping him do the right things.

But since he passed away, the siblings have spilt. They have copied their father's system of a lead grantor doing most of the decisions, with small discretionary funds for each of the other individuals. They rotate the lead role on an annual basis.

They feel that they are too small to justify hiring professional staff. This granting system is forcing the family away from a common philanthropic dream that would give them the "glue" they now need to replace their father's strong interpersonal force. It also places a huge burden on the trustees to research and identify projects and prepare proposals to present to the board.

The siblings also adopted their father's "venture philanthropy" policy of one-time funding, which means that there is no continuity with the organizations they fund, and they have to find new projects every year. Besides being more work than they can handle, it fosters a competitive dynamic among the siblings, institutionalizing a culture of different dreams and pet projects.

Right now, it seems that they are not operating as one foundation but really as three foundations. The absence of a common vision is reflected in a very general mission statement that doesn't convey much passion. They are very cautious about making everything very equal in every respect. This has meant that they cannot productively discuss inviting their spouses or children into the process, since their family situations are very different. "We seem to have lost the possibility of getting any satisfaction from doing something good in the community. Instead, the family is falling apart and the work is becoming more and more a source of conflict and a burden—another thing on my already too busy to-do list and something else to feel bad about not doing properly."

A collegial, well-functioning Collaborative Family Foundation does not necessarily have to be democratic. In particular, the authority hierarchy of generations was very evident in many of the best functioning foundations. The key is that each participant, and each generation, has a clear sense of its role, and is valued for its contribution.

Two parents and three of their children are involved as trustees or directors. They all have input into decisions, but it is clearly still the parents' show. The three offspring are all very attuned to the wishes of their parents, honor their roles as founders and prime trustees, and do not suggest projects that do not fit within their parents' vision. The daughter said the one time she brought something else to the table it was "a very unpleasant experience, and I wouldn't be likely to repeat it." The message was, "This is not yours to play with. Not yet."

Can a Well-functioning Foundation Actually Heal a Troubled Family?

We were pleased to find that the answer to this question was clearly "yes." In chapters 4 and 5 we saw that focusing on quality work may provide more benefit to family dynamics than the other way around. That is, foundations that try to structure themselves with minimal demands on performance, in an effort to attract maximum ease of "family togetherness," do themselves a disservice. Instead of creating an atmosphere of inviting acceptance, a feeling of nonimportance sets in. The resulting family dynamic is destructive, and can spread far beyond the foundation to other activities in common and to social interaction in general.

The foundations that take the work most seriously are in fact the ones that have the most positive impact on relationships. The participants develop a sense of true pride. There are few bonding experiences more powerful than real accomplishment as a result of challenging hard work. This is a sample of foundations that have *endured*, and their ability to do so may arise from this insistence on quality work more than any other characteristic. In more than a third of the cases, the family credits the foundation with fostering closeness and perpetuating family cohesion across branches, geography, and generations.

In the words of a nonfamily director, "The sisters are close in the sense that when problems arise in the family, they come together like a rock. If it weren't for the foundation, they'd probably have little contact. Watching this family work together, I've become a believer in what foundations can do to bring families closer."

For this foundation's third-generation executive director, the foundation is a vehicle for getting together and connecting with her parents' generation and her younger cousin. The involvement on the foundation particularly strengthened her relationship with her mother. They go on trips together, do site visits, and learn together. She says her mother is now her best friend.

It is important not to overstate the case. If a family is seriously dysfunctional with deep schisms and a culture that tolerates open antagonism, the potential for positive impact from the foundation will be minimal. But there were cases where the collaboration in grantmaking seemed to lift up the family and demonstrate a more rewarding way to relate. Some observations are in order:

1. The rewards may be a generation delayed in appearing. A second generation that makes a decision to work together despite their history and differences may foster a cousin generation that believes in collaboration and wants to preserve a collective legacy.
2. A strong and sensitive nonfamily executive is a very powerful advantage. No single characteristic is more closely linked to overcoming and improving family process than a trusted, objective, and psychologically skilled professional staff director.
3. Sometimes fate has to take a hand. A health crisis in a previously disinterested leader, the departure of a disruptive in-law or sibling, or a sudden change in the financial condition of the family can stimulate a new perspective.

This family had been split in two over a bitter father-son fight in the family business. When the company was sold twenty-five years later, the third-generation leader, brother to the banished ex-executive, completely restructured the foundation and invited his brother and his brother's son to rejoin the foundation. "That was then, this is now," he told his own son. "My brother has a right to be on the board."

The two branches have worked closely for the past twenty years, and the cousins, who also had not spoken during the twenty-five-year split, quickly became a well-integrated group. One reported, "The ban on seeing each other for all those years was really ridiculous. We missed out on a lot by not knowing each other as children." The collaboration has proven strong enough to satisfy everyone, even though the two branches have grown very different on politics and general outlook.

There was one lingering residue of the family conflict. The disinherited brother's wife was generally blamed for the crisis, pushing her husband to publicly challenge and embarrass his father. As a result, spouses are excluded from all family economic arenas, including the foundation. This policy is reinforced by the many divorces and strained marriages in the third and fourth generations.

Marty Ashton, the former head of the company and current president of the foundation, was never very close with his family. After the death of his wife, he found himself alone on his seventieth birthday. But shortly thereafter he experienced an epiphany after a serious health crisis. He began to experiment in the foundation with a new way of relating with his offspring. In effect, he was articulating a new approach to the mission, the dream, the organization, the leadership, and the future. For his seventy-fifth, after four years with the foundation, Marty took the whole family to Italy to celebrate his birthday and the fiftieth birthdays of most of his children. They all had a great time.

NOTE

1. Carter and McGoldrick (1999) and Nichols and Schwartz (2001) are good reference volumes for these themes.

8

DEVELOPING THE
ORGANIZATIONAL STRUCTURE

Many of the foundations in our sample were created without much thought to their needs as organizations. As often happened in the last century, the work of establishing a foundation was a few days' paperwork for a competent attorney. The designs were boilerplate and minimal; all of the attention was on tax relief and facilitating the donor's personal charitable contributions. The founders were decisive, entrepreneurial people: They faced few legal requirements and needed little organizational support to accomplish their goals.

But the field of philanthropy has matured. Although some advisors still tend to confuse family foundations with family philanthropy, most understand that there are many ways for families and the individuals in them to be philanthropic.[1] Professionals who truly care about nurturing the charitable impulse in families can guide the leaders through an informed discussion of available options. They can help families consider the personal, legal, and financial ramifications of personal giving, and of community and operating foundations. If establishing a private foundation is the appropriate choice, professional advisors can shepherd the process of setting it up from scratch. In the best cases this involves articulating the family's mission and dream within the proper legal format, and creating the organizational structures and processes that will allow the foundation to do its work.

Even though the current legal restrictions place greater requirements on foundations, once the foundation exists the organizational aspects are usually underdeveloped or neglected.[2] The same sort of "pragmatic inattention" often happens in the founding stages of family businesses. Entrepreneurs don't pay much attention to organizational structure, span of control, project support, information systems, human resources, or even budgets. They want to get the work done with minimum distractions and administrative costs.

However, businesses soon reach the point when they must pay more attention to their infrastructure. Potential employees want contracts and job descriptions. Customers want delivery assurances and to deal with a supplier that demonstrates dependability and professionalism. Most importantly, banks and other creditors want to see management and governance structures that are both adequate and realistic. By the time a business venture has found its niche, when its volume of sales is climbing into the millions of dollars and it is hiring significant numbers of employees, it must meet the basics of organizational design to survive.

Foundations do not often come up against the same constraints. There may not be any nonfamily employees for many years. The "customers" are unlikely to make any demands on the organizational formality of the foundation. And, of course, there are no creditors except for the donors. As policies are being drafted, the preferences of founders, family, and perhaps the grantees may be taken into account, but most often no one speaks for the organization. In fact, those who do raise issues of management, training, performance evaluations, governance designs, leadership criteria and terms, budgetary controls, human resources, and career development, may be accused of distracting the attention of the volunteer trustees and wasting resources. Even the most exemplary foundations are usually noted for their grantmaking, not their administration.

The research suggests that this is a mistake. Good grantmaking cannot occur in a vacuum. A great programmatic idea stands a poor chance in a chaotic, undermanaged meeting. The best talent in any generation is less likely to volunteer if they do not have confidence in the design and management of the system. How many hours are spent in inefficient committee meetings because no one has been trained in basic group facilitation techniques? How long do some foundations keep working with investment managers and attorneys who are performing poorly but are never held accountable?

As we described in chapter 1, the research team evaluated each foundation in the sample on a variety of performance and descriptive variables. The data from this study show a "constellation" of organizational strengths that to some extent differentiated the foundations

Table 8.1.   Organizational Performance and Family Dynamics Ratings
(Number of foundations in each category)

	Very Low	Low	Moderate	High	Exemplary
Clarity of Program	2	5	10	10	4
Grantmaking Vitality	2	5	11	10	3
Successor Development	4	18	4	2	2
Endowment Management	2	4	7	12	5
Quality Control	1	9	7	9	4
Clarity of Mission	2	4	10	8	6
Organizational Structure	1	7	8	9	5
Family Collaboration	1	9	10	8	2
Likelihood of Continuity	1	5	7	14	3
Next Generation Enthusiasm	3	10	9	4	4
Positive Family Dynamics	6	7	11	5	1
Conflict Avoidance*	2	5	10	13	n/a

* Conflict avoidance is scaled in the opposite direction from the others, with very low being the most preferred and high being the most problematic.

rated high on "likelihood of continuity" from those ranked lower. The entire array of scores is presented in table 8.1.

Overall the highest rankings were for endowment management, likelihood of continuity, clarity of mission, clarity of program, organizational structure, and grantmaking vitality (the averages for these characteristics were between moderate and high). The lowest rankings were for successor development and family dynamics (between low and moderate).

When we divided the sample according to their current governance stage, we could compare the Collaborative Family Foundations with the Family-Governed Staff-Managed Foundations. Staff control is, of course, higher in the staff-managed subsample, as is clarity of the mission, while family collaboration is somewhat higher in the Collaborative group.

But staff-managed grantmaking does not provide any observable advantage in grantmaking vitality, successor development and next generation enthusiasm, quality control, mission, or positive family dynamics—the two groups are nearly identical on those variables.

Staff-Managed Foundations were rated somewhat higher on likelihood of continuity and organizational infrastructure, and significantly higher on conflict avoidance. In this case, while there is no way to know from these data, it is likely that the staff-managed form was chosen because of the family's aversion to conflict, rather than the other way around. (Table D.3 in appendix D presents the mean ratings for all variables for the total sample, and then breaks it down for the twenty-one Collaborative Family Foundations and the nine Family-Governed Staff-Managed Foundations. Table D.4 in appendix D then presents the correlation matrix of all the ratings.)

The number of cases is small for this kind of analysis, but the picture is very clear. Good management is measured in a number of ways that go together: clear programs, clear mission, asset management, quality control, successor development, and organizational structure. All of them, with the exception of the reported quality of asset management, are significantly and positively related to the rated likelihood of continuity.

Less obvious, but even more important, they are also highly correlated with family collaboration, next generation enthusiasm, and positive family dynamics. *In these cases it is strikingly apparent that investing in good organizational infrastructure and good governance pays off in the odds of successful continuity into the future, and in the quality of the experience for the participants today.*

CONSTRAINTS ON
ORGANIZATIONAL PERFORMANCE

In chapter 5 we introduced the two primary reasons that trustees voiced for being cautious about professionalization and organizational development: cost and loss of control. We have discussed the issue of the balance of control between family and nonfamily staff in previous chapters. However, the issue of cost deserves further analysis.

Most of these families report some tension or conflict about how much to pay an executive director, or uncertainty about the reasonable cost of meetings, stipends to community board members, and travel expenses. Others worry about sending trustees to conferences. The concerns about money have direct effects on policy, on including non-family directors, and on staff size.[3]

As this foundation's annual giving grew from $500,000 to almost $5 million, they operated with a part-time executive director only. "We wanted to keep operating expenses to a minimum." When a new executive director was hired, he argued strongly that the board needed to also hire a program officer. The board agonized over the additional cost, and eventually agreed to another half-time position.

Many foundations do not feel comfortable with these kinds of expenditures. If they can get individuals to volunteer or accept token salaries, they do it. If they can get by without a computer system, a membership in an association, another telephone line, or a better administrative assistant, they postpone or deny those investments. They are trapped in the same ideology about infrastructure at this professional stage that they remember from the Controlling Trustee stage of the foundation in its earliest years. They treat themselves like bare-bones organizations, and do not consider the possibility that excessive frugality will lead to bare-bones performance.

In this typical scenario, the founder, "Iron Mac" McInerney, did the early grantmaking himself. After a few years, he invited his two children to join him, making recommendations about small grants and occasionally discussing the overall philanthropic agenda of the foundation. As Mac moved through his seventies, he became increasingly collaborative. He also had less time and energy for the details of grantmaking, at the same time as the endowment and scale of the disbursements was growing. When his daughter Margaret, an experienced social service administrator, offered to take over the role of "executive director," everyone was pleased.

Then, after two years as a volunteer, Margaret asked for an "appropriate professional salary." As she spent more time working for the foundation, she had less time for her career, and her income had taken a sharp drop. The board held a special meeting to discuss compensation. Her brother Mike objected to a salary because: (1) the trustees have personal funds and don't need money; (2) all the trustees give their time to the foundation, not just Margaret; (3) it would set a bad precedent for the third generation who might think they should be paid for their work; (4) the foundation should contain administrative costs; and (5) serving on the board should be considered a privilege. Mac's first response was to avoid conflict by paying the salary out of his pocket. But the family stayed with the issue. They researched the legal and practical implications of paying a family member by talking to other foundations and asking a consultant to spell out the pros and cons. In the end, they agreed to pay the salary from foundation funds.

In general, the staff of the foundations included in this sample were very aware of the consequences of underinvesting in infrastructure, but the boards seemed to accept it as good practice, even if it frustrated their own agendas. Sometimes the severe restrictions on operational spending meant that the board could not implement policies that it had designed for itself. There were many cases where bylaws required due diligence, site visits, and follow-up that were simply impossible given the level of staffing.

When this foundation reached its fiftieth birthday it was being led by its third generation, with annual giving of several million dollars but had only two part-time staff, a researcher and a secretary. The board, aided by a consultant, held its first review of mission and program and designed a system of priorities and strategic program objectives. However, the staff was too small to even make a start on implementing the new model, and the old grantees pressured the trustees into continuing traditional grants. As a result, nothing changed for ten more years, until the board, overwhelmed by the dispersal demands of its rapidly growing endowment, hired its first professional executive director. He was able to use organizational skill to enlarge the staff and formalize the processes. The debates on professionalization and organizational expenditures remain very heated among the trustees.

This foundation asks for reports on the use of its funds, but it has no system for rigorous evaluation of grants because it doesn't have the staff to do them. The trustees have no responsibility for following up on grants that they have stimulated. This group of younger trustees are primarily professionals, geographically dispersed, and not close as a family. The foundation is a peripheral part of their lives.

Are family foundations stingy, appropriate, or self-indulgent in their expenditures? The Council on Foundations has been tracking administrative expenditures for many years. They have consistently found that family foundations spend less on average than independent foundations on administrative activities, averaging about .5 percent of assets and 10 percent of grants.[4]

Table 8.2. **Administrative Expenditures as a Percentage of Gifts and Assets**

	Admin. Expenditures as % of Gifts	Admin. Expenditures as % of Assets	Gifts as % of Assets
Lowest Case	0.0	0.0	2.6
Highest Case	32.5	1.4	9.2
Average	11.8	0.56	5.2

That means that a foundation dispersing $1 million per year from an endowment of $20 million will spend about $100,000 on itself—rent, utilities, travel, publications, salaries and benefits, training, and public information. In contrast, among nonprofits in general the most efficient agencies are considered to be doing very well if their administrative expenses fall under 20 percent of their budgets—fully twice the expense level of the average family foundation. (Table 8.2 presents administrative expenses for our sample.)

The percentages for our sample are in line with the council averages.

We gained an additional perspective from the research team's assessment of the level of resources in each of the sample cases. Each foundation was assigned to one of four categories:

- *Underresourced* (inadequate staff to accomplish essential grantmaking tasks, low salaries, inadequate training and professional development, poor or barely adequate facilities and support systems, reluctance to support conference attendance, insufficient funds to engage professional resources).
- *Adequately resourced* (sufficient staff to perform essential tasks, but not intensive or strategic initiatives, competitive salaries, some staff development opportunities, adequate computers, software, phone systems, and so forth, some conference attendance).
- *Fully resourced* (sufficient staff to perform not only management but strategic and program evaluation tasks, attractive salaries, widespread encouragement of development—including participation in multiple conferences and regional associations of grantmakers, use of outside professionals and consultants as needed, active community liaison and education activities, sufficient compensation to eliminate financial hardship on active trustees).
- *Surplus resources* (more staff than necessary to perform functions, excessive salaries, luxurious facilities and infrastructure, generous funding for meetings, including elaborate recreation and very broad family attendance, significant perks for trustees and/or staff).

In the judgment of the research team, one quarter of this sample (7 cases) were allocating too few dollars to organizational support and infrastructure development. An additional third (11 cases) were only adequately resourced. The remaining twelve cases were judged to be "fully resourced," and none was rated "surplus resourced." Taken all together, this data presents a strong argument that these foundations are not only "efficiently" funded, but in fact thinly resourced.

In addition, it is clear that additional resources do pay off in improved performance. When we looked at the impact of the level of resource adequacy on organizational and grantmaking performance, we found that higher levels of resource adequacy are significantly positively correlated with clarity of program, grantmaking vitality, likelihood of continuity, successor development, quality control, clarity of mission, and organizational structure (table D.4, appendix D).

This conclusion stands in stark contrast to the recurrent public concern about foundation expenditures. The specter of self-serving family foundations is periodically raised as a justification for restricting administrative spending more severely. The cases of abuse are undeniable. There have been foundations that have overpaid for services, indulged themselves with facilities and luxuries, and spent more on doing philanthropy than on the actual grants themselves. We have also already made the argument that the public has a legitimate "donor's interest" in any foundation that takes advantage of tax abatement.

But in this sample at least, the story is very different. From these data there is no evidence that foundations are spending inappropriately. In fact, the danger is that many boards will be intimidated by the press attention and the stories of excesses, and be even more reluctant to make necessary investments in organizational upgrades in the future. Based on this study, we would have to suggest that the public has more to lose from understaffed and overwhelmed foundations doing less than exemplary grantmaking because their infrastructure is too thin, than from those that overspend on themselves.

ASSET MANAGEMENT

We found that asset management was the one arena where these foundations have become willing to pay the cost of quality service and were most likely to use professionals. In the early years, only ten of the foundations used professional investment managers other than family business employees to handle their portfolios, but today nearly all of them do. The total expenditures on endowment management equal the sum of all other expenditures combined. At first it seems as if these foundations place higher priority on the skills required to manage an endowment than on those required to fulfill the philanthropic mission and coordinate the family's dream. More likely this is an area in which many board members and trustees feel there is high risk and where they have few skills. The field has developed a large literature on endowment management and legal and financial issues in asset management, but it is still hard for nonfinancial amateurs to feel confident.[5]

By far the most common structure is an investment committee of the board, usually small and including the few trustees who are most experienced in money management, and a single investment advisory firm. There are some cases where the family does its own investment allocations. These are the families where the family business is directly involved in professional financial services. Even in those cases, some families feel that it is important to turn the foundation's portfolio over to someone else.

The Duttons are sophisticated investors and they know what they are doing as far as managing the portfolio. The nonfamily executive director views the foundation as an investment company: "Our business is to make money so that we can in turn give it out." The Duttons have a very active board committee and a lot of opinions about the way funds should be invested, but they have decided to hire outside professionals to do this work to reduce conflict and conflicts of interests amongst family trustees. "When the professionals don't perform, they are fired, and there are no hard feelings. It would be impossible to do that if a trustee was responsible for the investments or if any of us suggested an investment that later turned sour."

While there have been some important changes in the level of attention that these foundations have given to portfolio management in recent years, it is still an area where the trustees give themselves a critical evaluation. Most of our data was collected before 2001, and reflects a lower priority on asset management than we would probably find today. We know from our work in the field that the recent dramatic swings in equity markets have had a powerful psychological impact on many foundation boards. They expanded their programs along with the rapid increase in portfolios, and then they had to deal with cutting off longstanding grantees, ending multiyear programs prematurely, and shutting the door completely to new initiatives when the markets turned down.

But even in more placid times, many interviewees expressed anxiety and uncertainty about how to responsibly fulfill their asset oversight responsibilities. Except for discussions about "how much we have to give away this year," the endowment is not part of the general discussion. Most commonly, it is either "in-sourced" (delegated to the member or members of the board who are seen as having financial skills) or "outsourced" (delegated to a professional money management organization). Either way the majority of board members in the sample as a whole do not feel competent in overseeing endowment management, do not have a clear sense of reasonable expectations, and do not want to be responsible for having expertise in this area.

IMPLEMENTING IMPROVEMENT IN ORGANIZATIONAL OPERATIONS

The critical techniques for attending to the organizational health of the foundation are straightforward and no different from any operating system:

> Provide adequate staffing
> Develop effective financial controls
> Define operational policy
> Encourage training and development

We have commented on each of these categories for each of the developmental stages of the foundations. There are also two other general lessons that cut across categories.

As we saw in the previous chapter, an effectively managed foundation can actually help heal a dysfunctional family. It is dramatic to see the cases in this sample where some family dynamic problems were resolved not by directly focusing on the communication, history, or psychodynamics of the family, but rather by formalizing the grantmaking work. Once structures and policies are in place, the momentum of success can be remarkable.

This third-generation sibling group was frustrated and saddened about their inability to work together within the model of philanthropy that their parents had used. They decided to change their operation to rely on outside professionals, and in only a few years they were able to turn the foundation around. "We'll never again have family members as staff. We are just too competitive. Having a non-family person saves us from ourselves and allows us as a family to do our best work." The executive director says that she decided to "policy the trustees to death, so there wouldn't be any conflict—and it has worked miracles." The family agrees. "Her strategy was genius. We have clear policies on everything now, it works great, and she is there to remind us in a minute when we forget what we have agreed to."

While policies are a necessary first step in improving the organization's performance, we learned from comparing the foundations' written materials with their actual operations that creating a policy is not the same as implementing one. Most of the cases in this sample, at some point in their history, made great strides in design and policy creation in a "leap." Often stimulated by the intervention of a consultant, there was a flurry of activity in creating a succession plan for trustees, a governance plan about how the meetings will be scheduled and run, and criteria for various aspects of service. It was also common for only some of the new policies to be implemented. Surprisingly, a large number of interviewees were unembarrassed about saying that they were not familiar with their foundation's organizational policies, and did not think the other trustees were either.

This foundation, led by a new second-generation president, spent two years working on a job description for trustees. Over time, it became clear that implementing the new criteria for board service would leave two family branches without any qualifying candidates. Rather than reconsider the policy, they just ignored it. They also resisted spending anything on infrastructure or professionalization—training, administrative support, stipends for nonfamily trustees. Their operating theory was, "let's not become too professional—a family foundation should be fun work."

Designing policies and then forgetting them can have the same long-term impact as the founder's creating formal organizational structures and ignoring them. It is not just a statement that the current leaders feel entitled to do what they think is right, regardless of the formal rules. It suggests that the rules themselves are silly, or that following rules is unnecessary. That is a confusing message for new members of the organization. It is not possible to respect formal structure and procedure when you agree with it and circumvent it when you do not, without undermining the overall organizational integrity of the foundation. That in itself is a threat to continuity.

A second observation regards the allocation of development and training funds, especially for participation in professional organizations, regional groups, and conferences. Many participants said that in their experience, education and leadership development actually work. There are numerous stories of attendance at conferences or seminars providing a shot in the arm, both in terms of motivation and in pure skill development.

In the late 1980s, some of the second generation began attending meetings of the local regional association. Then all four of the siblings attended the Council on Foundations meeting four years ago. "It was a liberating act and the beginning of our collaboration. We all became excited about the possibilities of running the trust more professionally and continuing it as a family foundation."

The current executive director (a family member) really emphasized the role of the Council on Foundations conferences and networking with others in the region about philanthropy. She emphasized, "We learned so much." Her niece, the newest member of the board, also went to the council conferences so that she could learn about foundations. She said she was very nervous about going, but that it was the "best thing that could have happened. It was amazing to see the great variety of foundations, and that the issues were the same. I hung close to my aunt, but it was a wonderful introduction and really made me feel confident about my role."

Nevertheless, only ten of the thirty foundations relied on benchmarking or resources from formal philanthropic associations to guide their organization development. Only one-quarter of the sample were regular attendees at conferences and regional grantmaking forums, although all of those participants valued those experiences very highly.

The nonfamily staff were somewhat more likely to mention how much they gained from conferences and conversations with colleagues. However, they worried about confidentiality and protecting the privacy of the family, so they severely constrained their sharing efforts. Some of them stated that they assumed the family expected them to know, or figure out, how to resolve all difficulties and accomplish their tasks without exposing any problems outside the foundation.

This is a case where retreats, discussions, and the input of a trained facilitator or consultant could help many foundations to make better use of the experience of others. The balance could swing a little more toward interfoundation collaboration without risking embarrassment. That would be a benefit for the individual foundations and the field.[6]

In summary, foundations who deal most successfully with the challenge of organizational structure must address several critical tasks:

- Pay as much attention to the organization's needs as to the management of its endowment: provide truly adequate funding for staff, facilities, training, and operations.
- Resolve the dilemma of collaboration versus coexistence: find a balance between collaborative grantmaking and discretionary funds that responds to the diversity in the family without undermining the commitment to improving collaboration skills and evolving a core identity for the foundation.
- Do not accept poor management and ineffective group process, but invest in the training and skill development necessary to handle such mundane tasks as agenda setting, conflict management, decision-making rules, record keeping, and meeting logistics before they become destructive.

- Take their bylaws and policy documents seriously, making sure they reflect the mission, dream, and actual preferences of the group, and then implementing them consistently and fairly.

NOTES

1. The National Center for Family Philanthropy and the Council on Foundations publish many guides to families about their philanthropic options; for example, Born (2001); Foote (2000); Esposito (2002); Edie (2002a); Edie (2002b).

2. Bryson (2002) has written a very popular booklet on the most common pitfalls.

3. These are questions that a family business of comparable size would not entertain in the same way. While cost containment is also an issue in businesses, they are prepared for the "cost of goods sold." The best companies compete for executive talent and pay market-based compensation rates to get it. They invest in support systems, training, networking and trade associations, and technological infrastructure, because that improves their products and their service to customers. When there are problems, they spend the necessary funds to correct them.

4. These figures, taken from 990 forms, make use of the administrative expenditures assigned to the grantmaking functions, which average about half of the total organizational expenditures (the other half is allocated by the foundation to endowment management).

5. For example, National Center for Family Philanthropy (1999) and Esperti et al. (2003).

6. Some leading foundations have become more public about interfoundation collaboration and have invited colleagues to share program ideas, strategic planning, and research on grantees. The Edna McConnell Clark Foundation, for example, is experimenting with a "lead funder" program where they share their "due diligence" data with other foundations interested in common funding areas, and invites collaborators to participate in coordinated funding.

9

PREPARING FOR FUTURE GENERATIONS

The final task of each generation is to ensure the foundation's continuity by preparing the transition of their work to future generations. Surveys of family foundation trustees continually find that the top priority concern of current leaders is succession. Given that, we were extremely surprised at the low level of succession planning in these foundations.

Fewer than half of the foundations had any formal development program for prospective trustees or directors. Even the ones that had well thought-out grantmaking procedures, highly professionalized systems for managing their endowment, and clear rules of behavior for all leadership roles and professional staff, often behaved like ostriches regarding continuity.

In fact, some of the best functioning foundations from a grantmaking perspective were the worst in continuity planning. The distribution of ratings by the research team on the quality of successor development was as shown in table 9.1:

Table 9.1. Ratings of Successor Development Activities

Very Low	Low	Moderate	High	Exemplary
4	18	4	2	2

The successful grantmakers who speak with enthusiasm about their philanthropic work and with embarrassment about their neglect of continuity planning have good reason for both emotions.

FIVE REASONS THAT FAMILIES AVOID
SUCCESSION PLANNING

We tried to find in the data all of the possible dynamics which acted as impediments to aggressive successor development, and we came up with five reasonable hypotheses. These are reminiscent of the classical work on the resistance to succession planning in family companies,[1] but with some special twists in these foundations.

The first interpretation that emerged was a fear of opening a can of worms. If the current trustees felt they had a system that worked, they didn't want to jeopardize it by adding new players—especially from such a complicated pool as their offspring.

In this moderate-sized third-generation foundation, the senior trustees were reluctant to add anyone from the next generation. "Why should we change something that is working so well?" The current conclusion on the board is that "we're a family but we're also a foundation— it's a business responsibility. We have to focus on our current obligations." Another trustee summarized the discussion: "We have worked so well together, why invite trouble?" They realize that eventually they will have no choice, but for now they are just focused on the present.

A second, but related, explanation given in some of the most highly-functioning trustee groups was that the work is fun, and they wanted to hang on to it for as long as they could.

This foundation was managed by the first-generation parents for more than two decades. They invited two of their five children to attend, but they were not equal partners. Now the second generation is the board, and they are conveying the same message to their children. There are twelve members of the next generation, and they are a lively, bright group. They are very knowledgeable about the family business, and inheritance/estate planning. Furthermore, many of them have strong philanthropic values and have expressed personal interest in the foundation. The second-generation siblings are preparing their offspring for governance roles in the family business, but when it comes to the foundation, they tell them that there is a foundation, it does a lot of good things, and, right now, that's all they need to know.

A third reason for not revisiting the status quo is consideration for the parents. The foundation is in many families the "retirement package" for active leaders. It is easier to move an aging parent out of the controlling role in the family business if the foundation is available as the consolation prize. What is lost in developing successors is gained in the parents' fulfillment and the more active succession in the business and family office.

"They still find it meaningful and fulfilling. No one wants to take this away from them. Dad is not a man who lets go easily. Letting him hold on to something helped him let us take over other things."

Fourth, the reluctance of some families to address succession was a puzzle until we looked beneath the surface at the complicated dynamics as the branches become more differentiated in the second, third, and later generations. Almost without exception, the differences among branches began as distinctions of preference and style, and then evolved into a hierarchy of impugned "quality."

At one extreme, some branches would develop a reputation for high achievement, leadership, successful marriages, accomplished children, and business success. If they led the family company, it did well during those years. If they became entrepreneurs, their ventures grew. They built impressive houses in the best neighborhoods, sent their children to high-status colleges, and were often profiled in the society pages of the local newspaper.

At the other extreme, some branches couldn't seem to do anything right. Their marriages often ended in messy divorces. There might be drug abuse or alcoholism, and often one or more family members were diagnosed with mental illness (either by professionals or in the examining room of the family). In the family business, they had the reputation as either deadwood, who are shunted aside and forgotten, or impulsive spendthrifts, who needed to be cordoned off and controlled. If they passed through a series of marriages, their children were often lost to departed spouses, and their new stepchildren were never fully accepted as family members. Both of these forces complicated their branch continuity.

If family branches differentiate this way it creates increasing tension in foundation governance and continuity planning. Here the differences between the family business and the foundation are most important. Families almost never allow low status branches to control an operating company. The financial imperative overpowers any general bias toward equal opportunity. Once a sibling or cousin is labeled as a "loser" by the family as a whole, there will be high hurdles to limit his or her authority.

That is harder to do in a foundation. When there are no specific job descriptions, criteria, or performance measures for trustees and directors, it is much harder to justify excluding anyone. Especially if the founders describe the foundation as a "place for the family to work together," the right to participate equally is taken as absolute. Equality is the key here. All branches usually assume not only a right to be at the table, but to be there in equal numbers with everyone else. This is independent of the relative size of branches or of their position on the invisible hierarchy described above.

One consequence of this dynamic is that some families avoid continuity planning altogether, or manage to keep it always at a theoretical level. To talk about representation in future generations would force all these issues onto the table, and they don't want to risk that.

This family has talked about rules and criteria for trustees, but never acted. Two of the branches have significant problems with mental health disorders, substance abuse, and other serious problems. The executive director feels that if they truly adopted guidelines, they would end up with no representatives from those branches, "which would create conflict and resentment in the family, which they want to avoid."

Finally, in some cases it was not the senior generation that was reluctant to begin developing successors, it was the juniors. This is particularly true when the foundation was not an important part of the family culture when the offspring were young, and the parents have suddenly decided that now was the time to open the door.

This family developed a very collaborative partnership among siblings in the second generation after a long period of control by the founders. Now they are having a very hard time interesting the third generation. The executive director believes that, for the third generation, "the foundation is just another thing on their plate that they have inherited from their parents. There is a lack of interest, motivation, and, especially, time. Paying trustees to do some of the work will not accomplish much, since they are all independently wealthy. The discretionary 'initiative' fund hasn't seemed to motivate them either. The few third-generation members who have expressed any interest are already on the board."

OVERCOMING RESISTANCE

All of these dynamics are hard to overcome. Trustees do not need any more cheerleading about successor development. They hear it frequently from publications and at conferences and forums. The field has developed more material on succession than on any other topic, with the possible exception of asset management.

The resistances are powerful. What separates the "high continuity" foundations from the others is that they do succession planning anyway. The key seems to be that they do it not as a family process, but rather as an organizational requirement. They think as trustees or directors, not as parents, grandparents, aunts, and uncles.

This may be the most difficult part of the formalization package to put into place. The family can rely on professional staff and highly motivated leaders to initiate other organizational enhancement activities such as policymaking, record keeping, legal compliance, program descriptions, strategic planning, and staff development. Once the family has resolved the dilemma of family versus staff control, these tasks themselves are easy to endorse. Even reconsideration and reaffirmation of the mission, while personal, is also largely an intellectual and cognitive task—it invites people to talk about "what I think" more than "what I feel."

Successor development seems more dangerous. For all the reasons listed above, it is easier to avoid than to initiate. That is why it is so important for the senior generations to honor the organizational needs of the foundation even in the face of ambivalent emotions. The requirement goes well beyond the obvious fact that at some point senior family members will be gone and others will need to take over. The organization has continuity needs that require logical, fair, and proactive preparation.

Identify the Risks and Opportunities

The stories of these thirty foundations are completely consistent with the general literature on continuity planning. The best research on family companies and other family structures emphasizes that "laissez faire" approaches to successor development are risky, and associated with lower organizational success and family satisfaction. Case histories and survey research have articulated a number of reasons:

- Current success is no guarantee of future success, and the strategic choices of the past are not necessarily obvious to new generations. Any organization's particular strengths are best passed on to future leaders while the seniors are still active.
- Successors need training and competence-building to minimize "transition deficits"—the dip in operational efficiency that happens inevitably when experienced leaders withdraw.
- New leaders need the legitimacy that completing a rigorous development program provides, so that the entire family will empower them to act on behalf of all stakeholders.
- Successor development programs are also assessment and selection opportunities, for both existing and potential leaders to see what works, who excels, and how it feels to participate.

There are also other risks of avoiding successor development.

- There are no viable contingency options. Almost a third of the cases in this sample had to deal with an unexpected crisis or death at some point in their history.
- "Fending off" potential successors for too long is dangerous. By the time the parents are ready to be more inclusive, the offspring may have moved away or invested their philanthropic interests elsewhere.
- The very issues that the family is trying to avoid by postponing successor development may be the most important ones that need addressing: disputes over mission, the pressure of geographic dispersal, uneven competencies and commitment across branches, poor leadership, or inadequate staff support.

The particular design of successor development programs is beyond the purpose of this study. Only a few of these foundations had programs that even they found satisfactory. But some were coming to grips with the issue much more actively in recent years, and were making progress. We culled several critical lessons from these cases— a few exemplary, and others imperfect but with strong features.

Invest the Effort in a Comprehensive Design

Some families did not *prepare* for succession and continuity, they just started involving younger family members. At some moment, often triggered when the offspring reached a milestone birthday (21 or 25 or 30), they were invited to join the foundation. In a few cases, the contact was not so much an invitation as a summons.

This foundation is based on a strong identity with the family's church, and has needed to deal with a wide range of lifestyles in its sprawling, complex family. One trustee remembers,

> When I turned seventeen I was not very religious and very much a hippie. Out of the blue, my mother called me up and said, "It's time for you to start attending the meetings." I suggested that I might not be a good fit, that I was very busy with other things, but I didn't argue much. I lived in awe of my mother, and she wanted me there, period. She said, "All of the women in this family are strong," and that was that. I wouldn't say it was the best introduction, but I am still there and figuring it out as I go along.

While action has its rewards, it also can be risky. We have consistently concluded that personal commitment and choice are better processes for continuity than obligation. Sometimes the behavior of participating, no matter why it begins, leads the newcomer to find a place for her own reasons. As she said, "I am still there. . . ." But it is a safer bet to have a procedure of invitation, a "pull" rather than a "push," with a well-designed sequence of experiences that combine education and immersion.

Not surprisingly, some of the largest and most complex foundations have the most elaborate successor development programs. This is particularly true if the family believes in high involvement, consensus decision-making, and limiting the control of staff.

One of the most impressive things about the Jacobsen Foundation is the wholehearted way they bring in new members. Children from every branch are invited to join the foundation when they come of age (16, 18, or 21 depending on the rule at the time).

Those who are interested become apprentices for three years and are assigned a mentor. The mentor is usually a parent, but could be another member who was geographically and psychologically close to the apprentice. It is the mentor's responsibility to teach the apprentice about the foundation and its procedures and to encourage their involvement. The mentor is also responsible for answering questions and acclimating people to the culture of the broad extended family.

The Jacobsens also have a three-day training program for all new members that apprentices are required to attend. New members also attend area meetings and are encouraged to attend the annual meeting. They participate actively in the grant review process, reviewing grants alongside their mentor. The current senior generation are willing to step back from their leadership roles in order to give new members a chance to run committees and participate actively in the foundation.

After they have finished the apprentice program, they become active members. Many of them go on to take leadership positions at an early age. For example, one fourth-generation cousin became a committee chair right after finishing the apprentice program at the age of twenty-one; and another was elected to be a Trustee at twenty-four.

Take into Account the Resources and Limitations of Your Actual Family

While the large foundations have the advantage of plenty of room in the grantmaking process for new members and many candidates (their issue is *selection*), the smaller foundations are more concerned with finding adequate resources in a small population (they worry about *recruitment*). These smaller systems often find it especially important to tailor the successor development programs to the particular needs of the individuals involved.

Once the third generation at the Stein-Marek Foundation decided it was time for succession planning, they gave it their full attention. Initially they did it "by the book," reading stories of other foundations and adopting the most common practices. They decided on a minimum age (21), and limited access to direct descendants of the founders. They sent out a letter to all fourth-generation family members announcing the new apprentice program and asking if anyone was interested in getting involved in the foundation.

Those who responded were invited to attend the annual meeting and all board meetings, to participate in the discussions but not to vote. They also attend a private orientation session with the executive director (two to three hours) and one conference/seminar in the field of philanthropy. The foundation pays for the apprentice expenses to attend the meetings.

The first version of the program required the fourth generation to wait three years before they could become eligible to become directors. This was too long and the juniors were getting frustrated. After gaining some confidence with their own experience, the seniors shortened the program to one year. They also made some adjustments to accommodate special needs of some cousins (disabilities, graduate school schedules, child care).

The seniors are aware that in the first year or two they were somewhat dismissive of the input from their nephews and nieces, but relatively quickly the relationship between the generations had changed dramatically, both inside the foundation and in general. They are now finishing their second cohort in the program, thinking about a third round, and the seniors agree that the next leader of the foundation is expected to be a fourth-generation member.

Start Very, Very Early

The most basic approach to successor development in the majority of cases employed the fundamental transmission of family values through example. Similar to the assessment of successor development, the research team ranked only eight of the thirty foundations either "high" or "very high" on "Next Generation Enthusiasm for the Foundation."

The correlation between preparation and enthusiasm was very high. In every one of the highly ranked cases, the successor generation pointed to early experiences and informal modeling by their parents as the source of their commitment to philanthropy, more than formal training programs.

The first second-generation trustee in this foundation was only thirteen years old when her father died, but stories of his philanthropy influenced her desire to participate in community organizations. When she graduated from college, she spent one summer working for the foundation, doing site visits and writing reports on the agencies. She still considers it the most enjoyable job she ever held.

She remembers the year that the foundation reached the $5 million annual giving mark as a turning point in her determination to participate. She was suddenly aware of the foundation's growing influence, and she wanted to have a hand in the grantmaking. At first she started attending board meetings as an observer; later she was asked to become a director.

Now with children of her own in their teens and twenties, she says that she believes in teaching by modeling. "I talk with them about the grants that excite me. They see how much pleasure I get from serving on the foundation. I don't want to push them into philanthropy. I'd rather wait to see how they develop and what their interests are." She recently was thrilled to see her youngest daughter, without any suggestion or advice, make a gift to an organization she had heard about using her own money.

Balance the "Inclusion" and the "Performance"
Agendas of the Foundation

The foundations that are happiest with their successor development programs have found a middle ground between setting high standards and welcoming the broadest participation possible.

At the McInerney Foundation, the older generations have done a superb job of introducing the next generation to philanthropy in a way that is thoughtful, gradual, and comfortable for everyone. The second generation modeled charitable giving and volunteerism at home before their father started the foundation.

When his grandchildren reached adolescence, Mac began taking all four on summer vacations. Aside from spending time with them, he wanted the cousins, who lived far apart, to get to know one another.

These trips were important preludes to bringing the third generation together in the foundation. One of the cousins said, "If we hadn't known and liked one another before we started giving away money together, our ideological differences might have caused problems."

The older generations have been scrupulous about making third-generation participation voluntary. They invite the cousins to meetings, professional conferences, and give them money to distribute but they don't pressure them or ask for explanations when the kids don't participate. When they do participate, the board solicits their ideas and listens respectfully to them.

At present, two of the children are working, one is job hunting, and the other is a junior in college. Three of them make use of the discretionary funds available for them, one does not, because he did not want to comply with the preparation and reporting requirements. "It was a burden to me, not an opportunity, because I didn't have the time to research issues as much as I needed to come to the right decisions. But nobody hassled me or blamed me for saying, 'Not now.'" The kids also agreed that at this stage of their lives, they don't want to be publicly identified with the family foundation; the older generation understand and respect their wishes.

SUCCESSION AND CONTINUITY

Finally, in thinking about the appropriate successor development design for any foundation, it is useful to keep in mind some of the models and theory that have emerged in the past two decades of work with family-owned companies. In any system, successfully completing transitions—generations, leaders, product lines, services—requires a delicate balance of two opposing processes: succession and continuity. These two processes are sometimes confused and used interchangeably, but they are actually complementary pulls and pushes that create the dynamic tension that propels the transition forward.

Succession refers to everything that must change for the transition to be a success. That includes the individual leaders, or the whole generation in control. It may also be the new strategy, or emphasis, that changes the course of the organization's work. It requires the "letting go" of the old and the "taking over" by the new. Succession is the opportunity for the reinvigoration and redirection that comes with change. Without it, all organic systems would age past their ability to perform, and the system would die with its members.

Continuity refers to everything that stays the same through the transition. It may be the vision, the core values, the history, and the place of the system in its network. Continuity requires the socialization and education of the rising generation so that they understand what they are receiving, and the reasons that it has taken the shape it has over time. Continuity is the opportunity to reaffirm the legacy that provides the special meaning to current efforts. Without it, each change would be starting over and all past lessons would have to be painfully relearned.

Both of these dynamics carry powerful emotional charges, and both generate ambivalent feelings.

Succession raises both hope and anxiety: *hope* that new solutions can be found, that youthful energy will revitalize old routines, that the future will be better; and *anxiety* that there are no new solutions, that the new leaders are not up to the task, that the dangerous and untried new directions will be less successful than the techniques of the past.

Continuity arouses both security and frustration: *security* that there is a solid family legacy on which to build new efforts, a pride—sometimes nostalgically enhanced, sometimes realistic—in the reputation derived from historical accomplishments; and *frustration* with the constraints of tradition, the need to comply with the "dead hand of the past," and the burden of comparison with past moments of glory.

While organizations are constantly changing and evolving, and in some ways succession and continuity are built into every act in some small way, the intensity of these dynamics is enormously greater at times of major transition. Changing people forces the issue.

This suggests a connection between history and governance regarding the degree to which foundations are able to change. It appears that the typical balance between succession and continuity in foundations is different from that in operating businesses. In business, there is a primary attention on the succession part—the selection and training of the new leaders, the "letting go" and "taking over," and the political conflicts and strains that all of this causes. Good business performance requires the clear transfer of power and the new leader's ability to act. It is hard work to get the system to also focus on the continuity part.

On the other hand, in foundations it may be more natural to focus on continuity: legacy, original intent, mission, and respect for the hierarchy of age and generation in the family. That is, foundations may have more trouble dealing with the inherent discontinuity that accompanies the needed changes. If so, this has many implications for how to help families understand the transition process and attend to the necessary preparation and work.

For example, the foundations in this sample were very reluctant to address policies that affected changes in board makeup. Only twelve of them had bylaws which set term limits or a retirement age for directors. Even more dramatic, of those twelve, the rules were only actually enforced in four cases. Often the junior generation or the professional staff were uncomfortable about the breach of policy, but did not feel it was possible to bring it up.

Longevity may be a blessing for individuals, but it is a mixed one for institutions. Some leaders maintained their positions well into their eighties, which probably would not happen in their family companies and which creates a real problem for succession in their foundations. A generational leader of eighty-five has children in their fifties and sixties (and grandchildren in their twenties and thirties). Even if they are active in the foundation, the next generation's opportunity for real leadership is passing them by.

Staying on as director or chair of the trustees in one's seventies and eighties sends a message that the foundation is a personal arena, a platform for the demonstration of family hierarchies and status, rather than a continuity-focused working organization. This is independent of the skills of the leader, his or her energy and commitment, the family relationships, and the consensus within the trustee group on program and mission. Whether or not the senior leader is doing a good job, there are consequences of refusing to step aside.

If the middle generation is shut out of leadership, or even participation, during their high energy and productivity years, they may never return. That is a high price to pay for protecting parental egos.

Some foundations need to use their best creativity to design governance roles that honor the wisdom and experience of senior family members while moving authority and responsibility to the next generation. Then, having designed such a system, they need to find the courage to implement it.

This foundation has traversed a rocky road over its four generations, but it has persevered at modifying and modernizing its successor development program until all the current participants feel it is a model system. Three-year terms, renewable only once, are strictly enforced for all board members. Family members are actively recruited and welcomed when they reach the age of twenty-one, and they are greeted with an extensive and formal program of apprenticeships, mentoring, and training sessions. There is a gradual series of opportunities for involvement leading up to election to the senior foundation board. Most of the senior generation are no longer trustees, but instead participate as mentors and advisors. Perhaps as a result, the "next generation enthusiasm" for this foundation was among the highest in the sample.

In summary, the foundations that were the most successful in successor development:

- Treated successor development as an organizational imperative, not a family prerogative. That meant they overcame emotional resistances, and dealt with continuity alongside of mission, strategy, program, governance design, and the overall collective Dream for the future of the foundation.
- Educated themselves on exemplary programs from other foundations, but adapted their effort to the realities of their own families.
- Included both grantmaking education and governance education in their development program.

NOTE

1. The best summary is still found in Lansberg (1988).

10

THE PROMISE OF
GENERATIONS OF GIVING

Paul Ylvisaker, one the most thoughtful observers of family foundations, was keenly aware of the challenge facing family philanthropy.[1] Shortly before his death, he predicted that at least half of all family foundations would run into trouble within the first two generations, face more difficult problems in the third generation, and probably cease to exist before reaching the 100-year mark.[2] He was not a pessimist by nature, but he was realistic in his judgment that any institution set up to run in perpetuity faces great challenges. Over time, disagreements may increase, interest wane, and family members drift apart, threatening the survival of the foundation.

Fortunately, there are many examples of family foundations that have defied Ylvisaker's prediction—some represented in this study. Now in their fourth, fifth, and even sixth generations, they are vital institutions characterized by active, involved trustees and thoughtful grantmaking programs. Some emerged from long periods of stagnation or autocratic control to revitalize their foundations; others have been on a steady course, gradually becoming more inclusive in their governance, more strategic in their grantmaking, and more thoughtful in preparing the next generation for leadership.

The previous section summarized some of the conclusions from this research about practices that increase a family foundation's likelihood of successful continuity. In each of the four areas, there were clear differences between those cases that were thriving and those that were only continuing. Considering all thirty foundations as a group, we asked ourselves if there are general themes that emerge as guiding principles. What are the core lessons from this research on continuity in family foundations?

THE PURSUIT OF EXCELLENCE

Those who do family philanthropy well do not get enough credit. (Of course, it may also be true that those who do it badly do not get enough criticism.) The difficulty of the work is invisible to most people who have not tried it. The general public, or even the nonphilanthropic wealthy, may feel, "How hard can it be to give away money?" This denigration of the task leads to underappreciation of the skills and efforts of the leaders who engage in it.

It also leads to underappreciation and underresourcing of the organizations themselves. If the task is supposed to be so easy, why would it be necessary to spend money, to recruit extraordinary talent, to invest in training, to attend conferences and seminars and to learn from peers and colleagues, to purchase equipment and services, and to pay whatever is necessary to ensure adequate management? The general public may believe that, since the donors were personally wealthy, and sometimes their families still are, the organization has access to whatever resources it needs—even to the point of luxury. We found that the opposite is often true. The boards and managers themselves are reluctant and embarrassed to demand the level of infrastructure investment that would be considered automatic in business operations of comparable size.

We have emphasized that one of the reasons foundations are undervalued as organizations lies in the difficulty of measuring their impact. This represents a primary difference between family foundations and family businesses. Excellent or awful performance in the business—the wealth-generating or wealth-maintaining parts of the family—is apparent to all, and has immediate consequences for everyone's lifestyle.

Not so for a foundation. Foundation reputations are based more on what they are trying to do than how well they are accomplishing it. Showy successes are rare, and many families would be uncomfortable with too much visibility anyway. Poor management in the foundation may be disappointing, or frustrating, but typically not more. Foundations can continue for years without being held to any assessment of their effectiveness. The current grantees will not complain, and the community has little awareness and less leverage.

That puts tremendous pressure on these philanthropic families to oversee themselves.[3] As long as they are law-abiding, there is no structure that will police and enforce their performance. Instead, this is a moral obligation. The family has to step up and create its own commitment, *not just to do good work, but to do it well.*

Even further, doing it well goes beyond doing no harm, or giving to reputable recipients. It means doing it with purpose and energy and standards, being educated and knowledgeable about the consequences of every grant, following up, being adequately staffed, participating in networks and helping and encouraging philanthropic colleagues. Ultimately that is the way that today's philanthropists honor their ancestors and their family legacy. It is also how they honor the investment that the general public—most of whom are not at all wealthy—are making in their foundation.

The reward is that the primary beneficiaries of good organizational performance may be the family itself. The most important conclusion from this project concerning governance and continuity is an ironic reversal. Most professionals and practitioners in this field assume that good grantmaking grows out of good family processes. That is, families who manage their relationships well, contain destructive conflict, and have affection and respect for each other will be able to generate good grantmaking procedures and effective operations.

We found that it also works in the opposite direction. That is not to say that you don't need a threshold of good process—a basic ability to work together, to have meetings, to talk about the task. But good performance *creates* good emotional experiences and commitment, more often than the reverse. A serious investment—personal, financial, intellectual, and educational—in the development of the foundation, its mission, its leadership, and the way it does its work creates pride, and the best chance that all the cousins named Amy will get on their planes in San Diego and Buffalo to do the foundation's work for generations to come.

THE FUTURE OF GENERATIONS OF GIVING

We have entered a new era of private philanthropy. The enormous impending transfer of old wealth, and the explosive creation of new, have put us on the brink of a new generation of potential philanthropists who live in a very different world from the founders of these thirty foundations. What can they learn from their predecessors? Through all the complexity of the rich data from these cases, the basic conclusions are clear.

First, all of the organizational requirements of family foundations need more attention. Philanthropists and the field that supports them have been preoccupied with grantmaking. We need to give more attention to governance. The structure and processes of foundations as systems need more study, more guidelines, and more respect.

If such issues as trustee qualifications and training, sophistication of asset management, strategic planning, staff supervision, and investment in infrastructure have been seen in the past as private matters of family preference, they need to be brought into the light.

Choosing to be personally philanthropic is a wonderful and private thing, but creating a family foundation is a public trust. Like it or not, these foundations are significant organizations, and they require all the attention to management, strategy, structure, information systems, accounting, and formal process that are inherent in organizational excellence.

The families who stood out in this sample refuse to be satisfied with just continuity, giving only enough attention to the foundation to keep it going, meeting the tepid obligation to give away 5 percent of their endowment, the furthest that the public requirement will go (so far). They take their organizations seriously enough to hire adequate staff, to schedule meetings that are long enough to get the work done, to support conference and association participation and learning from others, to mentor the next generation, to use retreats and advisors to continually refine and upgrade their infrastructure, to monitor their investment performance with the same vigilance that they apply to their personal finances. They understand that they are not just grantmakers, they are organizational executives.

It is no shame if a family wants to be charitable but does not want all this organizational baggage. Luckily, the field of philanthropy is gradually catching up with the diversity of agendas and capabilities in its family participants. There is more than one way to operationalize a family's philanthropic dream. Donor advised funds, charitable remainder trusts, a new variety of programs at community foundations, and the old standby—personal contributions—should be seriously considered before embarking on a foundation. If some families became more knowledgeable and asked themselves to honestly consider whether they had the will and the time to run a foundation well before they signed the papers, it would save them hours and years of trouble later.

Second, each generation needs to choose whether it feels a primary responsibility to its present or to the future. If the governing group, whether a founder or those who have followed, commit themselves to accomplishing a particular philanthropic agenda, they can focus all of their energy on doing that as effectively and efficiently as possible. Others, family or not, may share the same agenda or be persuaded by it, but they would be clear that they are invited to join the work as implementers, not as redesigners. The foundation's focus—and its lifespan—would be determined by its program.

If, on the other hand, the first priority of the founders or leaders is to create an opportunity for people they care about to discover their own passions and to enact their philanthropic values, the task is a very different one. Then the leaders need to invest in collaborative agenda setting, in mentoring and training, and in the foundation itself.

The first path is charitable giving; the second is institution building. Both are noble ways to contribute, but you cannot gain the benefits of one by investing solely in the requirements of the other.

Finally, these family leaders should learn from the progenitors in these cases that, regardless of the intention of the founder, perpetuity is always a negotiation. It is not enough to create something of value; it must also be valued by those whose efforts are required to sustain it.

In every case, the foundations which had vitality in their grantmaking, enthusiasm in their younger generations, and enjoyment in the process of collaboration were those that invited voluntary participation without coercion or manipulation. They engaged the personal passions of all their members and wove them into an agenda for the organization. They understood that exploiting the opportunity for continuity, ironically, comes not by exercising control, but by giving it away.

As organizational leaders, they figured out how to evolve a collective enterprise that successors and staff wanted to perpetuate for their own reasons. As parents, they established opportunities for their children to experience the pride and sense of accomplishment that comes from making choices and commitments themselves.

The most important audience for the lessons from enduring multigenerational foundations may be those who are thinking about starting one. If these families could speak to "philanthropists in the making," they might encourage donors to recognize the true nature of the spectacular opportunity that they have been given, or earned.

It is hard to imagine any other moment when they will have the same chance to do the right thing on this scale for their families and their communities. For their families, making it possible for them to be genuinely selfless, to give of themselves without tangible reward, to save or enrich lives, to voluntarily contribute and to earn the right to feel profoundly proud. For the community, to return resources to their source, to accomplish in a small or large way a leveling of the playing field, and to uphold the very best of the democratic tradition.

NOTES

1. Esposito (1999) has edited a wonderful compilation of Ylvisaker's work.
2. Nielsen (1996), p. 179.
3. Fleishman (2004) offers an excellent and provocative perspective on this theme.

APPENDIX A:
INTERVIEW PROTOCOL

LEADERSHIP AND CONTINUITY
IN FAMILY FOUNDATIONS

The design for data gathering includes:

"Fact Sheet" completed by foundation staff or trustee
Review of historical documents
Semistructured interviews

This study is interested in both retrospective and current data. Therefore, the interview includes both historical and "today" questions. We are interested in getting the facts and descriptions with a minimum of interpretation and rationalization. The historical questions are designed to encourage respondents to "tell the story" of their foundation. A sequence of descriptions of "what happened" is much more valuable than the respondents' conjectures about "why" things happened or what they meant. In the same way, the questions about current operations are designed to get descriptive data, not interpretive explanations.

Given the constraints of time, the interviews cannot possibly explore all the areas that we would like to understand. This semistructured format means that the interviewer will need to choose the set and sequence of questions that are the best stimuli for the particular interviewee. Some respondents will be the best sources of historical data; others will know little about the past but have a unique perspective on the present. It is also not necessary to get the same data from all respondents. We may learn a lot from hearing each respondent tell his or her version of some stories (the "founding myth" for example), but may need to hear other stories only once or twice.

Below are copies of the Fact Sheet and the Interview Protocol.

LEADERSHIP AND CONTINUITY
IN FAMILY FOUNDATIONS

Foundation Fact Sheet

Please complete the following information sheet and return it to the researcher before the first visit or interviews. This information will help us prepare for the interviews and make them as efficient as possible. The form is a general one, so adapt it or comment on those items as needed to fit your situation. If some information is not available, we will try to fill in the blanks in the interviews.

Thanks very much.

1. Foundation Name

2. Foundation Address

3. Foundation Phone(s)

4. Year formed or incorporated

5. Name of donor(s) or founder(s)

6. Legal form of foundation (e.g., trust, corporation, etc.)

7. How many staff work for the foundation?_____
   Total FTE?_____

Please list the names, titles, and years of service for the individuals in senior staff positions.

Name	Title or Role	Years of service (e.g., 1990–present)

8. Please fill in the following chart for all family members who are currently involved with the foundation, as trustees, directors, staff, committee members, or any other significant role. (Feel free to attach a list in an already-existing format if that would be easier.)

Name	Age	Family relationship to founder (e.g., daughter, married to grandson, etc.)	Current role or title	Years of service (e.g., 1990–present)

9. Please list the nonfamily directors or trustees, and any nonfamily advisors or consultants who have played an important role in the development of your foundation.

Name	Title or role	Years of service

10. If possible attach or draw a simple family tree, that shows the family members from the founder(s) to the present.

11. Please check the most accurate category for the size of the total endowment.

   ___   <$10 million
   ___ $10–30 million
   ___ $30–100 million
   ___   >$100 million

12. Please attach other information that will help us understand your foundation, such as a mission statement, annual report, newspaper article, and so forth.

   Thank you very much for your help.

LEADERSHIP AND CONTINUITY
IN FAMILY FOUNDATIONS

Foundation Interview Protocol

I.   Interview characteristics: Respondent, time, place
II.   Foundation characteristics
    A. Endowment [confirm from Fact Sheet]
       1. Size
       2. Investment policies, restrictions, and goals
    B. Annual giving
    C. Organizational structure [confirm from Fact Sheet]
       1. Number, names, ages, family status, and generation of trustees
       2. Number, names, ages, family status of staff
    D. Location [confirm from Fact Sheet]
       1. Founding location
       2. Current home office
       3. Branch offices
       4. Funding or program geographic areas
    E. Schedule and format of meetings (attach typical minutes or agenda if available)
       1. Number and schedule of regular meetings
       2. Number and schedule of special meetings
       3. Committee structure and meeting schedule
       4. Record keeping and communication
III.   Asset Management
    A. Who has responsibility for the endowment?
    B. How are professional advisors and managers chosen and monitored?
    C. Are there specific performance criteria for portfolio management? How are they enforced?
IV.   History
    A. Founding
       1. Family context of the founding
          a) Who was involved, in what specific roles?
          b) Family and branch relationships among founders
       2. Business context of the founding (if any)
          a) Businesses that predated the founding

b) Businesses that continued (currently operating?), with indication of which family members are active in currently operating businesses
3. Endowment context (where did the original funds come from?)
4. Intent of the founders
    a) Original mission statement
    b) Inferred or informally communicated intent

The following section of the interview asks for a retrospective review by the interviewee of the "story" of the foundation's development. The data can be organized as either one description (there has been no change over time) or a series of descriptions representing different phases in the foundation's history.

B. Development
   For each "phase" in the foundation's development story, gather the following information:
   1. Years
       a) What are the dates and marker events for the beginning of this phase?
       b) What are the dates and marker events for the end of this phase?
   2. Board makeup
       a) Specifically, who were the trustees?
           1) From the family
           2) From outside the family
       b) How were they chosen?
       c) Who were the leaders?
       d) How participative or shared was the board's decision making?
       e) Who were not included?
   3. Staff
       a) Were nonfamily staff employed at this stage?
       b) How was the decision made to hire them?
       c) What qualifications were they expected to meet?
   4. Guiding purpose, mission, criteria for grantmaking
       a) Was there a clear and articulated mission?

        b) Were there restrictions or requirements on the type, location, and so forth of eligible grantees?

        c) How much unanimity was there about the foundation's mission?

           1) Between family branches?

           2) Between leadership and other trustees?

           3) Between generations?

           4) Between trustees and professional staff?

    5. Grantmaking

        a) How often and where were the meetings held?

        b) How participative was the process of grantmaking?

        c) Examples of typical grantees or projects of this phase

    6. Most complicated problems (probe for stories)

V. Mission

    A. What is the best current statement of the foundation's mission?

    B. Is it different from the original mission? If so, how was the mission derived?

    C. When was it last reviewed or changed?

    D. How is it communicated to staff and trustees?

    E. How is it communicated to the family?

VI. Continuity planning

    A. How are younger generation members introduced to the foundation?

    [Probe for: whether the foundation is discussed informally at home with children present; are young children aware of family support for grantee projects]

        1. What are the steps in the education or socialization for prospective trustees?

           a) Do they observe board meetings?

           b) Do they sit on junior or adjunct boards first?

           c) Are they sent to professional meetings, seminars, or conferences?

        2. What steps are taken to anticipate and plan for trustee changeovers?

           a) Is there a mandatory retirement age or other term limit requirement?

B. Trustee selection
1. What criteria govern trustee selection?
   [Probe for: whether trustees are chosen at large, or from constituencies such as family branches; are family members who work in the family business excluded or, alternatively, encouraged, to be trustees; what demographic factors are important (gender, age, generation, blood descendant versus in-law, etc.); how is geographic dispersal handled]
2. Who is responsible for nominating new trustees?
   [Probe for stories, especially ones that illustrate controversial dilemmas]
   a) Who is responsible for selecting new trustees?
      [If there are representation or constituency rules for trustees, probe for stories of the recruitment and selection process (e.g., how is representation divided among branches of different sizes, does one branch have any say in the representative selected from another branch)]

C. Staff
1. Is there a formal job description for the chief staff person (and other staff, if applicable)?
   [Probe for: how they were developed, by whom, when, how they are modified, opinion on how useful they are]
2. Who supervises the staff?
3. Are there formal evaluation and feedback procedures in place for staff?
4. Are there staff positions filled by family members?
   a) Are the criteria for employment different for family members?
   b) Is the evaluation process different?
   c) Is compensation different?
5. What role does the staff play in managing the family involvement, guiding the foundation, setting priorities, and organizing the trustees?
   [Probe for: stories of trustee/staff relations; evaluations of staff performance; how conflict between staff and trustees or other family members was handled]

    6. What responsibility does the staff have for preparing the next generation of family participants?

VII. Governance and grantmaking

  A. Role descriptions

    1. Is there a formal job description for trustees?
    [Probe for: how it was developed, by whom, when, how is it modified, opinion on how useful it is]

    2. Is there a formal job description for officers (president, secretary, committee chairs, etc.)?
    [Probe for: how they were developed, by whom, when, how they are modified, opinion on how useful they are]

  B. Grantmaking (How are grantmaking decisions made today?)

    1. What are the committees, if any?
      a) How are trustees assigned to committees?
      b) What role do the committees play in grantmaking?

    2. Proposals
      a) How and when are proposals solicited?
      b) How are they reviewed?
      c) How do staff and trustees work together in preparing reviews of proposals?

    3. Fund differentiation
      a) Are there different subcategories of funds?
      b) Who participates in decisions about "common pool" dispersals?
      c) Who has discretionary funds?
      [Probe for: if discretionary funds exist, how did they start; who has them and are they all the same size; is there any restriction on the individual's freedom to disperse these funds to grantees]

    4. Process
      a) Schedule of dispersal meetings
      b) How are grantmaking meetings organized?
      c) Opinion: How effectively does the decision process work? How could it be improved?

    5. Evaluation and follow-up
      a) Who has responsibility for follow-up with grantees?
      b) Are grants revisited in a following meeting?
      c) What is the policy on site visits?

C. Governance integration

    1. What connection, if any, does the foundation have with: [Probe for: individuals with membership or leadership roles in more than one system; common mission; use of the same staff resources; networking; community or public image and relations]

        a) Operating family businesses?

        b) A family office?

        c) Other foundations within this family?

        d) Other foundations outside this family?

        e) A Family Council?

        f) Government or public offices?

        g) Any other family structures?

D. What roles, if any, have outside consultants or facilitators played in the foundation?

VIII. Family Dynamics

A. Structure

    1. Who do you consider to be the members of your foundation family?
       [Probe: which generation is considered the "first"]

    2. Is the distinction between blood descendants and in-laws important in this family?

    3. How common is divorce and remarriage in this family? Are there many complicated "blended" families within the larger family?

B. Alliances

    1. Where are the most important alliances in the family?

    2. How have those evolved over time?

    3. How does this affect grantmaking (probe for stories)?

C. Conflict

    1. Where are the most important conflicts in the family?

    2. How have they developed over time?

    3. How do they affect grantmaking (probe for stories)?

D. Leadership

    1. Who are the leaders?

    2. How much authority do they exercise and where does it come from?

        a) Formal leadership role

         b) Age or generational seniority

         c) Special expertise

         d) Branch of family or other "political" sources

    3. How are potential leaders in the next generation identified?

  E. Communication

    1. How often do family members within each nuclear family typically talk to each other?

    2. How open and honest is the typical communication?

         a) How often do family members from different nuclear families within the same branch typically talk to each other? How open and honest is the typical communication?

         b) How often do family members from different family branches typically talk to each other? How open and honest is the typical communication?

IX. Closing questions

  A. Is there anything else that we haven't asked about that would help us understand the development of your foundation over time?

  B. Is there anything you can suggest from your experience (regarding governance, problem solving, or planning) that might benefit other family foundations?

  C. Whom else would you recommend that we interview? [If a name is suggested that is not on our list, probe for why he/she was mentioned.]

APPENDIX B:
AGGREGATED VARIABLE LIST

FOUNDING

1. Year Founded [#]
2. Legal Organizational Form [trust/corporation]
3. Primary Reason for Founding [tax/philanthropic values/family collaboration/community relations/other]
4. Secondary Reason for Founding [tax/philanthropic values/family collaboration/community relations/other]
5. Other Reason for Founding [tax/philanthropic values/family collaboration/community relations/other]
6. Lead Founder Age [#]
7. Previous Philanthropy [none–minimal/moderate/opportunistic/significant]
8. # of Original Donors [#]
9. Original Donor(s)
10. Source of Wealth [inherited/generated]
11. Founding Mission Statement [none/general-implicit/specific]
12. Grantmaking Restriction [geographic/program/recipient/size/term/other]
13. Original Endowment [$]
14. Managed by
15. Source of Funds
16. Staff [yes/no]
17. Grantmaking Support [foundation staff/family business staff/donor/board/family/advisor]

18. Operating Business [yes/no]
19. Other Foundations [yes/no]
20. Original Trustees
    Donor [yes/no]
    Spouse [yes/no]
    Offspring [yes/no]
    Extended Family [yes/no]
    Family Advisors/Friend [yes/no]
    Community Rep. [yes/no]
21. Percent of Males [#]
22. Percent of Females [#]
23. Key Advisors
24. Years in First Stage [#]
25. Transition Year [#]
26. Trigger [death of founder/withdrawal/entry–gradual increase in collaboration]
27. Posttransition Form [successor CT/spouse and 2nd gen./SP or CC/1st–2nd gen. collaboration/staff run]
28. Change in Endowment
29. First Dedicated Staff
30. First Staff—Year [#]
31. First Staff—Year of Operation [#]
32. First Female Director—Year [#]

CURRENT

33. Generations Currently Involved [1st/2nd/3rd/4th]
34. Age of Trustees [young adult <35/middle adult 35–50/senior adult 50–65/elderly >65]
35. Governance stage [Controlling Trustee/Collaborative Family Foundation/Family-Governed Staff-Managed Foundation]
36. Current Mission Statement [none/general-implicit/specific]
37. Grantmaking Restriction [geographic/program/recipient/size/term/other]
38. Current Endowment [$]
39. Source of Funds
40. Annual Giving [$]

41. Senior Staff Position [family/nonfamily]
42. Senior Staff Title
43. Family Paid FTE [#]
44. Family Unpaid FTE [#]
45. Nonfamily FTE [#]
46. Operating Business [yes/no]
47. Other Foundations [yes/no]
48. Current Trustees
    Direct Descendents of Founder(s)
    Extended Family (family who are not direct descendents)
    Family Advisors/Friends
    Community Representatives
49. # of males [#]
50. # of females [#]
51. Meetings per Year—Grantmaking [#]
52. Meetings per Year—Other [#]
53. Term Limit Bylaws [yes/no]
54. Term Limit Actual [yes/no]
55. Used Professional Facilitator [yes/no]
56. Used Professional Associations [yes/no]
57. Designated Next Generation $? [yes/no]
58. Percent Discretionary Giving [#]
59. Key Advisors
60. In-laws ok? [yes/no]

PERFORMANCE AND FAMILY PROCESS RATINGS
[very low/low/moderate/high/exemplary]

61. Clear Program
62. Grantmaking Vitality
63. Staff Control
64. Family Collaboration
65. Likelihood of Continuity
66. Successor Development
67. Asset Management
68. Next Generation Enthusiasm
69. Conflict Avoidance

70. Quality Control
71. Clarity of Mission
72. Organizational Structure
73. Positive Family Dynamics
74. Resources [underresourced/adequate/full/surplus]

FINANCIAL DATA

75. Administrative/Grants Ratios
76. Administrative/Assets Ratios
77. Grants/Assets Ratios
78. Administrative + Grant/Assets Ratios

APPENDIX C:
ANONYMITY AGREEMENT
WITH PARTICIPANTS

UNDERSTANDING OF ANONYMITY

The National Center for Family Philanthropy and Lansberg, Gersick & Associates respect and appreciate deeply the time, energy, and dedication involved by all participants in the "Leadership and Continuity in Family Philanthropy" research project. Families involved in organized philanthropy play important and often public roles in their communities. Your agreement to take part in this project indicates your commitment to yet another community—the community of organized philanthropy.

In order to ensure that your responses to the interviews are held in confidence, the National Center and Lansberg, Gersick & Associates pledge that they will do all that is possible to assure anonymity. Participating foundations and names associated with participating families (including donors, trustees, staff, and other family members) will not be released to any individuals or groups by the Lansberg Gersick research team or the staff of the National Center, either during or after the project. In write-ups and reports emanating from this project, the data will be presented in aggregate form or disguised in such a way as to protect the anonymity of the data sources.

However, participating families and foundations may tell others of their involvement in the project at their own discretion.

We thank you again for your involvement in this project, and look forward to hearing and learning from your experiences, and the experiences of your family.

_____

Signature of National Center Representative   Date

_____

Signature of Lansberg Gersick Representative   Date

_____

Signature of Foundation Representative   Date

APPENDIX D:
ADDITIONAL TABLES[†]

Table D.1. Correlations of Mission with Organization Performance

	Clear Program	Grantmaking Vitality	Successor Development	Quality Control	Org. Structure
Mission Statement	.514**	.335[a]	.348[a]	.382*	.239
Mission Clarity	.800**	.733**	.519**	.779**	.739**

*p<.05, **p<.01, [a]p<.10

Table D.2. Correlations of Mission with Family Process

	Family Collaboration	Likelihood of Continuity	Next Generation Enthusiasm	Positive Family Dynamics
Mission Statement	.475**	.347[a]	.209	.398*
Mission Clarity	.611**	.672**	.421*	.614**

*p<.05, **p<.01, [a]p<.10

[†]For readers who do not frequently encounter correlation coefficients, they are the measure of the association between one variable in the table (the row heading) and another (the column heading). Correlations can vary between −1 (the lower the score on one variable, the higher the score on the other—like the relationship between the length of the day and the length of the night) and +1 (the higher the score on one variable, the higher on the other—like the relationship between height in inches and height in centimeters). A correlation of 0 means that there is no relationship between the scores on the two variables (like the relationship between shoe size and favorite color). A correlation that is significant (that is, with a probability less than 5 percent that it would occur just by chance) means that it is likely that the two variables are associated in reality, and that if one of them goes up, the other goes up as well.

Table D.3. Performance Ratings of Collaborative Family Foundations and Family-Governed Staff-Managed Foundations

					Relative Performance 1 = very low, 2 = low, 3 = moderate, 4 = high, 5 = exemplary							
	Clear Program	Gntmkng Vitality	Staff Control	Family Collab.	Likeli- hood of Continue	Succsr Dev.	$ Mgmt	Next Gen. Enthu- siasm	Conflict Avoidance	Quality Control	Mission	Organi- zational Structure	Positive Family Dynamics
TOTAL SAMPLE	3.37	3.30	2.83	3.03	3.43	2.33	3.47	2.86	3.17	3.20	3.40	3.33	2.60
Collaborative Family Foundations	3.19	3.29	2.38	3.10	3.38	2.33	3.43	2.86	3.00	3.14	3.38	3.29	2.57
Staff-Managed Family Foundations	3.78	3.33	3.89	2.89	3.56	2.33	3.56	2.86	3.56	3.33	3.44	3.44	2.67

Table D.4. Correlations among Organizational Performance Ratings and Other Organizational Measures

Ratings	Clarity of Program	Grantmaking Vitality	Successor Devmt	Asset Mgmt	Quality Control	Clarity of Mission	Org. Structure	Adequacy of Resources
Clarity of Program	1							
Grantmaking Vitality	.63**	1						
Successor Devmt	.44*	.61**	1					
Asset Mgmt.	.36 a	.42*	.25	1				
Quality Control	.58**	.69**	.51**	.30	1			
Clarity of Mission	.80**	.73**	.52**	.25	.78**	1		
Org. Structure	.60**	.65**	.56**	.52**	.74**	.74**	1	
Adequacy of Resources	.72**	.60**	.44**	.33	.46**	.64**	.67**	1
Likelihood of Continuity	.54**	.63**	.52**	.30	.65**	.67**	.57**	.43*
Family Process								
Family Collaboration	.46*	.69*	.43*	-.01	.42*	.61*	.21	.30
Next Generation Enthusiasm	.34 a	.52**	.57**	.28	.35 a	.42*	.24	.13
Positive Family Dynamics	.41*	.62**	.30 a	.10	.51**	.61**	.28	.20
Other Variables of Interest								
Nonfamily Exec. Dir.		.32 a			.47**		.37*	
Community Reps on Board			No significant effects					
In-Laws on Board			No significant effects					
# of Grantmaking Meetings/Year			No significant effects					
Term Limits								

* = p<.05, ** = p<.01, a = p<.10

BIBLIOGRAPHY

Alda, A. 1996. "Giving well." *Initiatives.* (Winter). Boston: Philanthropic Initiative, Inc.

Andreoni, J. 1998. "Toward a Theory of Charitable Fund-raising." *Journal of Political Economy* 106: 1186–1214.

———. 2001. "Economics of Philanthropy." In *International Encyclopedia of the Social and Behavioral Sciences,* 11369–376. London: Elsevier Science Ltd.

Barrett, W. 2000. "How the Other Half Gives." *Forbes,* October 30, 104–6.

Boris, E. T. 1987. "Creation and Growth: A Survey of Private Foundations." In *America's Wealthy and the Future of Foundations,* ed. T. Odendahl, 65–126. Washington, D.C.: Council on Foundations and the Yale University Program on Nonprofit Organizations.

Born, J. 2001. "Discretionary Grants: Encouraging Participation . . . or Dividing Families." *Passages,* vol. 3.2, Washington, D.C.: National Center for Family Philanthropy.

———, ed. 1999. *Investment Issues for Family Funds: Managing and Maximizing Your Philanthropic Dollars, National Center Journal,* vol. 2. Washington, D.C.: National Center for Family Philanthropy.

———. 2001. "Supporting Organizations: Options, Opportunities, and Challenges." *Passages,* vol. 3.3, Washington, D.C.: National Center for Family Philanthropy.

Bowen, M. 1978. *Family Therapy in Clinical Practice.* New York: Jason Aronson.

Bryson, E. 2002. *Top Ten Ways Family Foundations Get into Trouble.* Washington, D.C.: Council on Foundations.

Byrne, J., with J. Cosgrove, B. Hindo, and A. Dayan. 2002. "The New Face of Philanthropy." *Business Week,* December 2.

Carland, J. W., et al. 1984. "Differentiating Entrepreneurs from Small Business Owners: A Conceptualization." *Academy of Management Review* 9(2): 354–59.

Carter, B., and M. McGoldrick, eds. 1999. *The Expanded Family Life Cycle,* 3rd ed. Boston: Allyn & Bacon.

265

Council on Foundations. 1996. *The Family Advisor: Mission Statements and Guidelines.* Washington, D.C.: Council on Foundations.

———. 2001. *2001 Grantmakers Salary and Benefits Report.* Washington, D.C.: Council on Foundations.

———. 2004a. *2003 Grantmakers Salary Report.* Washington, D.C.: Council on Foundations.

———. 2004b. *Foundation Management Series*, 11th ed. Washington, D.C.: Council on Foundations.

Edie, J. 1987. "Congress and Foundations: An Historical Summary." In *America's Wealthy and the Future of Foundations,* ed. by T. Odendahl et al., 43–64. Washington, D.C.: Council on Foundations and the Yale University Program on Nonprofit Organizations.

———. 2002a. *Family Foundations and the Law: What You Need to Know.* Washington, D.C.: Council on Foundations.

———. 2002b. *First Steps in Starting a Foundation,* 5th ed. Washington, D.C.: Council on Foundations.

Eisenhardt, K. 1989. "Building Theories from Case Study Research." *Academy of Management Review* 14: 532–50.

Esperti, R., R. Peterson, R. Goldman, and T. Rogers. 2003. *Giving: Philanthropy for Everyone.* Denver: Quantum Press.

Esposito, V., ed. 1999. *Conscience and Community: The Legacy of Paul Ylvisaker.* New York: Peter Lang.

———. 2002. *Splendid Legacy: The Guide to Creating Your Family Foundation.* Washington, D.C.: National Center for Family Philanthropy.

Fleishman, J. 2004. "Simply Doing Good or Doing It Well: Stewardship, Hubris, and Foundation Governance." In *Benefactors: A Critique on Contemporary American Philanthropy,* ed. P. Karoff. Boston: Philanthropic Initiative, Inc.

Foote, J., ed. 1999. *Resources for Family Philanthropy, Finding the Best People, Advice and Support, National Center for Family Philanthropy Journal,* vol. 1. Washington, D.C.: National Center for Family Philanthropy.

Foote, J. 2000. *Family Philanthropy and Donor-Advised Funds.* Washington, D.C.: National Center for Family Philanthropy.

Foote, J., and C. Norcott. 1999. "Managing a Family Philanthropy." In *Resources for Family Philanthropy,* ed. V. Esposito, 1–21. Washington, D.C.: National Center for Family Philanthropy.

The Foundation Center. 2000. *Family Foundations: A Profile of Funders and Trends.* Washington, D.C.: National Center for Family Philanthropy.

Gersick, C. 1988. "Time and Transition in Work Teams: Toward a New Model of Group Development." *Academy of Management Journal* 31: 9–41.

———. 1991. "Revolutionary Change Theories: A Multilevel Exploration of the Punctuated Equilibrium Paradigm." *Academy of Management Review* 16, no. 1: 1–26.

———. 1994. "Pacing Strategic Change: The Case of a New Venture." *Academy of Management Journal* 37: 9–45.

Gersick, K., I. Lansberg, and J. Davis. 1990. "The Impact of Family Dynamics on Structure and Process in Family Foundations." *Family Business Review* 3, no. 4: 357–74.

Gersick, K., J. Davis, M. Hampton, and I. Lansberg. 1997. *Generation to Generation: Life Cycles of the Family Business.* Boston: Harvard Business School Press.

Gersick, K., I. Lansberg, M. Desjardins, and B. Dunn. 1999. "Stages and Transitions: Managing Change in the Family Business." *Family Business Review* 12, no. 4: 287–97.

Gersick, K., D. Stone, M. Desjardins, H. Muson, and K. Grady. 2000. *The Succession Workbook: Continuity Planning for Family Foundations.* Washington, D.C.: Council on Foundations.

Glaser, B., and A. Strauss. 1967. *The Discovery of Grounded Theory: Strategies for Qualitative Research.* London: Wiedenfeld & Nicholson.

Goldberg, A. 2002. "Opportunity of a Lifetime: Young Adults in Family Philanthropy." *Passages*, vol. 4.1, Washington, D.C.: National Center for Family Philanthropy.

Hughes, J. 1997. *Family Wealth: Keeping It in the Family.* Princeton Junction, N.J.: NewWrx.

Kanter, R. 1979. "The Measurement of Organizational Effectiveness, Productivity, Performance and Success: Issues and Dilemmas in Service and Nonprofit Organizations." ISPS Working Paper No. 208, Yale University.

Karoff, P., ed. 2004. *Just Money: A Critique on Contemporary American Philanthropy.* Boston: Philanthropic Initiative.

Kerr, M., and M. Bowen. 1988. *Family Evaluation.* New York: Norton.

Lansberg, I. 1988. "The Succession Conspiracy." *Family Business Review* 1, no. 2: 119–43.

———. 1999. *Succeeding Generations.* Boston: Harvard Business School Press.

Lawler, E., et al. 1985. *Doing Research That Is Useful for Theory and Practice.* San Francisco: Jossey-Bass.

Levinson, D. L. 1978. *The Seasons of a Man's Life.* New York: Alfred A. Knopf.

———. 1996. *The Seasons of a Woman's Life.* New York: Alfred A. Knopf.

Levy, R. 1999. *Give and Take: A Candid Account of Corporate Philanthropy.* Boston: Harvard Business School Press.

Marshack, K. 1998. *Entrepreneurial Couples.* Palo Alto, Calif.: Davies-Black Publishing.

Moore, S., and J. Simon. 2000. *It's Getting Better All the Time: 100 Greatest Trends of the Last 100 Years.* Washington, D.C.: Cato Institute.

Murray, B. 2003. "The Succession Transition Process: A Longitudinal Perspective." *Family Business Review* 16, no. 1: 17–33.

Nadler, D., and M. Tushman. 1989. "Leadership for Organizational Change." In *Large Scale Organizational Change*, ed. A. Mohrman et al., 100–119. San Francisco: Jossey-Bass.

Nelson, R. 1987. "An Economic History of Large Foundations." In *America's Wealthy and the Future of Foundations*, ed. T. Odendahl, 127–77. Washington, D.C.: Council on Foundations and the Yale University Program on Non-Profit Organizations.

Nichols, M., and R. Schwartz. 2001. *Family Therapy: Concepts and Methods,* 5th ed. Boston: Allyn & Bacon.

Nielsen, W. 1985. *The Golden Donors*. New York: Truman Talley Books/E.P. Dutton.

———. 1996. *Inside American Philanthropy: The Dramas of Donorship*. Norman: University of Oklahoma Press.

Odendahl, T., ed., with E. Boris, J. Edie, R. Nelson, F. Ostrower, G. Rudney, and E. Steuerle. 1987. *America's Wealthy and the Future of Foundations*, Washington, D.C.: Council on Foundations and the Yale University Program on Non-Profit Organizations.

———. 1987. "Independent Foundations and Wealthy Donors: An Overview." In *America's Wealthy and the Future of Foundations*, ed. T. Odendahl et al., 1–26. Washington, D.C.: Council on Foundations and the Yale University Program on Non-Profit Organizations.

———. 1987. "Wealthy Donors and Their Charitable Attitudes." In *America's Wealthy and the Future of Foundations*, ed. T. Odendahl et al., 223–46. Washington, D.C.: Council on Foundations and the Yale University Program on Non-Profit Organizations.

Oster, Sharon M., and Katherine O'Regan. 2001. "Does the Structure and Composition of the Board Matter? The Case of Nonprofit Organizations," Yale School of Management Working Papers Series #04.

Ostrower, F. 1987. "The Role of Advisors to the Wealthy." In *America's Wealthy and the Future of Foundations*, ed. T. Odendahl et al., 247–66. Washington, D.C.: Council on Foundations and the Yale University Program on Non-Profit Organizations.

The Philanthropic Initiative, Inc. 2002. *Philanthropy for the Wise Donor-Investor: A Primer for Families on Strategic Giving*. Boston: Philantropic Initiative, Inc.

Porter, M., and M. Kramer. 2002. "The Competitive Advantage of Corporate Philanthropy." *Harvard Business Review* (December): 57–68.

Putnam, R. 2000. *Bowling Alone: The Collapse and Revival of American Community*. New York: Simon & Schuster.

Remmer, Ellen. 2000. *What's a Donor to Do? The State of Donor Resources in America Today*. Boston: Philanthropic Initiative, Inc.

Rudney, G. 1987. "Creation of Foundations and Their Wealth." In *America's Wealthy and the Future of Foundations*, ed. T. Odendahl et al., 179–202. Washington, D.C.: Council on Foundations and the Yale University Program on Non-Profit Organizations.

Sarason, S. 1972. *The Creation of Settings and the Future Societies*. San Francisco: Jossey-Bass.

Schervish, P. 1993. "Taking Giving Seriously." In *Taking Giving Seriously*, ed. P. Dean, 11–41. Indiana: Indiana University Center on Philanthropy.

Sievers, B. 2004. "Philanthropy's Blindspots." In *Benefactors: A Critique on Contemporary American Philanthropy*, ed. P. Karoff. Boston: Philanthropic Initiative, Inc.

Sonnenfeld, J. 1988. *The Hero's Farewell: What Happens When Chief Executives Retire*. New York: Oxford University Press.

Sonnenfeld, J., and P. Spence. 1989. "The Parting Patriarch of a Family Firm." *Family Business Review* 2, no. 4: 355–75.

Stanley, T. J., and W. D. Danko. 1998. *The Millionaire Next Door.* New York: Simon & Schuster.

Steinberg R., and M. Wilhelm. 2003. "Giving: The Next Generation—Parental Effects on Donations," unpublished paper, Center on Philanthropy at Indiana University, June.

Steuerle, E. 1987. "Charitable Giving Patterns of the Wealthy." In *America's Wealthy and the Future of Foundations*, ed. T. Odendahl et al., 203–22. Washington, D.C.: Council on Foundations and the Yale University Program on Non-Profit Organizations.

Stone, D. 1997. *Family Issues.* Family Foundation Library Series. Washington, D.C.: Council on Foundations.

———. 1999. *Creative Family Grantmaking: The Story of the Durfee Foundation.* Washington, D.C.: National Center for Family Philanthropy.

———. 1999. *Grantmaking with a Compass: The Challenges of Geography.* Washington, D.C.: National Center for Family Philanthropy.

———. 2002. "Difficult Discussions at Difficult Times." *Passages*, vol. 4.3. Washington, D.C.: National Center for Family Philanthropy.

———. 2004. "Defining 'Family' in Family Philanthropy." *Passages*, vol. 6.1. Washington, D.C.: National Center for Family Philanthropy,

Tocqueville, A. de 1837. *Democracy in America, Part II.* New York: G. Dearborn & Co.

Tushman, M. L., W. Newman, and E. Romanelli. 1986. "Convergence and Upheaval: Managing the Unsteady Pace of Organizational Evolution." *California Management Review* 29, no. 1: 29–44.

Ylvisaker, P. 1990. "Family Foundations: High Risk, High Reward." *Family Business Review* 3, no. 4 (Winter): 331–35.

INDEX

ABOUT THE AUTHORS AND THE NATIONAL CENTER FOR FAMILY PHILANTHROPY

ABOUT THE AUTHORS

Kelin E. Gersick, Ph.D.

Kelin Gersick is a cofounder of and a senior partner at Lansberg, Gersick & Associates (LGA), a research and consulting firm in New Haven that serves family businesses, family offices, and family foundations. He is a Management Fellow at the Yale School of Organization and Management and Professor Emeritus of Organizational Psychology at the California School of Professional Psychology.

Gersick is the lead author of *Generation to Generation: Life Cycles of the Family Business* (Harvard Business School Press, 1997), *The Succession Workbook: Continuity Planning in Family Foundations* (Council on Foundations, 2000), and many articles, cases, and commentaries.

Gersick's consulting work with family firms and family foundations focuses on the impact of family relationships on governance and business operations. He also maintains an active research program on family business and adult development. From 1989 through 1993, he served as co-editor-in-chief of *Family Business Review*. He is a frequent speaker at conferences, family business forums, philanthropic association meetings, and international symposia.

Gersick grew up in a business family in Illinois. Earlier in his career, he worked as an organizational consultant and a family counselor in Boston and in New Haven. He holds a Ph.D. from Harvard University and a B.A. from Yale University, and he has taught at Harvard and spent ten years on the faculty at Yale.

Michèle Desjardins, CMC, (Senior Associate) has worked internationally as a management consultant for Price Waterhouse and the Quebec Securities Commission. She works with family-owned and -controlled enterprises in North America and Europe on issues such as succession and continuity planning, development of governance structures and policies, family philanthropy and foundations, and career assessments and leadership development for successors.

Katherine Grady, Ph.D., (Senior Associate) is a specialist in leadership, career development, and family dynamics in family companies. In addition to her work with LGA, she is an Associate Clinical Professor at Yale University, where she has been involved in teaching, service, and research related to families and organizational development.

Howard Muson (Research Associate) has written numerous articles and case studies on family-owned companies. As editor and copublisher of *Family Business Magazine* for ten years, he interviewed many owners and managers of family companies as well as consultants, academic researchers, and other experts in the field. His articles have appeared in the *New York Times, Your Company, Town & Country, The Conference Board Magazine*, and other publications.

Deanne Stone, M.A., (Research Associate) is an advisor and author on the spectrum of issues facing family foundations: management, governance, grantmaking, and family dynamics. Her articles on philanthropy have appeared in publications of the National Center for Family Philanthropy and the Council on Foundations, and she is also a regular contributor to *Family Business Magazine*.

[A more detailed biography of all authors and selected publications are available at www.lgassoc.com.]

ABOUT THE NATIONAL CENTER
FOR FAMILY PHILANTHROPY

The mission of the National Center for Family Philanthropy is to promote philanthropic values, vision, and excellence across generations of donors and donor families. Our understanding and experience with the very personal act of giving ensure that these donors and their advisors have access to the highest quality information and the encouragement needed to:

- articulate, pursue, and achieve their charitable missions;
- understand and meet their governance and management needs; and
- have a significant positive impact on the lives and work of those they support.

The National Center is a nonprofit, 501(c)(3) organization.

For more information, please visit www.ncfp.org.